mref
W9-BSD-740
1986
E PLURIBUS UNUM
TUEBOR
SI QUÆRIS PENINSULAM AMŒNAM
CIRCUMSPICE
MICHIGAN
STATE
LIBRARY

MR. JEFFERSON'S DISCIPLE

MR. JEFFERSON'S DISCIPLE

A Life of

JUSTICE WOODWARD

By FRANK B. WOODFORD

Michigan State

EAST LANSING

MANUFACTURED IN THE UNITED STATES OF AMERICA
AT THE LAKESIDE PRESS, R. R. DONNELLEY & SONS COMPANY
CHICAGO, ILLINOIS, AND CRAWFORDSVILLE, INDIANA

To

ARTHUR M. WOODFORD

Foreword

TIME HAS BEEN passing over Michigan. Great men have lived and worked here, and prodigious changes have been wrought. It is now almost a century and a half since Justice Augustus Brevoort Woodward arrived in Detroit on the last day of June, 1805, to be confronted by a disconsolate population amid the burned-out ruins of their village. The beginning of his service to the Territory was certainly inauspicious and discouraging. A miracle of creation lies between that bleak prospect and the energetic city which we know and which continues to change before our eyes.

It is a good time, therefore, to look back to our beginnings and foundations, and survey the road over which we have come. All the difficult problems are not concentrated in our own day. The Founding Fathers had a few of their own which, in their setting, were more demanding and baffling than ours. It is desirable that we get a fresh and vivid view of what has gone into the making of this state and region, and of the men who labored so diligently for the public good.

Frank B. Woodford made a notable contribution to this end when he published in 1950 his fine study of Lewis Cass, "The Last Jeffersonian." This biography of Woodward enlarges that picture and fills in more of the details.

For this Mr. Woodford deserves, and has, our gratitude. These lesser historical figures do not have for our age the glamour that keeps the giants like Jefferson, Franklin and their circle steadily in focus. Yet their labors and their unremembered acts are of vital importance to our understanding of the making of America.

We discovered a few decades ago that we had been creating somewhat unconsciously something rare and precious in this land, and that the land itself had beauty and personality of its own. An outstanding example of this renewed interest was the project to tell the story of the growth of the nation around a framework of biographies of its rivers—those first frontier highways into the continent.

This device has its merits, and the public has responded to them. But men are more interesting than rivers, and a keener insight is gained through a series of related biographies of the men who used these rivers for a purpose. Mr. Woodford's books on Lewis Cass and Judge Woodward are pioneers in this rewarding field. If this example can be followed (perhaps Mr. Woodford will do more) we shall have a treasure shelf of the lives and works of the lesser known men who helped to make us what we presently are.

In this company Judge Woodward has a prominent place. He comes effectively to life before us in these pages, a restless, persevering man, tall, ungainly, lean and stooped, with a narrow face, a big nose, and long heavy hair, a confirmed bachelor, a tireless worker, a fearless disciple of Thomas Jefferson. His guiding political creed was: "The will of the People will be finally triumphant; and it can never be the desire of a free and generous People to fraternize with a band of slaves."

It was Woodward's fortune to live on the American frontier in an environment that had no great understanding of his culture, and many of his troublesome moments stemmed from this conflict. But he never faltered in his pursuit of his vision of planning a great and beautiful city for the future growth of Detroit, and he projected the concept and purpose of a university for the territory which, modified by time and experience, and finally relocated at Ann Arbor in 1837, became the University of Michigan.

It was a turbulent era, often wayward and crude, full of vexations and hardships; but here were soundly laid the foundations for the future. Mr. Woodford leads us through the period in company with the learned judge, with a sure sense and touch of the historian who is objective but appreciative, in a style that is lucid and precise, and in a volume of readable length.

The one surviving monument to the judge's name is Woodward Avenue, which appropriately leads to the Northwest. This book is another and is worthy of its subject.

July, 1953 HARLAN HATCHER
Ann Arbor, Michigan *President,* University of Michigan

CHAPTER I

"We Hope for Better Things"

1

A PANORAMA of shocking desolation greeted Augustus Brevoort Woodward when he saw Detroit for the first time. What had been a tiny, stockaded village was only a charred ruin. Back from the river, on its slight elevation, squatted the old fort, solid and undamaged. Between its ramparts and the shore where the town should have been there were only a few gaunt, fire-scarred chimneys pointing skyward like accusing fingers. Houses, barracks, stores and warehouses, church and fleshpots—all had disappeared.

Looking upon this grim scene, Woodward must have felt he was the victim of a bitter joke. Surely, he must have told himself, he had not traveled all the way from Washington City for this. Detroit was to have been, for him, a beginning—the start of a new career. The commission in his pocket said as much. It bore the signature of his good friend and patron, Thomas Jefferson, certifying his appointment as judge of the Supreme Court of the newly created Territory of Michigan, of which Detroit was the capital. Woodward had expected to start building a new government in the wilderness. Now it must have appeared that even the foundation had been swept away. Was it for this that he had exposed himself to the hazards of travel in the western country? Rivers and mountains, hot sun and chill rain, stifling dust and boot-top mire, bad food and scant rest in the flea traps that passed for inns: were these alone to be his reward?

He had gone to Detroit to accommodate Mr. Jefferson as much as anything. He would have preferred a consular post in Central or South America, and he had taught himself Spanish, anticipating such an appointment. But there was unrest in the West. Jefferson's enemy, Aaron Burr, was promoting some sort of enterprise along the Ohio and lower Mississippi. Some said he intended to detach those regions from the United States and to found a new western empire. He was extremely secretive about his plans; maybe he had designs on the Northwest, too. The president had explained all this to Woodward, pointing out that he wanted officials whom he could trust on the frontier. The post would be no sinecure. Jefferson had made that clear. But it would be an opportunity for patriotic service. It might lead to something better. Jefferson had an unshakable belief in the future of the West and he could be most persuasive on the subject.

It was a month or more since Woodward had set out from Washington for Harrisburg. There he had taken the great western pike, already thronged with a motley stream of pioneers, to Pittsburgh. A keelboat had carried him down the Ohio to Marietta or Cincinnati. (His exact route is uncertain.) Then he had followed the overland trail across the new state of Ohio to the mouth of the Maumee where he had boarded ship for the last leg of his trip to Detroit.

Somewhere along the way the immensity of the land, the immutable strength of the mountains, the irresistible sweep of the rivers, the vast mystery of the forests, must have gripped him. He began to understand what Thomas Jefferson meant.

As the vessel left Lake Erie and sailed into the Detroit River, it can be imagined that Woodward's feeling of anticipation mounted. On July 1, 1805, the day after his arrival, the act of Congress creating the Territory of Michigan would become effective. It was his mission—Woodward's and the other officials who had been named to act with him—to bring American law and civilization to this new land. Its people, more French than American, knew little about, and appreciated less, the blessings of liberty and equality preached by Mr. Jefferson's Democratic-Republican party. The inhabitants, he had heard, though unlettered and lacking the cultural graces of the eastern states, were, nevertheless, a gentle, hospitable folk, living in a rustic utopia which the new government should try to preserve. Woodward had read Locke, Hume, Rousseau and Voltaire. Man, he agreed, should be free. That was the first principle. In his natural state, or as close to it as the amenities of civilization permitted, man was a noble creature, endowed, as Mr. Jefferson had so eloquently stated, with the inalienable rights to life, liberty and the pursuit of happiness. Even the savages, lurking in the forests, could be made a part of this idyllic dream—they, too, were nature's unspoiled children. And possibly, in the midst of this pleasant existence which Woodward's imagination painted, a man might improve his fortune. Behind the eyes of the dreamer, there was a practical turn of mind.

Some such thoughts must have filled his mind and heightened his sense of expectation. This was a new, unfamiliar world. As the river narrowed, he saw on both shores, American and Canadian, the low, white farmhouses, secure behind their high, solid picket fences which served both as a defense against marauding Indians and free-wandering livestock. The French farms ran back from the river in "ribbons" with frontages of four hundred to six hundred feet. This arrangement brought the houses close together, giving the appearance of a continuous village street. Here and there along the path paralleling the river stood wayside shrines where the pious habitant, bound for the town market, could pause and pray, or gossip with neighbor Jacques or Jean-Baptiste. Where the occasional creek flowed into the main stream, windmills lazily swung their giant arms. Nature gave the countryside a benign look of peace, plenty and security.[1]

And then Detroit—or where Detroit should have been! The dream was rudely shattered; instead of the bustling town there was only the black scar of disaster.

2

No one has ever been able to explain exactly how it happened.

Tuesday, June 11, 1805 began like most other days in Detroit. At sunrise the garrison turned out and stood reveille in the fort, and the morning gun boomed flatly across the water. Smoke from freshened breakfast fires rose from the chimneys of the town; the merchants and factors opened their stores, took down the shutters and waited the arrival of the first noisy voyageurs, or the silent, shadow-like Indians, coming in to trade. More country people than usual entered the town through the east and west gates as the morning wore on. They came to attend a religious festival that was to be celebrated at St. Anne's. Most of the women and children of Detroit would also be there to hear Father Dilhet celebrate Mass, assisted by the rector, Father Gabriel Richard.

Antoine de la Mothe Cadillac had come down the lakes and founded the village one hundred and four years earlier. Since that time it had not changed much. It was small, compact and badly overcrowded. Its area was about three acres, laid out as a rectangle. Four north and south streets intersected an equal number which ran east and west. These avenues were narrow; none was wider than twenty feet, making it almost impossible for two carts to pass. The town was surrounded on three sides by a palisade, ten to fifteen feet high. The north side, away from the river, was open, but the pickets extended to the east and west corners of the fort, thus enclosing a broad area which was used for a parade ground and garrison garden. In the west limits of the village was the citadel—the barracks, cook houses and shops of the garrison. The troops at this time were not quartered in the fort. Directly east of the citadel was the government store with an enticing display of Indian trade goods. At the other end of town, near the east gate, stood St. Anne's. Between citadel and church were crowded the houses, stores, warehouses and shops—small, frame and tinder dry. Most of the five hundred or so inhabitants were French, descendants of the original settlers, although several Scotch, English and American merchants had established themselves. The town had two or three doctors and several craftsmen and mechanics necessary to the support of even a crude community. Detroit had its fleshpots, too. There were at least five taverns, and Margaret White maintained a scandalous establishment—"a common, ill-governed, and disorderly house" where sundry low characters met for "drinking, tippling, whoring, and misbehaving themselves . . ." A slaughter house, warehouses full of raw furs and open sewage competed odoriferously against each other.

About mid-morning, Robert Munro, the government storekeeper, was busy at his desk when suddenly a sheet of flame burst in the door and windows. Shouting a warning, Munro picked up papers, records and what goods he could carry, and sprinted to safety on the common outside the stockade.

"It has not been ascertained how the fire took place, but it is generally believed, it was by design, and by persons interested in the lumber trade," an official report stated. "Contracts had been previously made, for all the lumber at the mills, and which could be sawed this season, which was a novel arrangement in the Country." [2]

Another version has persisted—and more likely it is the true one—and it places the blame on John Harvey, a baker, or on his hired man Peter Chartrand. Having run out of flour, according to the story, either Harvey or Chartrand went to the stable adjoining the shop, to hitch up the cart to drive to May's mill for a fresh supply. The driver, whichever one it was, knocked out his pipe; a live coal was blown into the hay. Within a few seconds the fire fattened on the hay, straw and dry timbers and quickly spread to neighboring buildings.

The alarm, sounded by Munro and others, brought out all citizens, men and women, to fight the flames. James Dodemead, the fire warden, mobilized the early-morning tipplers who lounged in his tavern, and rushed them to the battle line with the town's decrepit fire pump. In their excitement, the fire-fighters made the mistake of dropping their suction pipe into a hatter's vat instead of running it to the river. Bits of fur and felt shreds promptly clogged it into uselessness. A bucket brigade already was at work; soldiers began pulling down houses to make a fire break. Across the river in Sandwich, John Askin saw a plume of black smoke rising from Detroit. Gathering up his sons and *engagees*, he piled them into his boat and steered for the American shore to do what he could.[3] But it was to no avail. The fire had its teeth firmly set into the combustible village, and there was no shaking it loose. Someone ran to St. Anne's and warned the worshippers. Father Dilhet finished the Mass in a hurry; then he and Father Richard carried the vestments and sacred vessels to a safe place. "The smoke and flames rose to a prodigious height and presented a spectacle that was both majestic and horrible," Pere Dilhet recorded.[4]

"In less than two hours the whole town was in flames, and before three o'clock not a vestige of a house (except the chimneys) was visible within the limits of Detroit," Munro stated in a report to William Henry Harrison, governor of Indiana Territory.[5]

A more detailed account of the disaster was published in the *National Intelligencer* of September 6, 1805. "About 300 edifices, of all kinds, were consumed, among which were nearly an hundred dwelling houses, the church, several stores, the citadel, with officers' and soldiers' barracks, contractors' stores, United States store, etc., etc . . . the old Block House, at the south end, escaped." Even the stockade was destroyed. Almost immediately beyond control, the fire was so fierce it ran against the wind. The narrow streets offered no refuge; the people, abandoning their property, fled to the fields outside the town or clambered into boats and canoes and pushed out into the river. It was a miracle no lives were lost; only two persons, an old woman and a child, were injured.

The miserable populace and members of the garrison gathered on the common, below the fort. Despairing, the citizens compared their losses. Naturally, the wealthier merchants had suffered the most. Joseph Thibault inventoried his loss at £7,711 7s; George Meldrum, £3,000; Robert Abbott, and the firm of Robinson Martin, £2,500 each. The church and presbytery, valued at £6,000 were completely destroyed. John Harvey, who had been the cause of it all, got off comparatively easy. His loss was only £400.[6] Contemplating the scene of misery and destruction, Father Richard is said to have been moved to murmur: *"Speramus meliora; resurget cineribus"*—"We hope for better thing; it will arise from its ashes." In time a new city, rising phoenix-like out of its dark despair, would adopt the priest's words for its official motto.

But Pere Gabriel had little time either for prayers or prophecy. He was off, almost at once, on a mercy errand, seeking quarters for the dispossessed in farmhouses up and down the river—on the Canadian as well as the American shore—and gathering food, clothes and blankets. Jacques Girardin, another village baker, had just finished kneading his dough and shaping his loaves when the fire started. The bread was in the oven which he didn't have time to light. Later, poking about the ruins, he found his bread, baked to a golden crusty brown by the intense heat. He distributed it to the hungry, dispirited crowd huddled on the common.

"The people," reported the *National Intelligencer,* "are scattered up and down the settlement, crowding the houses even to overflowing, occupying hovels and everything having the shape of an edifice, and several families are encamped in booths upon the public common and highways."

Eleven days passed before the arrival of Woodward, but the spectacle of desolation had not changed.

3

When Woodward reached Detroit on June 30, 1805, he found his work awaiting him. He was met at the landing by Frederick Bates, an amiable young Virginian, who was to be one of his associates on the territorial bench. Bates introduced the new arrival to James May who gave him lodgings in his house on the outskirts of town. The following morning, July 1, the homeless inhabitants of the town turned out for an open air reception. Woodward's fame, he discovered, had preceded him. A man who was on intimate terms with the president; who had rubbed shoulders with congressmen and ministers of state—famous characters known on the frontier only through the medium of an occasional fugitive newspaper from the east—such a man was worth looking at.

Woodward, they made it clear, was more than a curiosity. He was a community hope. He represented authority, and how Detroit needed that! For more than three weeks the citizens had bickered among themselves about when and how they should start to rebuild. Some, satisfied with things as they had been, proposed raising their new homes and shops on the blackened ruins of the old buildings, laying out a new town within the congested precincts of the old. Others demanded more room, insisting on spreading out over the common. Finally, in desperation, it was decided to do both—utilize the old site and appropriate as much of the common as was necessary to provide elbow room.

It was obvious to the thoughtful that it would be folly to rebuild without careful surveys and a pre-determined city plan. A town superimposed on the wreckage of the old one, even with additional space, would not be adequate. But there was no one with authority to make the necessary decisions and then enforce them. Despite the claims to the common, based on some vague, half-forgotten and unproved French grants, the land outside the old stockade was government property. It could not be taken for private use until the government had transferred title to the freeholders. With no visible government nearer than Washington, who would do this? Bates, who had lived for several years in Detroit, and who had suffered personal loss in the fire, had been appointed a member of the new territorial government—the Governor and Judges—but he had not taken his oath of office. Therefore, he could not speak with authority. Now Woodward was on the scene, bearing the prestige of important Washington connections. What would he say? Could the building begin?

Quickly Bates briefed Woodward on the situation; convincing him the old location would not do. The military made its wishes known. It desired no obstructions between the fort and the river. "If, in rebuilding the Town, such arrangements could be made, as to remove the buildings farther from the Fort, it would be desireable; which . . . may be done by an exchange of private for public lands," was the suggestion of headquarters.[7]

Like Bates, Woodward recognized that it was no problem for him alone to resolve. He had not been sworn in either; therefore he could not act. To the crowd assembled in William Macomb's orchard, waiting for him to assume the role of judge, he offered only common sense advice. The new governor, William Hull, and the territorial secretary, Stanley Griswold, who, with the judges comprised the full complement of government, were expected to arrive momentarily. Until then, no one had authority to do anything. Go back to whatever quarters they then occupied, Woodward advised; go back to the farmhouses of their friends and relatives where they had found refuge, or to the tents and makeshift lean-tos they had thrown up. A few more nights as they had spent the past twenty would not be fatal. As soon as Governor Hull arrived, decisions could be made. Bates nodded his agreement. The people appreciated the reasonableness of Woodward's suggestion. They agreed to do nothing for a fortnight.

True to Woodward's prediction, Governor Hull, accompanied by Secretary Griswold, arrived from Albany later that same day. The following morning, as his first official act, Hull administered the oaths of office to Woodward and Bates—the former, by virtue of a commission bearing the earlier date, becoming chief justice. The government of Michigan Territory finally began to function. Woodward assumed the role in which he would dominate the social and political life of this outpost of American civilization for many years.

4

The new government of Michigan Territory was confronted by serious problems. The disaster of fire was local and superficial. The real difficulty lay much deeper than the smouldering rubble that once had been Detroit.

The Territory's troubles could be traced back to the end of the Revolutionary War. Victory at Yorktown and the Treaty of Paris endowed the seaboard colonies with a vast hinterland between the Alleghenies and the Mississippi of which a substantial part lay between the Great Lakes and the Ohio River. On the basis of royal charters and tenuous colonial claims, often conflicting, New York, Massachusetts, Connecticut and Virginia each claimed the area as its property. But the new United States was jealous of these claims; the "have not" states regarded the West as a public domain in which confederation could be achieved through compromise. The claimant states, in the interests of harmony, ceded their rights to the national government.

This, in turn, created a new problem. The disputed area was rich in furs, navigable waters, timber and arable land. It was sparsely occupied, principally by Indians, although it contained some white settlements. Traditionally expansionist in their political viewpoint, Americans along the northern and middle seaboard instinctively looked upon the western territory as an arena for exploitation and growth.

By 1787 it became evident that parts of the Northwest would soon be invaded by settlers from the East, and a plan of government became imperative. A convention in Philadelphia was laboriously striving to frame a Federal Constitution. At the same time, Congress, meeting in New York, adopted an Ordinance for the Government of the Territory Northwest of the Ohio River. Known variously as the Ordinance of 1787, or the Northwest Ordinance, this charter was remarkable. Thomas M. Cooley declared it "immortal for the grand results which have followed from its adoption, not less than for the wisdom and far-seeing statesmanship that conceived and gave form to its provisions."[8]

The remarkable thing is that the members of Congress in New York were able to produce such a document as the Ordinance. Into it they wrote a provision prohibiting slavery for all time in the Northwest Territory. They stipulated that the Territory and its subdivisions should always remain part of the United States; they ordained freedom of religion, wrote a bill of rights, recognized the inviolability of contracts, and encouraged education as a moral essential of good government. Then they decreed that the Northwest, when its districts acquired prescribed populations, might be divided into not less than three nor more than five states.

The Philadelphia Convention completed its work in September, 1787, but the Constitution was not ratified until two years later. Meanwhile, the Confederation had made the Ordinance operative, and the first Congress of the new Union confirmed it. As its governing body, the president, with consent of the Senate, appointed a governor as executive, and three judges to exercise the judicial function. The governor and judges together would comprise a legislative board. The legislative body was given no original jurisdiction. It could only adopt laws already in force in the original states. Before becoming effective, new laws were to be reviewed and approved by Congress. Thus, there was no real self-government. It was there that the framers of the Ordinance fell short of the democratic ideal. While they provided an enduring and noble social document, it was not a fundamentally democratic one.

Not everyone agreed that the Ordinance was perfect. After having held territorial office, Augustus Woodward said: "I have always considered these territorial establishments, most wretched systems of government. . . . The evil appears to be in the system, and not in the men." [9] His opinion is substantiated by the later testimony that the Ordinance as it evolved, was a "most undemocratic and really extraordinary form of temporary government," stressing a co-mingling of executive, legislative and judicial duties in one group "contrary to the general spirit of the men who framed the Constitution with its divided powers." [10]

Perfect or not, the Ordinance of 1787 functioned. By 1799, the influx of settlers had provided a population large enough to warrant a popularly elected and representative legislature. A year later, Congress divided the Northwest Territory, creating Indiana Territory out of its western half. Ohio and eastern Michigan continued to be known as the Northwest Territory until 1802. Then, as Ohio prepared for statehood, a new alignment was made with all of Michigan and the remainder of the Northwest being assigned to Indiana. Thus the original Northwest Territory passed out of existence as a political unit, to remain only as a geographic or social abstraction. Whereas the people of Detroit and the neighboring settlements, or in the upper lakes region, had formerly looked to Marietta, Cincinnati or Chillicothe as their seat of government, they now turned to Vincennes where Governor William Henry Harrison and a new set of territorial judges ruled.

It soon became evident to the citizens of Michigan that this was not a satisfactory arrangement. Cincinnati and Chillicothe had been accessible; Vincennes was not. Governor Harrison and the territorial dignitaries made infrequent visits, but the people were, for all practical purposes, denied recourse to the courts. When Indiana Territory, in 1804, advanced to the second stage of government with a popular legislature, the remote citizens of Detroit did not learn of the change until it was too late to elect a representative from their district. The result was agitation for territorial status for Michigan.

"Suffer us to entreat you," Robert Abbott of Detroit petitioned Congress in 1804, "to have justice promptly and impartially administered; compel us not to wander seven hundred miles thro' inhospitable deserts, for the redress of wrongs, which the uncertainty of punishment, and the hopes of impunity, have, perhaps, in many instances caused us to suffer." [11] Abbott's voice, and those of his fellow townsmen, carried to Washington and produced results. On January 11, 1805, Congress passed a bill, effective "from and after" June 30, which established Michigan Territory. A major reason for that act was to provide an adequate administration of justice.[12]

5

As soon as Governor Hull arrived at Detroit on July 1, 1805, he inaugurated his government by the simple process of swearing in his co-officials, Secretary Griswold, and the two judges, Woodward and Bates. Hull himself had been sworn in at Albany on his way west by Vice President George Clinton. It made little difference that the vice president, according to Secretary of State Madison, "was incompetent to administer oaths." The fact that Michigan's first government began under a cloud of illegality might have been regarded as an ill-omen. However, a note of solemnity was added to the occasion by Captain Dyson, commandant of the fort, who trundled out his artillery and banged away with a ground-shaking salute.

Hull found temporary living quarters in a farmhouse a mile up-river from Detroit. His home had been in Newton, Massachusetts. His wife, his son Abraham, two daughters, Ann and Maria, and his private secretary, Elisha Avery, accompanied him to Michigan. The Governor, a native of Connecticut, was fifty-two. He had attended Yale where he first studied for the ministry, then for the law. As an undergraduate he had been the roommate of the immortal Nathan Hale. Like Hale, he joined the Continental army and by following Anthony Wayne in the heroic assault on Stony Point, won a generous measure of distinction. As an aide to Baron von Steuben, he helped reorganize Washington's army. After the war he was sent on two diplomatic missions, without notable success, seeking surrender of the western posts remaining in British hands. Later he traveled in Europe; on his return he became a judge in Massachusetts. Then, because of his war record, and because he was a Republican in a Federalist state, Jefferson appointed him governor of Michigan Territory. As it turned out, the appointment was an unfortunate one, both for Hull and the Territory.

Hull was a tall, handsome, courtly man, well educated, sensitive and, as it has been said, possessing an ideal judicial temperament. But he was no administrator; he was inclined to be imperious and arrogant, and he did not know how to conciliate those who opposed him. He was indecisive and, as he grew older, timid. The frontier with its uncertain peace, always in danger of being terminated by the British and Indians, made him uneasy. Eventually, when war did break out in 1812, Hull, mis-caste against his will in the role of military leader, ended an otherwise honorable if unspectacular career in black disgrace.

The chief function of the territorial secretary was to occupy the gubernatorial chair when the chief executive was absent from the Territory. Stanley Griswold, first to hold this office, was, like Hull, a native of Connecticut and a Revolutionary veteran. A political jack-of-all-trades, he had been a teacher, minister and editor of a newspaper in New Hampshire. His support of the administration brought him to Jefferson's favorable attention and won him his post in Michigan. He had a quarrelsome disposition; he regarded himself as the most able man in the new government, but did nothing to prove it. He "considered the clerical work of his office beneath his dignity," and soon became openly antagonistic to his colleagues. Within a short time, after Hull had "called on Mr. G. in pretty severe terms,"[13] and the officers of the garrison had viewed his disruptive activities with consternation, he was dismissed and left the Territory, unhonored and unsung. He was succeeded in 1808 by Reuben Atwater, a more even-tempered gentleman who possessed some ability, and who owed his appointment to the fact that his brother-in-law, Stephen R. Bradley, of Vermont, was president pro-term of the United States Senate.

On the judicial side, Woodward's only associate at the beginning was Frederick Bates. A third appointee, Samuel Huntington, of Ohio, declined to serve. Bates, a member of a Quaker family, was born in Goochland County, Virginia, in 1777. After clerking in a law office, he became a civilian employe of the Quartermaster Department and went to Detroit with Wayne's army in 1796. In 1802 he branched out for himself as a merchant; served as postmaster of Detroit, and a member of the land board. He had little legal experience, and his first act, after being notified of his judicial appointment, was to send to Albany for a copy of Blackstone. An able, frank and friendly man, he and Woodward became good friends. His tenure in Michigan was brief; because he was an expert on land titles, Jefferson transferred him in 1807 to St. Louis as secretary and land title recorder of Louisiana Territory. There he had a long and honorable career and in time became governor of Missouri Territory. His younger brother Edward, an equally capable man, became a power in western politics and eventually entered the cabinet of Abraham Lincoln as attorney general.

To fill the vacancy resulting from Huntington's refusal to accept the office, the president named John Griffin, a languid aristocrat, hypochondriac, and general incompetent. Griffin was the grandson of the Scottish Earl of Traquhair at whose castle in Peebles he was born while his father, Cyrus, was studying law at Edinburgh and London's Middle Temple. John was a graduate of William and

Mary College, and first held office as judge of Indiana Territory. Neither the climate nor his associations at Vincennes suited him. On October 3, 1805, his father asked the president to transfer John to Michigan. A Virginia neighbor of Jefferson's, a signer of the Declaration of Independence, and president of the last Continental Congress, Cyrus Griffin was a man whose requests were not to be disregarded. John was shifted to Detroit where he promptly came under the complete domination of Woodward to whom he deferred as "My Lord Chief Justice." His entire career in Michigan was succinctly summed up by William Woodbridge who called him "a man of respectable literary requirements, of good taste and manners, but with a mind lamentably inert."

The people of Detroit were cordial to, but not awed by, this group of officials who had been sent to rule them. There was much criticism of Jefferson's selections. Among them were no westerners, familiar with the problems of a French-American frontier society. There may be justification for that complaint, but experienced administrators and jurists were hard to find on the frontier in 1805. In making his appointments, the president was primarily concerned with doing the handsome thing for his political friends. He was performing a political function with the feeling, no doubt, that he was making the best possible choices, men of good character who would, he hoped, also display ability.

If Michigan failed to be impressed by the Governor and Judges, the latter certainly exhibited no enthusiasm for either the Territory or its inhabitants. Geographically, Michigan Territory as established by the act of January 11, 1805 had almost the same boundaries as the present State of Michigan. In all this vast area, above and below the Straits of Mackinac, there was a total white population of four thousand. Most of the people lived in Detroit or on farms nearby. There was a small settlement on the Raisin River known as Frenchtown. At Mackinac and Sault Ste. Marie there were trading posts, but in neither place was the population stable. From a dozen permanent inhabitants, more or less, most of the year, it swelled to several hundred when the trappers and Indians came in to sell their furs.

Outside Detroit nearly all the inhabitants were French, familiar only with their native tongue. Most of them were blissfully illiterate. Still, they were not lacking a homespun culture that was typically their own. Most of the men were farmers, and indifferent ones at that; but among them were some artisans and craftsmen. They affected a certain piety, but their morals, in many instances, were inclined to be somewhat free and easy. In the remote districts, the benefits of the church were beyond their reach; at Mackinac, most of the children were illegitimate half-breeds.[14] But despite their faults which did not stem from any natural degradation, they were a warm-hearted, high-spirited people, always ready to frolic when the fiddles were tuned and the peach brandy or cider was set out. Their self-dependence bred a contentiousness and sharpness of temper which made them as quick to quarrel as to play.

When the United States took possession of the Territory from the British in 1796, many of the leading, prosperous citizens of Detroit followed the Union Jack across the river to Sandwich in Canada. Enough American, English and Scotch businessmen remained to give the town a commercial flavor and a society with an air quite different from that of the habitant element. The merchant-trader group lived in relative luxury. They entertained frequently and lavishly, and broke the monotony of their isolation with banquets, balls, picnics, flirtations—and intrigue.

"In no part of the United States where I have resided is the expense of living so great as at this place," Governor Hull said. Secretary Griswold commented: "It is reduced to a certainty that this government cannot proceed without some additional pecuniary aid from Congress. Its seat is established at a place which combines all the disadvantages of an old and new settlement, without one of the advantages of either. Luxury, the relic of British fortunes formerly squandered here, and of a once flourishing commerce, continues its empire, though I am happy to think it is on the decline. Fashion, ceremony, and expense are great, far beyond the present abilities of the inhabitants."

Account books of the period bear out Griswold's complaint. Fine clothes, expensive and handsomely made furniture and household goods, including imported china, books, musical instruments, silver and pewter ware; fancy wines and foodstuffs fit for the gourmet's table, were regular imports from the eastern markets. It is significant that at this period, at least seven silversmiths flourished in this backwoods town, although much of their work was for the Indian trade.[15] In such a society, Woodward's annual salary of eight hundred dollars did not go far.

Adopting a paternalistic attitude toward the inhabitants from the beginning, Governor Hull displayed a tendency to underestimate them. The result soon was distrust on both sides.

"When it is remembered that the troops of Louis the XIVth came without women, the description of persons constituting the second generation will not be difficult to conceive," Hull wrote with patronizing superciliousness.[16]

Woodward never shared Hull's disdain for the French; yet to some extent he suffered from the attitude of other members of the government. Hull, he complained, lacked close contact with the inhabitants. The easterner, he said, who put on airs earned the contempt of the British, who applied the term "Yankee" as an epithet. "The French do not use this term, though they entertain the same ideas; and perhaps with still greater force," he said. "They have another term, which answers them the same purpose. It is the term 'Bostonnois' which they pronounce 'Bostonnais,' or 'sacré cochon de Bostonnais' is their most virulent term of abuse when they are displeased with an American, or with a person from the eastern states particularly."[17]

This, then, was the atmosphere and environment in which Woodward found himself. He could hardly have regarded them with enthusiasm, either from a personal or official viewpoint.

CHAPTER II

Mr. Jefferson's Disciple

1

A FEW DAYS after Augustus Brevoort Woodward came to Detroit there was a total eclipse of the sun. Obviously there could be no connection between the two phenomena. But some of the natives of his adopted city, particularly those of a superstitious turn of mind, may have thought his appearance on the scene was occasion for the sun to hide its face. Such was his impact upon the Territory of Michigan.

In 1805, Woodward was in his thirty-first year. He was born in New York in 1774 and baptized in the Reformed Dutch Church on November 6 of that year. The name Augustus was an after-thought of his own, adopted many years later, in place of his baptismal name of Elias. Perhaps he felt that Augustus was more elegant and better suited his personality than the plebian Elias.

The second son of John and Ann Silvester Woodward, Augustus —or Elias—was the descendant on his father's side of stalwart middle-class English stock. On the distaff side, he was related to a family of prosperous and influential Dutch burghers. His uncle, Elias Brevoort, was one of pre-Revolutionary Manhattan's leading citizens, and it was, no doubt, with an eye on his substantial estate, that Ann bestowed his name upon her unappreciative son.

In 1774 the Woodward family lived comfortably in a house at the northwest corner of Pine and Pearl streets. John was solidly established as a merchant and importer, and the scope of his enterprise, described in his card published December 23, 1773, suggests that his business was profitable. The advertisement called New York's attention to the fact that it could obtain "Irish linens, from 18d to 8s per Yard, Callicoes, cottons and Chintzes, Tabborets, Moreens, etc., to be sold upon very reasonable terms, for Cash, three or six months Credit, by John Woodward, At his store, near the Fly Market, who has for sale a Quantity of best New York Rum." A few weeks later, January 25, 1774, the *New York Gazette and the Weekly Mercury* carried the simple notice: "John Woodward imports materials."

Life might have continued to be pleasant and profitable for John had it not been for the turn that politics was taking. Such issues as the Quebec Act, the Navigation Act and the Stamp Act combined to implant disturbing thoughts in the minds of American colonists. These were viewed in certain quarters on both sides of the Atlantic as not conforming to the loyalties which all Englishmen owed their lord and sovereign, George III.

Along with many of his brethren of the merchant class, John Woodward took the radical side in the dispute. When war started, John organized a company of artillery and led it out to fight on the side of liberty. The result was hardship and ruin for him. He leased his shop from Robert Gilbert Livingston, member of a prominent family and a rich landowner. Livingston was a Tory who heartily disapproved of his tenant's political beliefs. Early in the seven-year period of British occupation, during all of which Woodward was with the Continental army, his store was repossessed by Livingston, and his stock was confiscated. Whether his family remained in New York during the war is not known. It is possible they found haven with the Brevoorts.

After the war, John apparently had difficulty re-establishing himself in business and the family's fortunes seemed to have been at low ebb from this time on. In 1789, at the age of fifteen, young Elias enrolled at Columbia College in the class of 1793. Undoubtedly this was accomplished through the bounty of his uncle. He must also have lived in the Brevoort home as an undergraduate because at this time the rest of his family moved to Philadelphia where John attempted unsuccessfully to build a new business.

Of young Woodward's college life little is known beyond the fact that he earned an A.B. degree, that he received an excellent classical education "and appeared eager, on all occasions, to display his knowledge." [1] Certainly he read widely as a student; he was well grounded in Greek and Latin, and he learned to speak French fluently. More important, he began to exhibit a lively inquisitiveness, a marked bent for scholarly investigation, and a hunger for information and knowledge that never dulled. At no time in his life, whether on the frontier or in more polished surroundings, was he ever without a generous supply of books.

At an early age, possibly during his college days, Woodward acquired the habit of keeping a small notebook in which he jotted down such thoughts and impressions as came to him, either from reading or from conversation. Some of these notations suggest a certain amount of soul-searching, and reveal an immaturity of mind. Apparently he considered them as a set of rules for personal guidance in society.

"I want no constant intercourse," he wrote; "no unwise familiarity. Of course I must be respectful but reserved, never rude, but never relaxed."

And again:

"An insatiable thirst of admiration is a silly weakness. Of what value is the enthusiastic admiration of another? A steady approbation of one's associates may prove highly serviceable to us, but mere admiration is of no value and is frequently the forerunner of contempt and disesteem. . . . He who commits an action which debases him in his own mind, besides its other evil consequences, lays up a store of future misery, which will haunt him as long as the memory of the deed remains."

This has the sound of a young man not wholly sure of himself. He begins to exhibit a sharper perception when, sandwiched in between notes on Adam Smith's *Wealth of Nations* there appears this observation: "Perhaps people never appear to more advantage than when they dare give the reins to their imagination and vivacity, and leave to others the care of being wise." That has the sound of a much more attractive Augustus Brevoort Woodward.[2]

In 1793, after his graduation, Augustus joined his family in Philadelphia where for the next two years he was employed as a clerk in the Treasury Department at a salary of $480. His father, too, at this time abandoned hope of ever again getting a foothold in business. He claimed the patriot's reward and obtained public employment, first in the office of the Register General; later as transcribing clerk to the Pennsylvania House of Representatives.

Augustus did not remain long in Philadelphia. In 1795 he was in Rockbridge County, Virginia, presumably teaching at Liberty Hall Academy in Lexington, and possibly studying law at the same time. In 1797 he was in Greenbrier, now in West Virginia. There he received word of the death of his uncle Elias Brevoort who remembered him in his will with a bequest of £150. With his inheritance in his pocket, he set out for the new city of Washington on the Potomac where he invested in real estate. At this time he described himself as a resident of Greenbrier.

While in Rockbridge County in 1795 an event occurred which had great influence on his life. He was received at Monticello and admitted to Thomas Jefferson's circle of intimates. It is unfortunate that Woodward left no account of their first meeting or the circumstances that brought it about. All that is known is contained in a letter written several years later to Jefferson in which he refers to being in Rockbridge in 1795, "just before I had the happiness of a first interview at Monticello." [3] This suggests that Woodward sought Jefferson out and asked permission to present himself at the home on the hill top near Charlottesville. But it does not entirely rule out the possibility that he was referring only to his first visit to Monticello, and that he and Jefferson may have met earlier —in Philadelphia, for instance.

This is only speculation. What is known is that the happy occasion to which Woodward referred was the first of many visits. He was a regular caller at Monticello whenever he was in the vicinity. It also marked the beginning of an enduring friendship that was to be the delight of Woodward's life, and which was not without value to Jefferson. Where one gained an idol, the other gained a worshipful disciple.

2

As a small-scale landed proprietor of Washington, Augustus Woodward's heart was where his treasure lay. Whatever it was that had taken him to Greenbrier lost its attraction and shortly before the beginning of the new century he changed his address to Georgetown in the District of Columbia. He had high hopes for neighboring Washington which at that time was emerging as something more substantial than just a plan on Charles L'Enfant's drawing board.

His acquaintance with L'Enfant imbued him with the Frenchman's enthusiasm for the new city. He could visualize the projected seat of government with its broad avenues, the parks and the handsome public buildings. Altogether he acquired ten parcels or groups of parcels of property upon which he paid taxes. Upon some of his lots, houses were erected. On the inside cover of his pocket notebook he pasted a copy of L'Enfant's plan for Washington (this was to come in handy later on in Detroit) with the location of his properties pricked out on it. One of his lots, No. 348, was close to the White House. The others were on or just off Pennsylvania avenue, midway between the White House and the Capitol site. On one of these, at Pennsylvania and Tenth, he eventually built a residence where he lived for a time with his sister, Maria. Thus, when the Federal government moved to Washington with its one hundred and thirty-six employes in June, 1800, Woodward had already acquired a solid interest in the town.

His stay in Georgetown was brief. He selected Alexandria as the logical place to hang out his shingle. Alexandria was then within the boundaries of the District of Columbia, and, as the seat of its law courts, cases originating in Washington were first tried in Alexandria. However, much of his practice was on the north side of the Potomac in the Maryland courts.

"The first court I attended [in Prince George's County, Maryland] was April 1799," Woodward wrote. He did not attend the September term that year, but he was on hand again in April, 1800, and "I attended every court since being eight courts.—The first cause I tried in prince george's was Sept. 18, 1801." [4]

On March 23, 1801, having first visited one of the barbershops on Pennsylvania avenue, Woodward arrayed himself in his best attire. This consisted of a long, loose-fitting blue coat with enormous brass buttons, a scarlet cravat, and buff waistcoat. The latter was worn open and from it "protruded an immense mass of ruffles. These last, together with the broad ruffles at his wrists, were invariably so soiled that it might almost be doubted whether they had ever been white. His pantaloons [if descriptions of him can be believed] hung in folds to his feet, meeting a pair of boots which were always well greased." [5] Thus impressively, if not immaculately, clad, he presented himself with ten other attorneys at the opening of the first session of the new court of the District of Columbia and was admitted to practice before it.[6]

If Augustus Woodward on this occasion—as well as on others—

fell somewhat short of being a macaroni, it must be acknowledged that whatever fame he ultimately achieved was not founded on his manly beauty. In fact, if we can trust his contemporaries, he might have qualified as the prototype of Irving's Ichabod Crane. Like the Sleepy Hollow schoolmaster, the ungainly and grotesque were about equally blended in him. He was tall, about six feet three or four, lean and stooped. His complexion was sallow, and the most striking feature of a long, narrow face was a big nose. He had a luxuriant crop of dark hair; this was his pride and represented the only outward evidence of vanity. He patronized only the best hairdressers. The absence of a competent barber in Detroit really distressed him. Once, being unable to find a barber who satisfied him, he asked a member of the Detroit bar to recommend someone who could trim his hair in the "improved fashion." The lawyer sent him to Austin E. Wing, no barber, but one of the town's leading businessmen. Wing obliged the judge, but the result was so unfortunate that for the next two weeks the sensitive Woodward found it necessary to hide his shame by wearing his hat indoors as well as out.

All who knew him commented on his slovenliness, but perhaps this was in emulation of Jefferson. If the president could advertise his democratic principles by receiving the British ambassador in a rumpled dressing gown and slippers, who was Woodward to try to outshine his beloved chief!

Actually, Woodward's appearance was a manifestation of an eccentricity in which he seemed to take a puckish delight, and which he went out of his way to stress. There were times when his conduct seemed as bizarre as his appearance, and it may be suspected that both were largely affected as a means of drawing attention to himself. What the world thought of his personal idiosyncrasies bothered him little. He considered himself above the public opinion of the frontier if not that of Washington. Self-confidence rather than self-esteem was his predominant trait, and if he was ever assailed by self-doubt the occasion was not made a matter of record.

"Whatever was odd and unreasonable," said Silas Farmer who devotes many pages of his monumental history of early Detroit to Woodward, "he was sure to do. If there was a thunderstorm, his chair was placed outside the door, and he would calmly sit and take his showerbath. His room, which was both office and sleeping apartment, was destitute of a bookcase, and many valuable papers lay in a heap in one corner, and clothing for the wash in another. Sweeping was never done, lest his books should be deranged, and they were where he left them, some on the floor, some on the chairs, and some on the table."

He made no profession of religious interest, but nothing that he ever said or did suggested that he was irreligious. In all probability he was as Jeffersonian in his attitude toward formal religion as he was in politics. He deplored sectarianism. Signing a charter for the incorporation of Detroit's First Methodist Society in 1822, he appended the following: "I should greatly prefer the union of all protestants under the name of evangelistic churches, as adopted in Germany and Prussia . . . to the retention of the existing sectarian distinctions." During his years in Detroit he was on easy terms with the clergy and religious groups; his intimacy with Father Richard was such that Father Dilhet concluded, mistakenly, that Woodward was a Catholic. If he failed to give any outward sign of religious feeling, if he never affiliated with any church body, he did not on any occasion display either impiety or looseness of character. Woodward was never known to use profanity, nor was his life ever touched by scandal or evidence of moral laxity.

The public impression of Woodward throughout his entire career was colored by his eccentricity. It was remembered long after his solid virtues were forgotten—or conveniently overlooked for political reasons, as was often the case.

"In your religious, your moral, political and social character we see no bud of promise to flatter us with the hope that any latent virtue may be found," declared one of his detractors in a diatribe published in the *Detroit Gazette* in the heat of a political controversy. "The portals of your narrow, selfish soul are as firmly barred against every generous or noble sentiment as the dark cave of Cerberus. You are literally without a friend. So disgusting is your character in every point of view, that it is really a matter of curious speculation how or by what strange fatality such a man could have been palmed upon this territory." [7]

No man could have been that bad. By an excess of abuse, his

political opponents sometimes made themselves ridiculous, but unfortunately for Woodward, his enemies often had the last word, and the libels have persisted to color the evaluations of posterity.

Yet, despite his foibles, and the abuse heaped upon him, even his most malicious critics were at times forced to concede his genuine ability. The term "genius" is often used in references to him. Farmer, who was neither fair nor friendly in his judgments of Woodward, had to admit that he was "really learned and accomplished," and "entertaining and agreeable in conversation."

"With all his eccentricity," Farmer said, "he would often manifest the most painstaking research, and endeavor to please his friends and gratify the public; but what he would do, or leave undone, could never be foretold."

He was called toady and time-server because he was respectful in his letters to Jefferson and Madison—men whom he genuinely admired. Yet the writer making this charge says "he could be courteous and affable if occasion required it." [8]

A judicious estimate of Woodward was made by Thomas M. Cooley, one of the most distinguished scholars and jurists to serve on the Michigan State Supreme Court. He said: "The chief justice was pronounced by one of his subsequent associates to be 'a wild theorist, fit only to extract sunbeams from cucumbers;' but this characterization presents only one side of his erratic and peculiar nature. He was a theorist, but not a mere dreamer; his ability was very considerable, and, in some respects, very substantial. In doing what he chose to do he was perfectly fearless." [9]

James V. Campbell, another Supreme Court justice of a later period, found little to admire in Woodward and accused him of "ridiculous vaporing and pomposity . . . of audacious impudence which, under the name of eccentricity, has sometimes characterized men of mark." Yet even Justice Campbell was constrained to admit that Woodward and Jefferson possessed many common characteristics and that "Judge Woodward was one of those strange compounds of intellectual power and wisdom in great emergencies." [10]

An objective consideration of the personal traits of Augustus B. Woodward leads to the conclusion that he delighted in posing as an eccentric; that he affected the attitude partly from contempt for the mediocrities by whom he was often surrounded in public life. At any rate, his idiosyncrasies alternately delighted and dismayed the citizens and succeeded in establishing him as part of Michigan's folklore.

3

When the Federal government moved to Washington, Woodward observed that "it came agitated by political conquest. It forgot its inconvenience and privation in the ardor of triumph." That was a reflection of his own exuberance, the feeling of stimulation aroused in him by being a part of the new city. He was there before it was the seat of government; before Abigail Adams hung her wash in the East Room of the President's Palace. He knew it when a public market occupied part of the White House grounds and the tree stumps stood in Pennsylvania avenue. He had a personal and financial interest in the new town. With characteristic energy and imagination, he went to work to make something worth while of that interest. Woodward never saw the things in which he had a part as anything less than tremendous. While Washington still consisted of little more than a few boarding houses and unfinished government buildings, it was already a cosmopolitan city in his eyes, emerging into an era of unequalled grandeur.

From the beginning of his residence in the District of Columbia —or Territory of Columbia as it was often called in those days— Woodward took an active and enthusiastic part in civic affairs, both social and political. He was hardly settled in his new surroundings before he donned the sword and single epaulet of an ensign in the District militia. He devoted much time to a committee to aid the poor. There were tea parties, dancing assemblies, fine dinners at Stelle's tavern or Tunnicliff's hotel. And he could trot back and forth between his own lodgings and those of Mr. Jefferson who, prior to 1801, was only the vice president and didn't have very much to do. He and Jefferson could sit comfortably, toasting their shins before a fire, while talking over their theories of government. At this time Woodward was reading the works of the Abbe Raynal, and no doubt he and Jefferson concurred with the French philosopher's opinion that any country was better for an occasional peaceful revolution. Something of the sort was needed, they must have agreed, to end the abuses of the Federalist Party and inaugurate the new era of the common man. In season, there were visits to Monticello and much exchanging of books.

Politics of the local variety interested Woodward. The Federal government settled in Washington with the constitutional authority to "exercise exclusive legislation in all Cases whatsoever over such District . . . as may become the Seat of Government of the United States." At first this authority was not actually exercised and the District found itself under the jurisdiction of two states and three counties. Its citizens, then as now, were political stepchildren; little better than wards of a national government. It was a condition which most residents of the District disliked, Woodward included. Was a man expected to live in the din of fierce political battles and have no part in them? Was he to own property and pay taxes, but have no vote for councilman, congressman or president? Not if Woodward could help it!

He became a leader of the faction which demanded the franchise as the republican American right, and clamored for a municipal government under the principle of home rule. Although at this time, 1801, Woodward professed adherence to no political party, he still was able to proclaim that "an original principle of republicanism" was to give "all those who are governed by laws, the right to participate in the formation of them."

Woodward undertook to furnish Congress with a plan. In a series of pamphlets entitled *Considerations on the Government of the Territory of Columbia,* he first defined and then defended a system of self-government. There were at least eight of these essays between 1801 and 1803; most of them were signed by the nom de plume Epaminondus. Woodward's style was lucid and sharp. Even after the passage of one hundred and fifty years, his ideas would probably have strong appeal for many of the present day voteless residents of the District. He insisted "that the government of the United States is under an obligation to exercise exclusive legislation over the seat of the national government, as soon as it can conveniently be done." [11]

Congress examined the matter, and it was tentatively proposed that the whole body of laws of Maryland and Virginia be adopted for the District. This received little attention because it was obviously inadequate, making no provision either for administrative machinery or fiscal responsibility. As an alternative, Woodward suggested an amendment to the Constitution to permit the District to have representation in both the Senate and the House of Representatives, and a voice in the election of the president and vice president. For the District itself, he proposed a territorial form of government. This would include a legislature elected by the citizens to whom the right of universal suffrage would be extended. A governor with veto power would be appointed by the president. Congress could repeal any law adopted by the District legislature.

This was going even further than the concept of territorial government which was laid down in the Ordinance of 1787, but the circumstances were different. The power to legislate over the District, Woodward felt, had the same inherency as the constitutional right of Congress to regulate forts and arsenals. But even here he noted a difference, "no less great as to mode, than as to time." Those who lived on military reservations must, because of the nature of the establishments, be prepared to give up some part of their suffrage.

"But far different is the situation of a respectable national metropolis," he pointed out. "This is from its nature susceptible of a population of one or two million souls. This body of people is as much entitled to political freedom, as much entitled to the enjoyments of the rights of citizenship, as any other part of the people of the United States. There can exist no necessity for *their* disfranchisement; no necessity *for them* to repose on the mere generosity of their countrymen to be protected from tyranny; to mere spontaneous attention for the regulation of their interests. They are entitled to a *participation* in the general councils, on principles of equity and reciprocity. They are entitled to a domestic government, free and energetic: a government founded on the principles of republican representation; and capable of regulating *all* their concerns, without waiting the leisure of a body, who are not only ignorant of their local affairs, and liable to eternal deception, but whose attention is totally engrossed by other subjects."

If you refuse to grant the District autonomy, he warned Congress, "the man of science, the man of business; the industrious mechanic, the enterprizing merchant, the eminent professional character, will avoid its limits. They will all consider it as holding out the destiny of contempt; instead of the honors which a seat of national government should present to the emulation and competition of generous minds."

If the principles of republicanism are discarded at the seat of government, he declared, "then has our country become retrograde in the path of political wisdom, and our position will be altered from the *front,* which we have hitherto occupied, to the rear of the nations of the civilized world."

Congressmen read these essays, first published in the *National Intelligencer* and republished in pamphlet form. And Congress divided along partisan lines—the Federalists generally advocating close executive control; the Republicans holding out for as simplified a governmental structure as possible with the greatest degree of self-determination. There can be little doubt that Woodward discussed his plan with Jefferson and had the vice-presidential approval. The House, where the Republicans were strongest, reported a bill out of committee that embodied most of Woodward's points. But the Federalist Senate had a different idea. From it came a measure, finally adopted by both chambers on February 27, 1801, which avoided the territorial question entirely. The government of the district was put in the hands of three judges, appointed by the president, with power to levy taxes. No legislature was created; the District continued under the laws of Maryland and Virginia.

This was not satisfactory to Woodward or to those who thought as he did. The congressional act of February 27, 1801, he insisted, by withholding local autonomy, contravened "the inherent and inalienable rights which appertain to *all men,* in *all places,* and at *all times.*" It was "an impolitic concession to the maxims of arbitrary and despotic authority."

He was willing to concede that there might be technical flaws in his, or any enlightened, plan. But a good beginning furnished a sound foundation for improvement. "Every institution founded in wisdom, and so beneficial in its operation as to preserve the confidence and affection of an enlightened and scrutinizing people, may be expected to endure with the nation to which it belongs, or until the character of that nation sustains an essential deterioration. Every provision on the contrary, which cannot withstand complete investigation, which has been originally but a compliment to current prejudice, a concession to prevalent error, may be expected to fall, as soon as any judicious pioneer shall turn on it the penetrative and exploring eye of public reason. In our arrangements on this subject, we must, however, be satisfied with the degree of light which is afforded us. Perfect wisdom, perfect certainty, perfect durability, are beyond our expectation; but by cautiously attending to first principles, and by correctly applying them, we may progress so far, that our successors will have only the task for *improving,* and not the more arduous operation of *undoing* previous measures." [12]

Then he stated what might well be considered his political credo: "The will of the People will be finally triumphant; and it can never be the desire of a free and generous People to fraternize with a band of slaves."

After Jefferson's inauguration, attention again was turned to organization of a District government; there was even some sentiment for giving it back to the donor states. But all that could be accomplished was to grant a charter to the city of Washington, with far greater autonomy than the District of Columbia enjoyed. Woodward had made no recommendations in this regard, but when the bill became effective in 1802, he quickly took advantage of it. The charter provided for a mayor, appointed by the president, and a six-man council, elected by those who could qualify by property ownership for the franchise. Despite his non-partisan professions, Woodward won nomination on the Federalist ticket, and when the election was held June 7, 1802, he was elected a member of Washington's first council, to hold office for a year.[13]

He began at once to find fault with the municipal government that he served; he saw an inconsistency between a city with self-determination and a District without it. The result, he dourly predicted, would be ruin for men of property and substance. While he served out his single term (he did not seek re-election) he felt no gratitude toward the party which put him in office, and controlled the city's politics.

He was not indebted, he felt, to the Federalists, and "his honest convictions," he publicly declared, using the third person, "make him wish that the Federalists may never regain their ascendancy in this government."[14]

From that time on, there was never any question of his adherence to the political principles of Jeffersonian Republicanism.

4

The Washington bar of 1802 consisted of only eleven members. With the city growing and its population increasing, with real estate speculation, there was business for all. Woodward got his share. He was diligent and he possessed a good legal mind. Clients came to him. He was soon being referred to as "literally the first lawyer in Washington." In 1802 his legal fees were $3,566.66; a substantial sum for that day and place, and indicative, surely, of his prosperity and standing in the community. His income may have been augmented by rents and profits on land transactions, although the necessity for meeting fairly substantial mortgage obligations kept him short of cash. He banked in Georgetown, and his balance, as far as incomplete records show, rarely was more than one hundred dollars. Usually it was considerably less.[15] But at least his financial condition belies the statement that he received his judicial appointment to Michigan Territory because "President Jefferson took pity on his poverty."[16]

Woodward had a deep and abiding respect for his profession and a sense of obligation to it. He was careful and studious and, as a practitioner and later a judge, he had no patience with slovenly preparation, and only contempt for the advocate who relied on thimblerigging, obfuscation and nimbleness of wit to win cases.

"Advocates in general do not take sufficient pains with their causes," he said, severely. "They are more copious than vehement; and many of them sacrifice glory to vanity, by lengthening out their pleadings that they may engross more attention from a public audience. But it is not enough to show one's self; it is necessary to be held in admiration when one wishes to become celebrated. Nor ought it to be concealed that literary men, who are accustomed to write with more care, have a marked superiority over advocates whenever they assume their profession."

This thought, jotted down in his notebook, contains a key to Woodward's own character, and offers an instance of the self-analysis to which he appears to have been addicted. It stresses the importance in his own mind of literary ability, giving it, perhaps, priority in his catalog of talents over the routine practice of law.

Careful as he was, able as he was, not all of his causes had happy endings. On August 16, 1802 he wrote Jefferson announcing a visit to Monticello to intercede for a client, James McGurk, who had the misfortune to be the first man to be executed in the District. Woodward, in turn, became the first attorney to lose a capital case in Washington.[17]

The McGurk case became a celebrated affair in the new city, and provided considerable local excitment. James McGurk had been accused—justly it appears—of the murder of his wife. Despite Woodward's eloquent plea to the jury of the circuit court of the District, McGurk, a rather notorious local character, was found guilty and sentenced to be hanged. The date set for the execution was August 28, but Woodward's journey to Jefferson's home was productive, and while he failed to win complete executive clemency, either in the form of a pardon or commutation of sentence, he did obtain a sixty-day stay of execution. That was the best he could do, and on October 29, McGurk was taken from the jail on C street, to a gallows which, according to tradition, was erected at Maryland and First streets. When the body was taken down it was buried in Holmead Cemetery, but respectable persons whose relatives were interred there, were outraged by what they considered a pollution of consecrated soil. By stealth, McGurk's remains were taken up and removed to a sort of potter's field known as the Slashes. When this was discovered, the body of the executed man was taken back to its original plot; but almost immediately those who had removed it in the first place, spirited it back to the Slashes. By this time everybody concerned was tired of the game, and the travel-weary mortal remains of McGurk were left, unmolested, in the Slashes.[18]

Not all of Woodward's practice was of so macabre a nature; most of it could be described as the routine business that comes the way of any diligent, well regarded counsellor. One case in particular earned him considerable distinction, gave him standing with Congress and even some degree of national prestige. This was his representation of Oliver Pollock before a committee of

Congress to press a long-standing claim for reimbursement of funds advanced to the patriot cause during the Revolution.

Pollock is one of the lesser known heroes of the War for Independence. It has been stated that his financial assistance "surpasses the contribution of any other person to the direct cause of the Revolution." It also has been said with equal emphasis that "lacking the financial support and advice of this trader, planter, and diplomat, the cause of the American Revolution west of the Alleghanies would have run a different course." [19] That the Northwest was won, and that it became a part of the United States, was the result, largely, of the efforts of Oliver Pollock. Yet, despite his great services, he was to taste the ingratitude of which republics can be capable.

Pollock was a native of Ireland, emigrating to Pennsylvania in 1761 when he was about twenty-four years old. He was of that breed of men with a natural bent for business and the golden touch. Whatever enterprise he turned to prospered. He began trading operations out of Philadelphia with West Indies ports, and with New Orleans where he established his headquarters in 1768. The following year, when Spain took possession of Louisiana from the French, Pollock was in a position to supply the Spanish army. He had the good sense to accept contracts which did not allow for the customary profiteering. As a result, he won the friendship and confidence of the Spanish authorities and, more important, the privilege of free trade throughout Louisiana. Before long, Pollock had considerable wealth; his mercantile interests became extensive; he acquired large land holdings near New Orleans on which he established profitable plantations, with slaves to work them.

At the outbreak of the Revolution, agents from Virginia appeared in New Orleans, seeking supplies for the patriot forces. Through Pollock's influence with Spanish officials, ten thousand pounds of powder were shipped to the colonies. At the same time, Pollock formally offered his services both to Virginia and the Continental Congress. He became the agent of both in Louisiana.

From time to time other consignments of supplies and munitions moved from New Orleans, up the Mississippi and Ohio Rivers to Fort Pitt, the American bulwark against the British on the western frontier. With Detroit as their base, the British unleashed their Indian allies in a wave of frightful terror throughout the Ohio valley. It was especially directed against the new settlements in Kentucky. To check this Indian menace, to win the rich western country for America, became the goal of several far-sighted patriots, among them the Virginian, George Rogers Clark. He conceived of checking Indian aggression by capturing Detroit. But he was astute enough to realize that a frontal attack on that distant post was not militarily feasible. Instead, he submitted a plan to Virginia authorities, calling for an expedition against the Illinois country which was not strongly held. Once Vincennes, Kaskaskia and the other Illinois posts had fallen, it would be easier to move on Detroit. The campaign was approved and by the end of 1778, American forces were in control of the strategic triangular area formed by the confluence of the Ohio and the Mississippi Rivers.

Large quantities of supplies were needed for Clark to effect his conquest; it took a continuing flow to enable him to hold it. From New Orleans, Pollock dispatched boatload after boatload of food, powder, blankets and clothing up the Mississippi, following, as he said, "the dictates of my own Zeal . . . deaf to every motive except an ardent affection for our righteous cause." Pollock made purchases out of his own funds. As the demands on him increased, he mortgaged his lands and slaves. Altogether he advanced more than $300,000, much of it pledged by his personal credit. Thus, Pollock helped give the United States an inland empire. But the victory was an expensive one for him. Peace found him a ruined man. His Spanish creditors pressed him for payment—he was even imprisoned for a while in debtor's jail in Havana—and he appealed to Virginia and Congress for relief.

From time to time, between 1782 and 1801, Pollock did receive some adjustment of his total claims of nearly $140,000. Although the validity of his claims was recognized by the government, an impoverished treasury would not permit payment of the debt. Later, he became disturbed by the opinion, held in some quarters, that the obligation contracted by Virginia was not binding on the Federal government. To help secure recognition of his rights as much as to obtain payment, he retained Woodward in 1801.

Woodward went to work with typical energy, preparing exhaustive briefs which he published and circulated in order to create a public opinion favorable to Pollock and which, he hoped, would influence Congress.

"The disbursements which occasioned those bills," Woodward wrote, "were made in aid of the conquest of the Illinois country by General Clark, under the authority of the state of Virginia. The state of Virginia afterwards ceded that conquest to the United States, and the latter took all consequent charges. So that on the double ground of the original embarrassment having been produced by the previous absorption of his funds by the United States, and on that of the whole benefit having resulted to them, it cannot be disputed that though the transaction originated with Virginia, if Mr. Pollock is entitled to recompense, and has never received it, it is to the United States he is to look for it." [20]

Referring to the hardships Pollock had undergone and the sacrifices he had made, Woodward said: "If the disaster of being arrested and detained at the Havanna, and having credits embargoed, originated in a solemn stipulation with government, and was virtually occasioned by its inability and failure to comply with a public contract, is not that government under a moral obligation, and duty of honor, to make an adequate atonement?"

Pollock, he said, was not seeking compensation for services rendered; he was too much the patriot for that. All he wanted was the repayment of what he had spent. "Silent without a murmur when his country was distressed, he now requires what he conceives a matter of right."

"When the call of private justice is forcible and clear, there would be no virtue in republican government, if it were capable of neglecting it," Woodward declared in summation. "To yield to the conviction, to propagate, and enforce it, is infinitely honorable and laudable. It is a sublime act of virtue; such as the opportunity to perform is not of daily occurrence. It is here that the legislative character feels its genuine importance. It is consolatory to the human mind. It is grateful to the friend of mankind, and to the friend of free government. It demonstrates, that, however, for a time, right may be impeded and obscured, it will not fail to prevail at last. It evinces that every magnanimous and generous sentiment, which, in the nature of things, ought to be expected from governments, can be realized from the rulers of a free people." [21]

In the end, Woodward's arguments, his eloquence and the justice of Pollock's cause prevailed. He eventually received all but approximately $9,000 of his claim.

More important from Woodward's standpoint, his participation in this case undoubtedly aroused his interest in the Northwest, and was a factor in prompting his acceptance of public service in that section of the country when Jefferson offered it to him.

CHAPTER III

Woodward Plans A Dream City

1

THE GOVERNOR AND JUDGES wasted no time getting down to business. The day after his arrival, Governor Hull met the citizens, received an address of welcome, and replied in lofty English which few of the French-speaking inhabitants understood. For their benefit, Father Richard later translated the speech. A proclamation was then issued designating as a single county all of Michigan Territory to which Indian title had been extinguished. A territorial seal was designed and adopted. Those preliminaries out of the way, Hull, Woodward and Bates resolved themselves into a land board and got to the chief business at hand: planning a new town to replace the one destroyed.

That was urgent. Although it was only the first of July [1805], decisions had to be made promptly so the people would have time to rebuild their homes before winter. At a public meeting, Hull added his arguments to those previously advanced by Woodward and Bates in behalf of abandoning the old town plan in favor of a more suitable one. By this time the burned-out citizens, perhaps expecting a miracle from their new officials, were muttering at the delays. Nevertheless, they were persuaded to wait a little longer until the land board could present definite recommendations.

Hull and Woodward concluded that any new site must include at least part of the common—the area between the former east line of the stockade and the western limits of the Askin, or Brush, farm, and the open country behind the fort. "All the farms front two or three acres on the river and extend forty acres back," Woodward stated. "Between the line of Askin . . . and that of McComb [the first farm west of the stockade] . . . there is only a space along the bank of the river of about twenty-five hundred feet. . ." This was all the river frontage available on which to rebuild, and it included the area directly in front of the fort. Lots fronting on the river were the most desirable; everybody wanted access to the water. The water lots in the old town had "value which words cannot describe and money scarcely represent." This being the case, every foot of river frontage would have to be utilized—and still there would not be enough. The idea of keeping the ground between river and fort unoccupied would have to be abandoned. "The Fort itself or the garrison in it are of no view of importance to the place, and will inevitably be abandoned by government," Woodward pointed out.[1]

It was agreed by the Governor and Judges, then, that all of the common and old village site would be used, and a tentative plat of streets and lots, subject to correction by a completed survey, was roughed out. The lots would be much larger than the original ones; they could contain at least five thousand square feet each. People crowded out of their old locations would be given new donation lots on the common, or permitted to buy any excess they desired over the basic allotment for two cents a square foot. The original town had only sixty-nine proprietors. Each of these could exchange his old claim for a new lot; in addition, a donation lot was to be given every person, proprietor or not, over the age of seventeen years who was a citizen of the United States, and who had resided in Detroit prior to the time of the fire. All this, of course, was subject to the approval of Congress and the president whose consent Hull and Woodward pledged themselves to obtain.[2]

This arrangement was described to the public on July 19. Several impatient proprietors had begun to rebuild on their original foundations. Others didn't much care where they built as long as they could get started. Twenty or more claimants who had suffered losses in the fire agreed to accept the land board's plan. Some were doubtful of the authority of the civil officers to enforce any kind of plan; others simply weren't interested. Several families, not caring to spend a bitter winter in tents or "bowers" appropriated whatever site appealed to them, and began to construct houses. They paid little attention to the tentative plat which had been suggested.

Woodward and Hull realized that no satisfactory arrangement could be enforced until Washington had approved it. No local surveyor being available, the territorial officials hired Thomas Smith, His Majesty's surveyor, who came over from Canada to lay out a general plan, and determine how much of the public domain would be required. A generous helping was taken. Not only the section along the river was staked out, but the whole width of the common between the Askin and Macomb farms for about three miles north, to a line even with the northerly limits of the private farms was claimed. Beyond this, behind the farms and the common, a vast area known as the Ten Thousand Acre Tract was requested. It was anticipated that in time this could be sold off in small parcels to private purchasers, the proceeds to finance construction of a jail, council house and other necessary public buildings.

Something was still lacking in this general survey. There was no attempt to locate new lots and streets, or to plan a symmetrical development of the whole area. There was a splendid opportunity to lay out a spacious city according to pre-determined, scientific planning; a city not only designed to accommodate the needs of the present, but capable of future expansion. But who was to prepare such a design?

All eyes turned to Judge Woodward; he had discussed such matters with Mr. Jefferson; he had watched L'Enfant laying out the city of Washington. He expressed a familiarity with the street arrangements and the parks and public buildings of European cities where scientific town planning had been successfully attempted.[3]

His colleagues appointed Woodward a committee of one to lay out the new Detroit. Always prepared, he had only to open the pocket notebook he had brought with him from Washington. There, on its inside covers, was pasted L'Enfant's plan of Washington. Using this as a guide, he was ready to go to work.

2

"Along with the present efforts of any action, in order to judge of its weight, we must put in the balance also its future consequences, and consider on one side the satisfaction and honor; and on the other the evil and disgrace that may attend it."[4]

These words in Woodward's memorandum book might have

been put there to condition his mind and steel his soul against the task he had assumed. To the public, it must have seemed there was no great problem in laying out a town. They had only to turn their backs on the river, and for two thousand miles to the west, and for at least that far to the north, there was nothing but empty space; plenty of land just for the taking; room a-plenty on which to build houses and barns, grow corn or pasture cattle. Why, then, all this talk about streets and alleys? Any kind of ground plan would do if it permitted easy communication within the village. Certainly this frontier town had no need to be rebuilt in the image of Washington, the nation's capital.

Woodward's vision matched his enthusiasm. Detroit, he preducted, would share generously in the future development of the Northwest, a region he foresaw "thriving with people, characterized by industry and abounding in the productions and arts which minister to the convenience and comfort of man. . ."

"I have ever believed," he told the people of Detroit, "that your new metropolis . . . is destined to have no common name among the cities which embellish the continent of North America, and that the melancholy conflagration of 1805 may by a judicious improvement of the calamity be almost converted into a blessing. The rapid increase which under many discouragements the short period of two years will have produced is a pledge of what may be expected as soon as by the encouragement of the general government the interior recesses of these pleasant and fertile regions are laid open to the irresistible energies of American enterprize." [5]

It was regrettable that the townspeople could not see the future as clearly as he, but he was not deterred by public apathy or opposition from going ahead with his grand design. If he could not have support, he would proceed without it.

"All the attachment of the inhabitants is to the old spot," he said resignedly. "They have none of those expectations with respect to the prosperity of their country, which are so common elsewhere. . . They value all the ground within the vicinity of the old town enormously rich, and all the rest at scarcely worth anything. . . They have seen what their country has been for a hundred years past and by this alone they judge of what it is likely to be for a hundred years to come." [6]

It was a year and a half before Woodward's plan was completed. He had the assistance of a new surveyor and cartographer, Abijah Hull, a nephew of the governor.

Woodward's plan for the city consisted of "an equilateral triangle having sides of four thousand feet each, and divided into six sections by a perpendicular line from every angle bisecting the opposite side, with squares, circuses and other open spaces of ground where six avenues and where twelve avenues intersect, with lots of 5,000 square feet, with an alley or lane coming to the rear of every lot, with subordinate streets of sixty feet width, with a fine internal space of ground for education and other purposes, with grand avenues to the four cardinal points of two hundred feet width, and with other avenues of one hundred twenty feet width. . . The town shall consist of similar sections to be successively laid out, extending the plan for some miles up the River Detroit, and some miles down by gradual process, without inconvenience, whenever the growing city or public interest might require it." [7]

Stated another way, the plan contemplated at intervals of four thousand feet, large circular plazas one thousand feet in diameter. These were to be connected and intersected by the north-south and east-west grand avenues, each two hundred feet wide. From each of the hub-like plazas or "circuses," eight other avenues would radiate like the spokes of a wheel. These were to be one hundred and twenty feet wide and connected, at intervals, by sixty-foot streets. The grand circuses were intended to be sites for public buildings, churches, schools—all the space to be landscaped, adorned with fountains and statuary, and lined with trees. The base of the first unit paralleled the river for four thousand feet. The apex of its triangle was at the present Grand Circus Park, and the intersection of the avenues which would have bisected its angles can still be seen at the Campus Martius. This first unit was designed for a population of fifty thousand. It could easily be enlarged by adding a second, or any desired number of additional units merely by making one side of the original triangle the base of a new one.

It is no wonder that the rustics of Detroit found Woodward's idea beyond their comprehension. It still represents an advanced idea in scientific city planning. Writing in the *Art Quarterly,* Buford L. Pickens says:

"Here was the direct solution of a different problem, that of platting a city on flat, level ground fronting on the almost straight river bank, and making provision for unlimited expansion in any direction, especially anticipated along the river. The wide, straight avenues which radiate from the five and one-half acre circular parks form the organic skeleton of communications linking all parts of the city, and constitute a superb application of the Baroque discovery in spatial art—the rond-point. The streets are designed with a fine regard for their relative importance as traffic arteries. . . It is amazing that Woodward could foresee and prepare for the needs of a large modern city, which he seemed to understand far more clearly than do its citizens today."

The same writer suggests that Woodward's expandable plan was the first example of mass production in a city which has made a science of mass production.

"In its method of planning, its convenience of access, its regularity, order and love of mechanical reproduction, Woodward's master plan of 1807 provided a startling matrix for modern Detroit," Pickens declares.[8]

After eleven years, Woodward's plan was abandoned. But in the heart of the modern city there can be clearly traced its original outlines. Half of one grand circus remains; the streets radiate from it like the extended fingers of an open hand. Had the plan been retained, Detroit today would be the happiest of large cities; its traffic complexities and frustrations would be no more than minor annoyances. During the past twenty years, Detroit taxpayers have spent millions of dollars to attain in their downtown district something approximating what Augustus Woodward originally envisioned.

One hundred years after Woodward presented his plan to the people, Frederick Law Olmstead, Jr., son of the pioneer in modern civic design, and himself a leading city planner, stated:

"Nearly all the most serious mistakes of Detroit's past have arisen from a disregard of the spirit of the Governor and Judges' [Woodward's] Plan."[9]

3

Officials of the Territory were badly mistaken if they believed a scheme for distributing land to the homeless or planning the city beautiful would sweeten the tempers and soothe the patience of the inhabitants. It was neither parks, grand boulevards nor lovely vistas in which they were interested. They wanted assurance that their titles would be recognized by the Federal government. That was something neither Hull nor Woodward nor anyone else could give them.

Not only the proprietors of the town made life miserable for the harassed Governor and Judges. The farmers, up and down the river, wanted their titles certified, too. Most of their property originally had been purchased privately from the Indians. In many cases it was done without sanction, or in direct disregard of orders of the French government. The descendants of these farmers had nothing to show that would prove their ownership. Observing the way the new territorial government was shuffling the claims of lot owners in the town made the others fearful that a similar adjustment might be their fate. Angry habitants insisted on recognition of their ancient claims.

These farmers acted through the grand juries which represented almost the only medium of public opinion. One grand jury appealed directly to President Jefferson that "Our patience is now exhausted, as every expectation of reform in those we complain of is entirely at an end.—We are compelled reluctantly to appeal to the source from whence our oppressors derived their power.—Our dependence and consolation, are in your known magnanimity, benevolence, and Justice:—from them we confidently expect relief.—"[10] The militia companies sent representatives to Detroit, some of them coming from as far away as Michilimackinac, to urge Hull and at least one of the judges to go to Washington and lay their plight before Congress.

Hull and Woodward were aware of the predicament of the people, both in the town and country. They would gladly have resolved it if they could. The suggestion that the two officials go to Washington was accepted. It was agreed that Woodward would proceed directly to the capital, exert all his influence on the president and Congress to get a land bill adopted, and Hull would join him there as soon as possible.

They each departed for the East in October, 1805, Woodward traveling by way of New York, and Hull going first to Massachusetts to attend to personal business. Woodward carried a communication signed by Hull and himself, dated October 10, 1805, urging Congress to confirm the land titles which the Governor and Judges had tentatively and unofficially recognized. Explaining in detail the conditions they found on their first arrival in Detroit, they retraced the steps that had been taken to meet the situation.

"A town was accordingly surveyed and laid out, and the want of authority to impart any regular title, without the subsequent sanction of Congress, being first impressed and clearly understood, the lots were exposed to sale under that reservation. . . As soon as the necessities of the immediate inhabitants were accommodated, the sales were entirely stopped, until the pleasure of Government could be consulted. As no title could be made, or was pretended to be made, no payments were required, or any moneys permitted to be received, until the expiration of one year, to afford time for Congress to interpose. The remaining part was stipulated to be paid in four successive annual installments. . . It therefore now remains for the Congress of the United States either to refuse a sanction of the arrangement made, or, by imparting a regular authority to make it, or in some other mode, in their wisdom deemed proper, to relieve the inhabitants from one of the most immediate distresses, occasioned by the calamitous conflagration." [11]

Other arguments were advanced, based as much upon expediency as justice. Unless low-priced land could be acquired with confidence, settlers would not come to Michigan Territory. The British authorities in Upper Canada offered generous land inducements to newcomers, but "such, however, is the inestimable value of liberty to man, that notwithstanding these, and if possible, greater inducements to the settlers, the undersigned venture to predict a marked superiority to the american side . . . if the old claims are at once adjusted, and the country laid open to the acquisition of a new title."

The Indians also were to be taken into account. If the American "is not considered as an enemy, he is at least regarded as a character with whom they are to struggle, and, if in no other, certainly in a pecuniary view." The Indians were closely allied with the French inhabitants by ties of friendship, trust and sometimes blood, and would judge the sincerity and good intentions of the American government to an extent, at least, by the way it treated the habitants. "An honest and fair adjustment of land matters would give more strength to the country than a thousand disciplined soldiers."

Bolstered by these arguments, and employing a persuasiveness that was hard to resist, Woodward began his assault on bureaucracy. Months passed, and Congress and the administration were slow to act. Relief for Michigan was delayed while committees studied and congressional orators debated. Despite discouragement, procrastination and broken promises, Woodward worked doggedly, pleading with the president and cabinet members; button-holing congressmen whenever and wherever he could corner them. As evidence of his personal sacrifice on behalf of the people of Michigan, he complained bitterly that he spent three hundred dollars for wine to quench congressional thirsts before he could get action. It wasn't that members of Congress were hostile to Michigan Territory's needs; it was simply that there were more urgent matters nearer than the far frontier.

Hull joined Woodward in Washington, but the delays discouraged him. While Woodward hung obstinately on, the governor started a slow and leisurely journey back to Detroit. He was in no hurry to get there; he was actually afraid of the reception he might receive when he returned from an uncompleted mission. From Albany he wrote Secretary of State Madison: "Instead of returning to a greatefull, contented and happy people, I expect to find them uneasy and dispairing. Believing they have no interest in the Country, they will feel little attachment to it. . . I have made great personal sacrifices in changing my situation, in the hope of being usefull. In the full expectations, that arrangements would have been made, for the improvement and increase of the Territory, I am now removing with my family and all my future prospects to the Country—gloomy indeed are those prospects—surrounded by a Savage foe, in the midst of a people, strangers to our language, our customs and manners, without legal titles to property, and no measures adopted by which they can be obtained, and not an acre of land to be offered to new settlers!" [12]

But the situation wasn't as grim as Hull pictured it. Unknown to him, Woodward's persistent efforts brought success nine days before this gloomy letter was written. On April 21, 1806, Congress at last enacted the land title legislation which gave Michigan Territory almost everything it had requested.

4

The news that Congress had acted favorably preceded Woodward to Detroit, and on his return home he found himself something of a hero. But the public enthusiasm didn't last long. There were more delays, the result of petty squabbles and politics among the members of the land board, and bickering on the part of citizens who were dissatisfied with the location of their lots or the amount of land awarded them. Woodward objected to the people's inclination to erect their new houses wherever they pleased. He insisted that the rebuilding should conform to his new ground plan. As a result, not a single house was built in 1806, and up to May, 1807, only nineteen deeds were awarded.

"These delays cannot be justified," Silas Farmer stated; "indeed there can be no question that had there not been a settled purpose to delay action, plans might have been adopted, lots staked out, and proprietorship agreed upon, much earlier. And all such action would have received whatever of congressional sanction was necessary. . . The most valuable lots were sold to and taken up by persons who were not sufferers by the fire, nor even residents of the town when it occurred. The Governor and Judges sought, by various methods, to compel the people to purchase lots, and the donation lots were offered rather as a sort of bonus than as a gift." The general feeling, at least as far as Woodward was concerned, was that he was more interested in planning a city than in relieving distress. Woodward was aware of this feeling. "None of us," he admitted, "have given satisfaction to the people."

The great mistake the Governor and Judges made was their failure to share the responsibility of the land adjustment with the citizens. From the beginning they acted arbitrarily, reserving all decisions to themselves. In 1802, before the new government was appointed, Detroiters were allowed a limited measure of home rule with a popularly-elected mayor and council. Under the Governor and Judges, Detroit was reincorporated, but the mayor and council were placed so closely under the control of Governor Hull that the citizens refused to take part in the municipal government.

The home rule law was soon repealed, and not until 1815 was any further degree of local autonomy granted. Had the representatives of the people been permitted to participate in the allotment of lands, all blame for confusion and delay would not have fallen on the Governor and Judges.

"The history of William Hull and Augustus B. Woodward since they took upon themselves the Government of this Territory, is a history of repeated injuries, abuses, and deceptions," the citizens complained; "all having a direct tendency to harass, distress and impoverish, if not absolutely to expel the present inhabitants,—and to accomplish private and sinister schemes. . . They have been guilty of unfeeling cruelty and barbarity by preventing those naked and homeless sufferers by the conflagration, from accommodating themselves with buildings during one whole year, and many of them during another year,—and several to this very day [1807],—thro' their systematic measures of speculation. . . They have by their intrigues and ridiculous manoeuvres, sunk themselves into the deepest contempt,—and they are actually at this time, a reproach and bye word among the people." [13]

Actually, Woodward was not as black-hearted as this indictment painted him. He deplored as bitterly as any the failure to give the public a voice in its affairs; he was sincerely distressed by the delays. He even drafted and signed a memorial to Congress asking for home rule for the Territory. "Attached as we are to the principles of a republican Government," he wrote, "we trust they [Congress] will be too sensible of its value, to withhold every degree of self-Government any longer than it can possibly be avoided." [14]

Despite his sympathetic attitude, criticism and ill-feeling centered more upon him than his colleagues. Although carrying out the town plan was the joint responsibility of the Governor and Judges, it was popularly ascribed to him alone because he was the author and it was known as the Woodward Plan. Therefore, he bore the brunt of public resentment.

The principal property owners of "the Northeast Coast"—now the Grosse Pointe district—resolved that "we greatly dread the consequences of the fluctuating and dangerous measures which have always been agitated by Judge Woodward, who makes use of the Territorial money to erect bridges behind the City of Detroit, and to digg wells and make pumps on the domain for the animals of the woods." Many people could see no sense in platting subdivisions back of the town proper; they preferred to use the common to pasture their livestock. Farmers with land adjoining the domain had visions of their property being cut up into avenues, parks and circuses of Woodward's devising. The prospect depressed them. Some citizens found fault because the lots on the common were too small. They preferred the land laid off in small farms of six to twelve acres. These "would have made us good meadows or pastures for our cattle . . . but the lots you are now attempting to sell are not worth the deeds and recording," the public protested.

The belief was general that both Hull and Woodward were feathering their nests by speculation when they acquired property of their own. Hull was one of the first to build a new house. He chose a lot on Jefferson avenue, then the main thoroughfare, paralleling the river. Woodward was accused of erecting a monument to himself when he gave the main north-south street the name of Woodward avenue.

"Not so," he replied, tongue in cheek. "The avenue is named Woodward because it runs wood-ward, toward the woods."

The chief bone of contention lay in the decision of the Governor and Judges not to award donation lots to resident aliens. There were several in Detroit, persons of substance and influence. At first Woodward favored treating them like the other inhabitants, but the land board overruled him and he gave in. One of those who felt himself unjustly treated was a Scot, John Gentle, who operated a river-front store and did a little smuggling on the side. His fire loss was estimated at £500, but not being a proprietor he was not entitled to a fire lot. In 1807 he applied for a donation lot, at the same time filing application for citizenship. Woodward refused to naturalize him on the ground that he was only seeking it as a subterfuge to acquire property. Gentle, who possessed a vitriolic tongue and a facile pen, was enraged. He unleashed an attack on Woodward to the latter's life-long mortification and damage. There was no newspaper in Detroit or Michigan at the time; the journal most generally read was the Pittsburgh *Common-*

wealth. Gentle submitted a series of articles to this paper, all berating the Governor and Judges, and with special emphasis on the misdeeds of Woodward. Some of the articles were re-printed in the Philadelphia *Aurora* and attracted national attention. Supplementing his journalistic efforts, Gentle posted handwritten broadsides around Detroit, excoriating the Governor and Judges. Regarding Woodward's plan for the new town, Gentle had this to say:

"After a few days spent in preparing their apparatus, the judge began his operations on a height contiguous to the fort. There he placed his instruments, astronomical and astrological, on the summit of a huge stone [this boulder originally stood in the Campus Martius, opposite Detroit's present city hall] which shall ever remain a monument to his indefatigible perseverance.

"For the space of thirty days and thirty nights he viewed the diurnal evolutions of the planets, visible and invisible, and calculated the course and rapidity of the blazing meteors. To his profound observations of the heavenly regions the world is indebted for the discovery of the streets, alleys, circles, angles and squares of this magnificent city—in theory equal in magnitude and splendor to any on the earth.

"But the most arduous and tedious performance was the laying out and measuring the marshes a mile back from town into streets, lots, circles, and grand squares, measuring and unmeasuring them, arranging and deranging them, for the space of two full months or more. The patience of the people was at last exhausted; and they became so clamorous at last that the Governor and Judges were constrained to rest from their labors and agree to make a division of the lots.

"The inhabitants were told to go and choose lots, and if more than one chose the same lot, the legislature would decide which should have the choice. They reasoned against this mode of decision, because they well knew it would not succeed; the legislature was applied to for a decision, and a dispute took place between the legislature and the people. In consequence, as was intended, this mode of division was abandoned.

"By way of killing time, the judge went to work again with his instruments, and measured the commons over and over for about three weeks more . . ."

Gentle concluded by calling Woodward "a perfect quid."

So it went on; article followed article, for months. Salted with enough truth to make them sound plausible, the ridicule hurt. Attempts were made to quiet Gentle. He was attacked in his own house by friends of the Governor and Judges, and he was indicted for libel. Although he pleaded the truth, the truth then could not be offered as evidence and he was found guilty. To escape punishment he moved across the river to Canada. From there he continued his clamor.

The *Commonwealth* and *Aurora* pieces were read far beyond Detroit. Bates, who in 1807 had gone to his new post in St. Louis, was alarmed for his friend's reputation.

"Should not these impertinences in the *Urora* be answered," he asked Woodward, "or are they too trifling to be regarded? Yet believe me they have an effect on the minds of many. Our Michigan proceedings were censured with some severity at Washington, and some men even of sense and understanding affected not to be satisfied with them." [15]

At first Woodward refused to notice the Gentle attacks, but finally he felt it necessary to reply. He used the same mediums for his answers—the *Commonwealth* and *Aurora*. Even before Bates' warning he had written to Madison, defending himself against charges that he was speculating in Detroit lands.

"I have no personal interest, direct or indirect, in the new town; or in any of the questions which are agitated in the adjustment of titles, and distribution of donations," he declared. "The Governor is in a different situation. He has purchased a piece of ground, and built himself a house . . . I firmly believe the Governor's conduct in this purchase upright and just. It is at the same time both patriotic and necessary. His situation requires him to have accommodation and shelter, and being possessed of wealth, it is an advantage to the country of which he is an officer, that a portion of his private resources should be applied to the erection of a house for his own accommodation. That in which he dwells is mean and comfortless beyond description. If he has any other concern relative to property in this country I am ignorant of it," he said.

Woodward then admitted he had helped the surveyor, "both on paper, and on the ground . . . It is not true," he added indignantly, "that thirty days and thirty nights were employed in taking observations." [16]

The Gentle articles made no impression on Jefferson. But they were believed by many people in Michigan, to the everlasting damage to Woodward's reputation. The things most commonly remembered about him today are the things Gentle wrote.

5

The Woodward Plan remained in effect for eleven years. It was legislated out of existence partly because of greed, partly because of public pressure, and partly because a hundred years is too long to wait for a dream to come true.

The Governor and Judges voted in 1817 to abandon the Woodward Plan. Of the men who originally authorized it, only Woodward and Griffin remained in the government. Hull was gone and Lewis Cass was governor. James Witherell had replaced Bates on the Supreme Court. By 1817 Cass had become the dominant figure in the territorial government. He was an able, aggressive man with a vision of his own.

The opposition to the plan came from farmers whose land adjoined the city. Cass was one of these; he had bought the Macomb farm soon after his appointment by President Madison in 1813. Detroit's population was growing by 1817. Owners of the large private tracts wanted to subdivide and sell lots. They did not want to be restricted by platted boulevards and grand avenues cutting across their property at angles, slicing it into odd-sized and odd-shaped parcels. And they did not relish the competition of public lands being made available to buyers who wanted only house lots. It was to the advantage of everyone to divide the Ten Thousand Acre Tract into small farms that would more readily attract settlers and bring revenue into the Territory's treasury. Single small lots could be purchased from the proprietors.

A thin subterfuge was used. The Governor and Judges—Woodward dissenting—decided the congressional act of 1806 authorized the laying out of a "town." Applying the New England definition of "town"—or of a New York township—it was claimed that the term did not mean "village" or "city." By this reasoning, it was a "village" Woodward planned; not a "town." Therefore, he had not acted in strict accord with Congress' intentions and the whole project was null and void. This was legal semantics, but the majority voice prevailed. What was left of the common was sold off in one hundred and sixty acre tracts.[17]

Woodward's protest was loud and eloquent. It can be read today as the sad reminder of what might have been.

"Nature has destined the city of Detroit to be a great interior emporium, equal, if not superior, to any other on the surface of the terraqueous globe," he wrote, sorrowfully. "The commerce of seven immense Mediterraneans,—Ontario, Erie, Huron, Michigan, Superior, Cuinissique, Arabasca,—connected by noble rivers with the Atlantic ocean at two points, New York and Quebec, and stretching on the other side to the Pacific and even to the hyperborean ocean, must glide along its borders. In such a case the art of man should aid the benevolence of the Creator, and no restricted attachment to the present day or to present interests, should induce a permanent sacrifice of ulterior and brilliant prospects.

"It requires no extraordinary vigor of penetration, and no protracted perseverance of investigation, to apprehend the errors which within a few centuries have been committed in Europe, and even on our own continent, on the subject of cities; and to deduce the proper inferences from the information. None of the great cities of Europe,—Lisbon, Paris, London, Dublin, Moscow,—can boast an antiquity, by a retrogressive computation from the present time, of eight centuries, to the period when their magnitude, resources and accommodations were inferior to those of the present city of Detroit. If then in that period, of some in less, they have grown to their present opulence, splendor and celebrity, what may not the same period, prospectively regarded, bring about with respect to the city of Detroit, with superior natural advantages to any of these, and under a government more free, and ten times more enlightened? In half that period . . . this phoenix of the world, now rising from the ashes of its parents, may transcend the present glories of those great and celebrated marts.

"Are cities built in a day? Can you throw them down, when your ground-plan is found contracted and inconvenient, and erect new ones on a better ground-plan, among the ruins of the old? What would it not cost to throw down the existing cities of London, Paris, Lisbon, New York, and to erect in their places new ones on an improved ground-plan? Which of them is competent to meet such cost? What nation is adequate to meet it? Where is the spirit, the resolution, the patience of privation, the good taste, the patriotic enthusiasm, requisite for such an enterprise?

"No, cities are the work of time, of a generation, of a succession of generations. Their original ground-plan must remain, and cannot be changed without the height of inconvenience, trouble, and expense. A proper and prudent foresight can alone give to a great city its fair development. Order, regularity, beauty, must characterize its original ground-plan. It must have a capacious grasp. No petty interests ought to be permitted to enter into collision with its permanent welfare. Uniformity of plan, amplitude of avenue, of square, of plan, of space, of circus, free circulation of air, and variety of decoration and embellishment, are not to be hoped for, if one age shall determine on its limited and contracted view of things that a city can never reach beyond a certain limit. Enough and more than enough, ought to be allowed to give it a full expansion and growth." [18]

Nearly one hundred and fifty years have passed since Woodward gave that warning, and Detroit is just beginning to understand what he meant. Perhaps it is too late now, but Detroit has not yet caught up with his conception.

For that matter, what modern American city has?

CHAPTER IV

"Commotions and Ferments"

1

In all the history of governments, it would be hard to find one with a less auspicious beginning than that of the Territory of Michigan. Because of initial errors, it lacked the confidence and understanding of the public. To make matters worse, petty jealousy, back-stairs conniving, and bickering split the administration into almost as many factions as it had members.

The people themselves displayed a perversity which made the task of the Governor and Judges more difficult. An early instance occurred in August, 1806, when the grand jury expressed alarm at the threat to community morals from Detroit's waterfront fleshpots. Voyageurs from the north in town for a spree, joined mariners and soldiers in keeping the streets noisy and the bright lights burning. The fun started Saturday nights and continued through Sundays, to the scandal of the respectable element.

"In order to put an end to that brutal excess which occasions disorder and scandal on those days which are consecrated by law to the worship of Almighty God," the grand jury implored, "we pray that all persons convicted of being intoxicated or drunk on Sundays, may be subjected to a fine. We observe with regret that many of the youth of this country are much addicted to the ruinous practice of gaming. We demand, for the general welfare of this country, that all public hazard games, and public hazard game houses, should be abolished, particularly on Sundays." It was recommended also that horse racing in the village streets be prohibited.

The Governor and Judges were limited to the adoption of laws already in force in the states. Searching the statute books, all they could find applicable to the local situation were the Connecticut

"Blue Laws" whose reputation for harshness had penetrated to the western frontier. The people reacted violently to the suggestion that they be adopted in Michigan. An orderly, peaceful village was one thing; a New England Sabbath was something else. Sunday, after Mass, was a day of traditional festival for the French, an occasion for feasting, visiting and dancing. They were willing to curb the town's riotous immorality, but they did not want to spend the day seated quietly before their doors, the fiddles silent and the peach brandy jugs corked. For even entertaining such a thought the Governor and Judges became tyrants and oppressors. The outcry against them became so loud that those harassed gentlemen dropped any further consideration of the Connecticut laws, and sin, it may be presumed, continued to enjoy the freedom of the city.

One of Hull's first official acts was to create a territorial militia. As commander-in-chief, he pinned the two stars of a major-general on himself. Woodward was appointed colonel of the First Regiment, composed of Detroiters. With Indians in the woods and British regulars stationed across the border, a local defense corps was necessary. Hull permitted himself to be carried away by his martial enthusiasm. In a general order issued October 3, 1805, he prescribed uniforms for his territorial army which would have made drab by comparison the brightly plumed household guards of a European monarch. Officers of Woodward's regiment were to wear dark blue coats, "long and faced with red, with a red cape, white buttons, and lining, white under cloathes, and silver epaulettes." Add to this, cocked hats with black plumes, red tipped; red sashes, swords, pistols and bear-skin holsters, and the birds of the Michigan forests might have hidden themselves in dowdy chagrin.

The privates were to be only slightly less gorgeous. At their own expense they were ordered to obtain knee-length blue coats, "white under cloathes in summer, and white vests and blue pantaloons in winter; half boots, or gaiters, round black hats, black feathers tipped with red, cartridge belt and bayonet belt black." [1]

The French farmer or woodsman who lived and worked in buckskin or homespun, found this uniform beyond his means. There was no cloth in the Territory for such costumes, so Hull had quantities shipped from the East, and sold to each militiaman. Most of the men couldn't afford such elaborate outfits and there was much grumbling. There also were the inevitable rumors that Hull was acting as middleman to his own profit. To add to the discontent, Hull ordered out detachments to rebuild the town's stockade and strengthen the defenses. The people wanted protection, but they hardly expected they would be required to go to such lengths to obtain it.

Woodward entered upon his military duties with customary enthusiasm. He accepted his commission with a flourish—"with his humble acknowledgements for the unmerited rank and honor." Soon he was laying out battery positions which failed to meet Hull's approval. The two men quarreled and the governor revoked Woodward's commission, whereupon the latter publicly declared the whole enterprise was pointless and retired to non-military activities.

The rift between Woodward and Hull over the militia widened as the result of the establishment of a territorial bank. This, perhaps, was the most serious error committed by the officials. Compounded of equal parts of gullibility and a distorted estimate of the economic importance and prospects of the Territory, the effort was a foreordained failure. Moreover, collapse of this undertaking brought both the government of the Territory and the Territory itself into disrepute.

During Hull's eastern trip of 1805–6, he met a group of Boston financiers to whom he must have looked like a lamb ready for shearing. No doubt he painted a picture of Michigan in the most glowing colors. These men were interested in the fur trade. To them, a bank of original issue in the lake country would have been useful, provided they could control it.

"Currency," says Charles Moore, "was scarce in this isolated community, and trade was conducted mainly by barter. The advent of the British had driven out the Spanish and French coin, and when the United States came into possession the sources of money supply were the payments made to the garrison, and the meager salaries paid to the governor, the judges and the territorial secretary, together with the coin brought in by the traders of the American Fur Company, who were the bankers of the forest." [2]

This situation, in a village which in 1806 boasted fewer than two score houses and buildings, where mercantile business was carried on largely through credit arrangements with eastern banks and merchants, and where scarcely a copper coin could be found to rattle in a pewter bowl, hardly justified a full-fledged banking institution. But the idea sounded good to Hull. He saw it as a way to advance the Territory's importance, and to catch up with Canada which, on that border at least, was economically ahead of Michigan. He was easily persuaded to lend his influence, not overlooking the possibility of personal gain.

"A very rich and respectable Company of Merchants, in Boston, have agreed to make an establishment in our Territory to carry on the fur Trade," he wrote Woodward in the spring of 1806. "They will place a Capital of one hundred thousand Dollars in the business in the first instance.

"They have petitioned our Government for a Bank—I have ventured to give them such assurances, that they will immediately make all their arrangements—all the shares are now Subscribed for excepting one quarter part, which is left for the People of the Territory. . . It is imposssible, that a Company of more wealth, intelligence, & Spirit could have been formed. . . "[3]

The original encouragement seems, from this letter, to have come from Hull. At least he was in direct negotiation with the promoters. When the news got around, others shared his enthusiasm. From Woodward's expansive viewpoint, a bank for Detroit was entirely logical. He easily convinced himself that it would concentrate in Detroit the fur trade for which Michigan had always competed with the Canadians. As a result, it was not difficult to obtain from the Governor and Judges on September 15, 1806, a charter for the Detroit Bank.* The act by which it was granted was forwarded to Washington for the approval of Congress.

Without waiting for congressional action, the bank opened for business. Its organization and structure were unique, all circumstances considered. The promoters sent their man, William Flanigan, from Boston, to be cashier. As a matter of policy they picked a local man for president. Their choice was Judge Woodward who

* The Detroit Bank, or the Bank of Detroit, as it was sometimes called, should not be identified with a modern institution of the same name.

was quite willing to add the prestige of heading a financial institution to his many other accomplishments.

The Detroit Bank was first capitalized at $100,000 of which only $19,000 was paid in. At least sixteen Detroiters were subscribers, including Woodward who, as president, bought one qualifying share on which he paid an initial—and only—installment of two dollars. The Territory itself put up ten per cent and the controlling interest, as could be expected, remained in Boston. The charter had a life of thirty years.

Neither the term of the charter nor the capitalization satisfied Woodward. Preferring things on a much grander scale, he managed to have the charter extended to one hundred years and the capital increased to one million dollars. "Short periods," he said of the charter, "opened always a door for intrigue and corruption for renewal." Justifying the increased capitalization, he added: "Popular sagacity and good sense, though perhaps not always competent to express these ideas with precision, yet is always competent to act on them, and always does act on them, and that with the greatest precision. Governments need therefore never attempt to regulate the quantity of coin, or of bank bills in society. The good sense of society always regulate both, without any aid, and much better without aid than with it." This was carrying republican principles in the field of applied economics a step further than even Jefferson ever evinced a willingness to go.[4]

With a charter and capital structure which would compare favorably with most banking houses on the seaboard, it became necessary to furnish impressive quarters. To do this, and to provide an advantageous location, Woodward butchered his own city plan by cutting up a lot to give the building, equipped with iron doors and constructed at a cost of eight thousand dollars, a corner site with frontage on two main streets.

With the iron doors open for business, the real purpose of the syndicate soon became clear. It was not to encourage the fur trade or to improve the condition of the Territory, but to circulate paper money in the East—so far away from the point of issue that it would be difficult to determine the discount rate or present it for redemption. Within a few weeks $165,000 worth of scrip had been printed, and put in circulation in the East by the Boston promoters. It was peddled at a discount of from ten to twenty-five per cent. With this scrip disposed of, the printing presses began turning out more, until within a few months the eastern seaboard was flooded with a total of $1,500,000 of virtually worthless paper money.

Of course this had been obtained by the promoters in the first place as a loan or series of loans, backed only by notes and without any discernible collateral. Having thus milked the institution, the original backers proceeded to dispose of their stock. Gradually the scrip began to drift back to Detroit and was presented for payment. This was refused, there being no specie on hand. The secretary of war cautioned the commandant against paying the Detroit garrison in notes of the bank.

Woodward, as president, was apparently so involved that he dared not admit anything was wrong. Hull, who was largely responsible for the entire affair, hastened to wash his hands of it. He even exhibited signs of panic when Secretary Madison ominously ordered him to forward copies of the territorial law "respecting the erection of a bank."

"Until very lately I believed the views of the Applicants were pure," Hull replied in a letter of self-vindication, "and the management of the institution would have been such, as to have promoted the Public Interest." He expressed the hope that holders of the bank notes would be indemnified. "I have made this statement because it has been suggested that those who passed the Law, were influenced by other motives, than those of the public interest." [5]

This thought had occurred also to President Jefferson, but upon investigation he took a charitable view. "The Governor committed a great error in the bank institution, and at first a suspicious one," he stated. "But we have found that he took a very small interest in it, and got out of it as soon as he found he was wrong. in everything else his conduct has been correct & Salutary. that there was much roguery in the institution of the bank, I believe, of which he was the dupe." [6] At a later time, Woodward expressed the belief that Hull had originally been interested in the bank for speculative reasons.

Secretary Griswold, always the opportunist, tried to make political capital of the discomfiture of Woodward and Hull. He found enough citizens of Michigan willing to join in demanding the impeachment, or at least removal, of both Hull and Woodward. Meanwhile, Congress vetoed the Michigan act of incorporation and by 1809 the bank, unhonored and unsung, passed out of existence.

Still, the bad taste lingered. Woodward, Hull and Griffin, who had given the bank its charter, had to defend themselves. Even when he should have known better, Woodward insisted that the bank was solvent. The officers of the Territory jointly signed a letter to the president attempting to show clean hands.

"Our *Sole* object," they wrote, "in the institution has been to give facilities to american enterprize in a department of commerce heretofore restricted to a foreign Nation, and with respect to which the present has appeared to us the crisis of Sucessful competition." [7]

No action ever was taken against Woodward or Hull, but the feeling created by the bank, particularly in the East, persisted for many years. The fiasco was responsible, to some extent, for the slow economic and social development of the Territory. Remembering the worthless scrip that had been foisted on them, eastern capitalists and eastern settlers by-passed Michigan during a decade in which it could advantageously have used both.

2

"I owe it to Judge Woodward," said Hull in a letter to Madison in 1805, "to say that I have received great assistance from his talents, his zeal and industry." [8] That was almost the last occasion of record on which the governor had a kind word for the chief justice. Within a short time he was using a different tone in a letter to the secretary of war.

"You undoubtedly have some knowledge of the Character of Judge Woodward–Every thing in this Territory was perfectly tranquil, untill his arrival–Since that time he has been doing all in his power to create parties and excit tumult–Thank God, his influence is small, and he has few adherents–As long as it was possible, I lived on friendly terms with him–At length, I found him insidious, and doing all in his power to injure me–I dismissed him from my confidence, removed him from a military Office. . ." [9]

For his part, Woodward accused Hull of "lack of tact, energy and firmness" and complained that the people had "thrown off the ties of civilized society to such an extent that the Governor and government were but feathers blown by the wind."[10]

These acidulous comments served to highlight the fact that the period from late 1806 to 1812 was one of deterioration in the administrative and legislative functions of the territorial government, almost to the point of chaos. There was a continuous clash of personalities and an open fight for the dominant position in the government. The distrust, recrimination and striving for advantage were to the discredit of all involved. Neither party ever appeared willing to compromise. There were unresolved viewpoints on the land bill and the town plan; the distrust which grew out of the bank added fuel to the flames. Griswold, with his constant petty intrigues, seeking to displace Hull and gain the governorship for himself, fanned the fires. Soon it became apparent that there were three parties or factions: Hull's, Griswold's, and Woodward and Griffin comprising the third. As long as the latter pair stood together—and it was said they acted with "insolence and malice"—they had matters tightly under their control. As a voting majority of the legislative board, they exercised an effective veto power over Hull.

This was somewhat modified with the arrival of Judge James Witherell who succeeded Bates. A phlegmatic man, Witherell did not share Woodward's mercurial enthusiasms. Lacking color and imagination himself, Witherell nevertheless had integrity and a good legal mind. He assumed the role of balance wheel.

Witherell often voted with Hull, and now it was Woodward's turn to find himself blocked. He early introduced a series of basic laws which were known as the Woodward code. But when Woodward was absent from the Territory, Hull and Witherell repealed them all in one enactment and wrote an entirely new legal code. One act, adopted at this time, made it punishable to conduct an unauthorized banking business. This was aimed directly at Woodward who, at the time, still held the presidency of the Detroit Bank.

Angered by this treatment, Woodward refused for a while to attend meetings of the legislative board. This prompted Griswold to write: "Very little doubt exists here that this unhappy man has for some time past been endeavoring by his own strange conduct, to impede this present system of territorial government, and make it appear as 'a wretched system.'"[11] Griswold was particularly incensed because Woodward had recommended abolishing the office of secretary after Griswold had been indicted for attempting to persuade members of the militia to desert. Woodward also let it be known that he regarded Griswold, the former clergyman, as a religious fanatic intent upon stirring up trouble and resentment among the French Catholics.

So matters proceeded from bad to worse. As a means of retaliating against Hull for the repeal of the Woodward Code and the adoption of the anti-bank bill. Woodward drew up a list of resolutions severely critical of the governor. Presenting them to the legislative board, he accused Hull of spreading exaggerated rumors of Indian threats, of arming a band of escaped slaves, and making improper use of the militia.

The real basis of Woodward's distrust of Hull had its origin in a dispute about validating the territorial laws. Several of these had been signed only by the governor. Woodward contended, probably with justification, that inasmuch as the power to legislate was placed in the hands of the Governor and Judges as a body, all acts should be signed by each member of the board. Woodward was willing that laws should be adopted by a majority of the members, but once adopted, he insisted, they had to be signed by all. Hull's contrary opinion and his single-handed actions in regard to these laws stirred within Woodward the fear and suspicion that the governor was attempting to set himself up as a dictator, and that his constant use of the militia was simply proof of his determination to support himself, by force if necessary, against any opposition. Woodward's suspicions in this regard very likely were unjust. Hull's behavior probably reflected bad judgment rather than evil intent. The governor managed to block adoption of Woodward's censoring resolutions by having himself appointed a committee of one to reply to them.

Woodward reported to Madison concerning the factional dissension in the territory. "The discord is both great and bitter," he wrote. "It seems to have resolved into a mere struggle between the governor and the secretary. . . I have not the attachment of the ardent and violent on either side; but experience most malignity from the partizans of the latter. Nothing less than an impeachment is to serve for me." [12]

Each sought to have the last word. Hull wrote to the president with his account of the state of affairs in Michigan. "I respect him," he said of Woodward, "as a scientific man; and he may be useful where he cannot take the lead. He may suggest many brilliant things, which after being pruned, and qualified, may be useful. His misfortune is, that he cannot level his mind, to the common—ordinary occurrences of life. The experience of past times, is no lesson to him, and his ambition appears to be, to surprize mankind, by the singularity and novelty of his schemes." [13]

This was a more penetrating analysis of Woodward's character than even Hull guessed.

Periodically, Woodward escaped from this heated atmosphere to a quiet retreat which he had found at Frenchtown, on the River Raisin. There he issued occasional blasts at Hull and Griswold, regarding them as a pair of evil genii, responsible for all the partisan feeling. He failed to realize his own contribution to it.

"The high and serious discussions . . . which subsist between the two first officers of our government . . . seem to present almost insuperable barriers to society and confidence," he wrote of Hull and Griswold on March 8, 1808. "I have found it an embarrassing and almost impossible task, to avoid the enmity of their respective adherents; according as I happen to be successively suspected of favoring the one or the other.

"The only mode I could adopt was to avoid, as far as practicable, particular intercourse with both. For sixteen months past I have had no intercourse with the secretary, and for about eight months none with the governor. While I condemn, in the most unequivocal manner the malice which the secretary bears towards the governor, and the low intrigues to which he has resorted to injure him, and collaterally all who have entertained the least friendship for him, I am at the same time very sensible of a number of important indiscretions in the governor's conduct. I say *indiscretions;* because if I thought there was more than indiscretions, I would not hesitate to say so, either to the general executive, or to the public." [14]

Griswold's efforts to undermine and replace Hull resulted in his own downfall. When the terms of the two officials expired in the spring of 1808, Hull was reappointed; Griswold, to his dismay, was not. In his place, Reuben Atwater was sent out as secretary—a safe, unassuming, and presumably unambitious man. Apparently Hull thought this was the time to extend the olive branch. To Woodward, still rusticating on the banks of the River Raisin, he sent a request that the chief justice preside at his inauguration and administer the oath of office.

If this was a peace gesture, Woodward rejected it rather brutally. In a long, involved and somewhat specious reply, he told Hull that he would not officiate, and gave his reasons. The original Ordinance of 1787 provided that the governor of the Northwest Territory should be sworn in by the president of Congress. There no longer was such an officer, Woodward pointed out, and the law had not been amended to authorize anyone else to perform the duty.

"In short, Sir," he told Hull, "the law requiring the oath to be administered by a particular officer, that officer having ceased to exist . . . it appears to me that no person now possesses the authority." That included the president, the vice president and the speaker of the House of Representatives, he said.[15]

If this was intended as a deliberate affront, certainly that is the way Hull took it. He found a justice of the peace to swear him in. Having heard about the affair, Jefferson remarked that "Woodward's scruples are perplexing. and they are unfounded."

The chief justice, Hull declared, was sulking because everyone did not share his "devotion to his darling child, the plan of the City of Detroit."

As time went on, Woodward became more firmly convinced that Hull intended to supplant the civil government with a military dictatorship. From Washington, where he had gone early in 1809, he wrote Griffin:

"A more steady executive would have made a wonderful difference in the state of affairs. Turbulence, vexation and fickleness are too often the concomitants of those who wear the sword, not with the holy enthusiasm of defending liberty, but from the minor passion of military eclat."[16]

The manufacture of false Indian alarms as an excuse to keep the militia semi-mobilized was, he insisted, an attempt by Hull "to subvert this government by force." He promised to resist such efforts by "what I trust will not be an unbecoming, but which will certainly be a firm opposition." The government of the Territory, he added, was not the one established by Congress, but one which had been created by Hull. "And I dare not give you my aid in carrying it into execution," he warned.

Hull defended his use of the militia, declaring the danger from the Indians was very real. Woodward, he observed, was as nervous as anyone else. "He ought further to have remembered," the governor replied with some spirit, "the cautions and preparations which for a long time he made for his own safety and the safety of his property; that everything belonging to him was kept constantly locked up in his saddle bags, and on various alarms, he appeared on the parade with his hair standing on end with his saddle bags, instead of arms in his hand." [17]

In all this period of near-anarchy, which continued from 1806 until 1812, the officers of the Territory shared with the people the unhappiness they had created for themselves. The thought and hope uppermost in the mind of each—Griswold excepted—was to be transferred elsewhere. Hull believed for a while that he might be removed from office, and he sought to forestall such a personal calamity by asking for an appointment to the army. Griffin exerted all his influence, unsuccessfully, to obtain a transfer to one of the southern territories. Woodward sought appointment as governor of Illinois Territory, but nothing came of it. For better or for worse, he had to remain in Michigan.

3

The ill-will, the distrust and the suspicion which existed among the members of Michigan's territorial government were, naturally, transmitted to the public. Governor Hull, Judge Woodward and each of the others had his friends and supporters. As the members of the legislative board fought among themselves, their quarrels spread among the people. A constant stream of complaint, charges and counter-charges, defense and explanation, flowed between Detroit and Washington. As it continued to pour out of the mail pouches, one may believe that the president and his cabinet became heartily sick of it. Bates, visiting in Washington in 1808, sensed the feeling of exasperation toward the Michigan disputants. "The complaints from Detroit had already made an impression on the minds of the President and the heads of departments," he informed Woodward. "Some of the members of Congress mentioned something about impeachment . . ."[18]

Peter Audrain, the venerable register of the land board and close friend of Woodward, revealed the fractious nature of the people in a communication to the chief justice.

"This unhappy place," he said, "is more than ever torn by factions, assaults, batteries. The Magistrates have been these several days buried in binding people to keep the peace." As an example of the measures necessary to preserve order, Audrain cited the case of George McDougall, a justice of the peace, who was required by another justice to give his word that he would refrain from whipping George Hoffman, the Detroit postmaster, "for 12. months." After that, presumably, Hoffman had to defend himself as best he could, without benefit of law.

"Merciful Heaven!" old Audrain lamented, "would these political dissensions had never existed; the parties in contention can never derive any advantage from it. They must have a poor opinion of us at Washington, or else we are little, or perhaps badly known."[19]

Audrain, who combined his talents as conscientious public servant with those of an inveterate gossip, mischievously reported that when Hull and Griswold, although barely speaking, were invited to a St. Patrick's Day party at Richard Smyth's new tavern on lower Woodward avenue, "mirable dictu they both attended, dined and got gay."

The situation became such that the military officers, usually aloof to civil disputes, became alarmed. They reported in a round robin to the secretary of war that "commotions and ferments" were being excited among the inhabitants, and that the laws and public officials were being brought into disrepute "to the danger and injury of the United States."

Hull and the judges were criticised for holding their meetings at any convenient place and at unscheduled hours. Sometimes they gathered in a tavern, quite often at Smyth's which was cynically referred to as the seat of government. The people were not offended because a tavern was used; it was the fact that the convenience of the surroundings created a public expense. Refreshments naturally were called for to slake thirsts acquired in line of duty, and the bill was sent to the public treasury. On October 28, 1806, the monumental James May (besides being a leading merchant, he weighed more than three hundred pounds) presented the Territory with a bill of £1, 10s for a dozen bottles of cider, six "black bottles" and "three pint tumblers, double flint cut." (Does the latter item represent breakage?) Eventually a council house was erected at the present intersection of Jefferson and Randolph streets, and government business was transacted in an atmosphere somewhat more free from temptation.

Dissatisfaction was often expressed at the methods employed in adopting laws. The Ordinance of 1787 required the Governor and Judges to use the laws of the "original" states. This was often difficult because the compiled statutes of all of the states were not available; laws of different states relating to the same subject were frequently in conflict, and acts needed for a specific purpose in Michigan did not appear in other states. Then the question arose as to the meaning of the term "original states." Did this bar the use of laws of the newly admitted states such as Vermont, Kentucky and Ohio? Or were the Governor and Judges limited to the use of laws of the thirteen states?

This provision of the Ordinance was a loose one, and the territorial legislative board, often in a quandary about the proper course to follow, found it necessary to improvise. This led to criticism. "They parade the laws of the original states before them, on the table," said one objector, "and cull letters from the laws of Maryland, syllables from the laws of Virginia, words from the laws of New York, sentences from the laws of Pennsylvania, verses from the laws of Kentucky, and chapters from the laws of Connecticut; as far as necessary and suitable to the circumstances of Michigan. If the author were allowed the same privilege, he could easily adopt a law to hang the governor and judges of Michigan, for cruelly mangling and wilfully mutilating the good and wholesome laws of the original states."

On the whole, the board did its best, acting from necessity rather than choice. If it erred too greatly, final ratification was up to Congress which could, and often did, reject improper or unwise statutes. Modern authorities are in agreement that criticism of the Governor and Judges for acting on their own initiative was "baseless" and they were justified in giving "liberal interpretations to the provisions which had conferred their legislative powers." [20]

"Every measure of any of the constituted authorities of the Country, whither it be of a legislative, executive or judicial nature, whither of the general or local government is attempted to be controuled with violence and passion by persons who are entrusted with no powers to act on the subjects," Woodward angrily declared. "The Opinions of those on whom the responsibility really rests, are resisted with personal insults. A public officer is called upon here, not only to do his part of public duty, but to defend himself privately against the low animosities of turbulent, uninformed men for so doing. He cannot walk or turn a corner in the streets, without being assailed by the most vulgar and insolent abuse." [21]

Lawlessness resulting from disrespect for the members of government shocked Woodward and affronted his judicial dignity.

"A Gentleman of the first influence of the country has declared in the streets of the town that the first law that is passed that does not please him, he will kick the government to hell," Woodward reported. "A justice of the peace tells a Citizen if he builds a house he will set fire to it, and he remains charged with the custody of the peace."

Woodward felt the "disorderly and riotous" conditions resulted from a lack of executive firmness, but the suspicion also grew that public resentment toward himself was being deliberately stirred up. He served notice that he would not remain a passive victim of low intrigue.

"It has frequently been insinuated to me privately that a great storm is rising, and that it is directed against me. I stand in a situation to repel with disregard all the efforts of those who have assumed the direction of it; but in consequence of these admonitions I have looked around, I trust with an eye of intrepidity, to discover and meet my enemies.

"I have found," he went on, "two sons of a British drummer,

who think they have a hereditary right to make a noise in the world, and an Englishman who came to this Country in exhibiting a monkey on his back, for money, and who taking it into his head that men are animals equally easy to lead, has assumed a kind of dictatorship here."

(To whom Woodward had reference is not clear. Perhaps John Gentle and his brother Adam were the "sons of a British drummer.")

One summer day in 1808, Woodward was stopped on the street by Major John Whipple, an army officer and a friend of Governor Hull. Annoyed by a ruling in a case then pending, he proceeded to berate the chief justice. With half the town watching the fun, his anger exploded and he shouted that Woodward was "a damned rascal."

This was more than the judge could stand. He cloaked himself in his judicial dignity, signed a warrant charging Whipple with assault, and placed him under twelve dollars bond to appear at the September term of court. Whipple pleaded guilty and was fined fifty dollars. The incident later was used against Woodward who was unjustly accused both of issuing the warrant and trying the case. Actually, he acted with propriety. When the matter came into court, it was heard by Judge Witherell. Woodward was marked "absent." It was, perhaps, a picayunish affair, but Woodward felt that respect for the courts must be upheld. He was "firmly of the opinion that the Territory possessed no sovereignty and that any criminal offenses were against the peace and dignity of the United States. Moreover, being on the frontier, among a population adhering to the United States only by the most brittle ties, he felt that respect for national authority should be enforced and upheld at all cost." [22] By no means, in his opinion, could the civil authority be permitted to suffer at the hands of the military.

No sooner had Whipple been fined than he was pardoned by Hull. Thus, if anyone acted improperly it was the governor who failed to support another, equal branch of government. His action was noted severely by the grand jury as indicating "a strong propensity to assume powers with which he is not legally cloathed." This presentment was accompanied by a memorial to the president demanding Hull's removal from office.

Attempting to explain the pardon, Hull lamely attributed it to a desire "to leave everyone happy." If he exceeded his authority, he said, it "was an error of the head & not of the heart." [23]

Another attack on Woodward, more violent, occurred in 1811. It was illustrative of the undisciplined attitude toward authority, so typical on the frontier.

On June 10, 1811, Woodward was assaulted by Whitmore Knaggs who, like Major Whipple, was a partisan of Hull. A half-wild backwoodsman, Knaggs had been kidnapped as a child and raised by the Indians. His return to civilized life did not remove any of his rough edges. Hull found him useful, and gave him a militia commission, and appointed him assistant superintendent of Indian affairs, in which capacity he dealt directly with the savages and kept the government informed about their movements and state of mind. Because of his close association with the governor, Knaggs made Hull's troubles his own. So, when Woodward severely censured Hull in a legislative board session for "seducing Negro slaves from their Canadian owners and supplying them with arms," Knaggs determined to avenge his friend and patron.

What happened was graphically related in a deposition to the grand jury by George Ewing Wilson of Massachusetts, a visitor to the Territory, who was an eye-witness to the affair.[24]

According to Wilson, he was calling at the home of William Forsyth where, on the afternoon in question, a party or reception was being given. Several guests were present, including a number of ladies and Judge Woodward. While the festivities were at their height, Knaggs, accompanied by John Anderson of Frenchtown, came to Forsyth's and summoned Woodward who was in the parlor with the ladies, to step out on the gallery. When he appeared, Knaggs "profanely berated and threatened Woodward; shook his fist and then struck him on the chest, knocking Woodward back against the bannisters."

Woodward was not lacking in physical courage, and he possessed the strength and ability to defend himself in a brawl. According to Wilson's testimony, he recovered his balance and struck back, giving as good as he received.

"They then went to it," the witness stated, "finally falling down at the end of the gallery."

The other gentlemen present attempted to separate the combatants, but Anderson "stepped forward and ordered no one to interfere, and called out 'don't touch; don't interfere; let them alone; let them fight it out'." Eventually the spectators did manage to get between them. According to Wilson, Knaggs "jumped and tore about a good deal," and soon departed with Anderson, "the former being very bloody."

Woodward remained in possession of the field, the honors all his. Wilson states that after the excitement subsided, the judge "staid and took tea with the company."

Woodward was justifiably incensed at this affront to his private and official person. He issued a warrant for Knaggs' arrest, charging that he had been assaulted "with force of arms, to-wit: with clubs, etc. . . . and him did then and there strike and wound." Knaggs was indicted for assault and battery by the grand jury, and appeared in court with his attorney, Elijah Brush, the most eminent, perhaps, of all the members of the Detroit bar.

Brush was surprised to find Woodward, flanked by two justices of the peace, ready to conduct the arraignment. An objection was made to Woodward's presence and it was suggested the matter be referred to one of the chief justice's colleagues. Woodward took this motion under advisement, granting a few days' adjournment. But Griffin and Witherell declined to act. Later, according to Brush, Woodward "expressed a full conviction not only of the legality, but of the correctness of his proceedings; and observed that it appeared to him too humiliating to be laying his complaint in the first instance, like a private individual, before one of his associates, neither of whom had thought proper to notice it officially, and much more so before a single magistrate, when he was legally vested with the authority of issuing the warrant himself."

Knaggs' counsellor accepted this ruling without protest. He was bound over for trial and the jury found him guilty. The court records fail to disclose what the sentence was, but it has been stated that it was not severe. While Woodward appears to have sat on the bench during the trial, he took no active part in the proceedings, leaving the duty of presiding to Judge Witherell. Later, he started a civil action against Knaggs, asking $20,000 damages, but the suit was never tried.

Of course the faction opposed to Woodward promptly unloosed a storm of criticism for his handling of the Knaggs case, and the usual barrage of complaint flooded the mails to Washington. Woodward defended himself against his critics as vigorously as he had against his original assailant. He made it clear that he was not acting from motives of petty spite or revenge. The attack on him, he insisted, was an attack on duly constituted authority; Woodward felt that in his official capacity he stood as a symbol of the dignity and might of the United States, and neither could be violated or affronted with impunity. He stated his position in a letter to Henry Clay, explaining his stand in both the Knaggs and Whipple cases.

"I flatter myself," he declared, "that in repelling the assaults directed on myself, in subjecting to the course of justice the immediate offenders, and in defeating the malice of their ignominious authors and abettors, I have been so fortunate as to have alike sustained my personal and official rights, and the honor of the Republic which I serve." [25]

Where a breach of the peace occurred, Woodward added, the public, rather than the individual became the injured party. Under those circumstances, "though the judge or justice may also incidentally sustain injury, yet he may act." [26]

This justification was strengthened by the opinion of Brush which, in view of the attorney's professional standing, carried considerable weight.

"I am . . . convinced of the legality and regularity of the proceedings of judge Woodward relative to Mr. Whitmore Knaggs," he stated. "In fact I may say that the general conduct of judge Woodward in his judicial capacity, from the first institution of this government . . . has for the most part met with my decided approbation. . . . Possessing a discriminating mind, and sound legal attainments, he has uniformly exhibited at all times, and on all occasions, a strict and undeviating integrity, assiduity, temperance, and urbanity, marked with a degree of politeness, not always to be met with in a judicial character." [27]

Being rare, such kind words must have been balm to a spirit often sore from calumny and abuse.

Coming from Brush, this was a significant tribute.

4

Twice during the early part of his Michigan regime, Woodward was threatened with impeachment. In neither instance was the matter seriously pressed. The demands for his removal attracted more attention in Michigan than they did in Washington where talk of an impeachment really counted. In 1807, a removal petition signed by three hundred residents of the Territory cited the delay in settling land titles, the bank, and accused the chief justice of having made "a mockery of Law and a prostitution of justice."

Not knowing how such charges might be received in Washington, Woodward forwarded proof that the removal petition had been signed largely by illiterate habitants who had no real understanding of the document to which they were putting their signatures and "X's." "Whatever maxims of morality sway the bosoms of others, ingratitude and unjust political persecutions, constitute no ingredients of the Canadian [i.e. French-Canadian]," he wrote Ephraim Pentland, editor of the *Commonwealth*. Not one in ten of the habitants, he insisted, knew what they were signing. "They have been imposed on by being told that it was simply a petition respecting their lands." [28]

Discovering how they had been hoodwinked, the honest Frenchmen apologized to Woodward, and a citizens' committee, deploring the fraudulent use of the petition, reported: "Having maturely deliberated on, and duly considered the charges . . . [we] are obliged by every sentiment of morality and justice . . . to say that we consider them scandalous, abusive and productive of the greatest moral evil . . ." [29] Jefferson dismissed the matter as a tempest in a teapot, and attributed the uproar to Griswold. He and a few others, the president said, "have conducted themselves in the most atrocious manner." [30]

From St. Louis where he was sheltered from the storms of Michigan politics, Bates wrote Woodward: "I believe an enquiry at this moment would be greatly to your advantage. An impeachment would establish your name and character throughout the union. A glorious opportunity would be thereby afforded you of silencing forever those silly calumniators." Bates wondered why anyone could care to put up with the "bawlings" of the "cross brats" who were making life in Detroit so miserable for his friend.

"Can it be possible," he asked Woodward, "that you are coolly resolved to drag out your existence at Detroit? Will you not, one day, be an inhabitant of Louisiana? Where all unsouthern gentry will bring their negroes, as they cannot take them to other territories; and where, to greater advantage than in any other part of the United States, infant establishments may be made, which will increase and mature with the population and opulence of the country?" [31]

Early in 1812 another complaint was made about Woodward, this time directly to the House of Representatives. Available records indicate it was based on the Knaggs case. The *National Intelligencer* for May 5, 1812, reporting the transactions of the House for the previous day, had the following item:

"The Speaker laid before the House a packet which he had received from Detroit, in Michigan territory, inclosing a number of papers, amongst which is a presentment of a Grand Jury to the Superior Court in Sept., 1811, complaining of the non-execution of the law, and of alleged misconduct on the part of one of the Judges (A. B. Woodward, Esq.) and sundry papers illustrative of these complaints, together with a letter from the Judge whose conduct is complained of, all addressed to the Speaker of the House."

Woodward was aware that there were those in the Territory who would have liked to see him impeached, and there is evidence that they were actively working toward that end. Lewis Bond, one of the Territory's leading political figures, had commented some months earlier to the effect that "I am aware that Woodward can only be removed by impeachment, but I am also of opinion that sufficient ground exist to effect that." Bond indicated that Senator Worthington of Ohio, had been making inquiries and "has requested me to give a correct and candid statement of the Conduct or rather Misconduct of the Michigan government." [32]

The impeachment never got beyond the back-of-hand whispering stage, although it has been suggested that more might have come of it had not the impending events of the War of 1812 made the conduct of Woodward and the territorial government in general a matter of secondary concern to Congress. Certainly Woodward must have felt relieved when he read the final sentence of the *Intelligencer* report of May 5.

"This packet," it stated, "which is voluminous and of rather unimportant contents, was ordered to lie on the table."

Perhaps it was relief at this disposition of the matter which prompted Woodward's breezy comment that the government "knows too well how much it costs to try a judge to listen to a territorial impeachment."

Relations between the members of the territorial government, and between them and the public, lead to the conclusion that as a legislative body the Governor and Judges were almost a complete failure. It is difficult to fix the responsibility for the unfortunate situation which existed. It was shared by many. Governor Hull failed as an executive leader. He was unable to remain aloof and detached from the petty jealousies and intrigues which inevitably assail a man in his position. Hull lacked firmness and decisiveness; a kindly nature and courtliness of manner were not enough on the frontier. What was needed were the iron and fire of an Andrew Jackson, the earthiness of a Sam Houston. Hull simply did not measure up, and because he saw everything, as it was said of him, through the medium of his fears, his end was ignominy and disgrace.

As a legislator, Woodward did not attain the stature which might have been expected in the light of his natural talent and experience. His great weakness was his impatience—both with people and events. Woodward saw everything in the clear light of ultimate achievement. He was more the architect than the mason building slowly on solid foundations. His flamboyant impetuosity led him to quick conclusions—which may have been correct ones—but his arrival left him standing solitary and lonely; it took too long for his associates and the public to catch up to him. The slow pace of territorial advancement discouraged him; he had a tendency to sulk when his vision was not immediately shared by others. Above all, it took him a long time to realize that the French habitants who were steeped in an ancient tradition essentially medieval in character, were not prepared for the enlightened republicanism he offered them.

The weaknesses of Woodward and Hull, while considerable, were not as serious as the inherent structual defects of the system under which they were required to function. This is recognized by students of the territorial government who find much in the administration of the Governor and Judges that reflects to their credit.

"The territorial legal structure of Michigan was chaotic," observes William Wirt Blume. "Laws of the old Northwest Territory became part of the code of Indiana when it was established as a territory; Michigan inherited these, and there was a wide difference of opinion even among the judges themselves, whether these statutes were or were not applicable in the new territory . . . There was no copy either of the Northwest or Indiana laws in Michigan in 1805 or for some time thereafter . . . The legislative power presented many problems of interpretation that were extremely difficult to solve." [33]

That is undeniably true. But later, when the legislative board had received the statutes of other states, upon which it was permitted to improvise for its own Territory, it failed to offer any sound legislative program looking toward the economic, social and political progress of Michigan. The single notable exception was the solution of the land title problem. Otherwise, during the entire administration of Governor Hull, there was no important legislation to encourage road building, education, or the advancement of political maturity. This neglect, abetted by the administration's failure to keep out of small intrigues, had a serious effect on the Territory's development. While migration was already surging west and southwest, it by-passed Michigan. Failure of the Territory to develop at the same rate as other sections of the West very nearly cost the United States the possession of one of its potentially richest and strongest components.

This was the state of affairs on October 4, 1811, when Governor Hull left Michigan for an extended leave of absence. He returned in the summer of 1812, not as civil governor, but as a military leader, under circumstances and facing events which were to bring about his complete ruin.

CHAPTER V

"Justice in the Land"

1

AUGUSTUS WOODWARD may not have been an unqualified success as a legislator. But in his capacity as judge, presiding over the Supreme Court of Michigan Territory, he performed with considerable ability and earned a well-deserved measure of distinction.

"Although in general the affairs of Michigan Territory were poorly administered during the period under consideration [1805–1812], the Supreme Court of the Territory, in spite of adverse conditions, managed to conduct its business in an orderly and fairly dignified manner," says W. W. Blume. "It provided the people of the Territory with an administration of justice according to law which under the circumstances, should have given, and which in most instances did give, general satisfaction."

The court was the real and almost exclusive expounder of American principles of democracy on that frontier. It was a bulwark of protection for individual and collective rights, privileges and security.

Woodward dominated the court. He and Bates worked well together during the latter's brief tenure. Griffin was content to nurse his physical aches and pains and to long for greener pastures. In all other ways he was perfectly willing to follow Woodward's lead, although the chief justice "apparently had very little respect for Judge Griffin . . . and he continually bullied him and controlled him to his liking."[1] The pair formed a majority on the bench against which the saturnine, completely realistic Witherell could not prevail. Knowing the futility of trying he rarely made the effort—only when Woodward was absent from the Territory could he successfully assert himself. Actually there never was such conflict in the court as there was in the legislative meetings. When it did appear, as it was bound to at times, it was given an emphasis beyond its importance.

"As a judicial officer," it has been said of Woodward, "the important and ludicrous affairs of the Territory were assigned to him for determination. Sometimes he acted vindictive, even absurd, and again he made decisions that were exceedingly just, though unpopular." [2]

"The work of the court," says Blume with a more kindly tone, "was conducted in a careful and orderly manner according to the orthodox procedure of the time. The opinions of Judge Woodward reveal a knowledge of law that was both extensive and penetrating." [3]

No judge could ask for a better verdict upon himself than that!

There was no delay in organizing the court and putting it into operation. The first session was held July 29, 1805. The Supreme Court, as the Territory's highest tribunal, actually served a dual purpose; it was, as its name suggests, the court of last resort for cases arising out of the common and statutory law of the Territory; it was also a United States court of broad jurisdiction. From the territorial standpoint it assumed "exclusive jurisdiction in all cases where the title to land was in question, original and concurrent jurisdiction where the amount in dispute exceeded two hundred dollars and appellate jurisdiction in all cases whatsoever." [4]

At the outset the Territory was divided into four judicial districts with a district court in each. These districts were those of Detroit, encompassing the area along the Detroit River; Erie, in the southeastern part of Michigan, including Frenchtown and nearby settlements; Huron, which was along Lake St. Clair and the St. Clair River and north to Saginaw Bay; and Michilimackinac which included all the Territory north of Saginaw Bay.

The district courts had local judges, appointed to preside over them, but the law required that one of the territorial judges should attend each district court session. Woodward regularly presided in the Erie district; he was holding court in Frenchtown as early as September 2, 1805 in the house of Jean Baptiste Jereaume on the north bank of the River Raisin.

The district courts had original jurisdiction in all civil cases involving more than twenty dollars. They also had probate powers.

Below the district courts were the justices of the peace, the number depending upon the need. In 1810 the district courts were abolished; all cases of less than one hundred dollars were given to the justice courts, and all others to the Supreme Court. This system continued until 1815 when county courts were established with jurisdiction between the justices of the peace and the Supreme Court, and with power to hear appeals from the former.

There was always agitation for circuit courts, but these did not appear until 1827, after Woodward had left the Territory. The reason was a lack of business for them, and because the Supreme Court judges were reluctant to undergo the hardships of riding circuit in the remote wilderness. Because of their dual role as legislators, the judges could not be long absent from the legislative board. Griffin particularly resisted the idea of leaving the comforts of Detroit for the perils of the backwoods. "His old Dread and horror of the possibility of being obliged to sit alone on the bench —Without Woodward at his elbow to *think* for him," was the way one member of the bar interpreted Griffin's unwillingness.[5] There is no record that Griffin ever presided over a district court outside of Detroit.

At first the powers of the territorial Supreme Court were not clearly defined. It became necessary for the judges to evolve a body of law applicable to the nature of the community and the circumstances which presented themselves under Michigan's imperfect social and economic development. In a sense, this represented an assumption by the court of a power not specifically authorized by Congress.

The fountainhead of territorial jurisprudence lay, of course, in the Ordinance of 1787 which assured the people of the Northwest of "judicial proceedings according to the course of the common law."

The problem of the court's reach was confused by the question of just how much ground the common law covered. Before Michigan Territory was established, the inhabitants had, at one time or another, lived under French edicts and custom, the English common law and statutes of Great Britain and Upper Canada, and the statutes and ordinances of the Northwest Territory and Indiana Territory. Blume points out that the first laws adopted in

Michigan contain only faint evidence of any assumption on the part of the Governor and Judges that the laws of Indiana Territory were carried over and remained in force in the new territory. Lacking the specific recognition, no initial effort was made to repeal or amend the Indiana laws which were based, in part, on the laws of the Northwest Territory. Yet, even without recognition, the fact remained that they existed and provided potential precedent if invoked. No wonder that the people of Michigan Territory "were confused and distracted by the complexity of the laws." [6]

Woodward, as chief justice, felt it incumbent upon himself to clarify the situation and eliminate some of the confusion. Prior to American occupation of Michigan on July 11, 1796, the laws of Upper Canada had been in force in the Territory. As a first move, Woodward ruled in 1807 that these no longer applied. Within the next two or three years, after the legislative branch had written its own statutes, it was time to go a step further. On September 16, 1810, an act was passed which abolished all but the English common law and the territorial statutes and Federal laws. This act provided that from that date there no longer would be in force "the *Coutume de Paris* or ancient French common law" or "laws, acts, ordinances, writs and decrees of the ancient Kings of France . . . and decrees of the Governors or other authorities of the province of Canada and the province of Louisiana," or the laws of the Northwest and Indiana Territories.[7]

The English common law was retained to give support to the adopted laws because, as Woodward expressed it: "The United States of America derive So much of their government and jurisprudence from the Celebrated and potent island on the western Coast of Europe, by Whose enterprise and perseverance the Northern part of this hemisphere has been principally Colonized, that it is difficult, even at this day, to decide ordinary Cases, without a reference to the laws and policy of Britain."

To erase from the books of an American community all the laws of foreign powers might appear to be a curious and unnecessary gesture. Why it was done, at Woodward's instigation, has been the subject of speculation. A clue is offered by Professor Blume. In 1794, Great Britain and the United States made treaty arrangements for the British evacuation of Michigan. These were finally carried out in 1796. The treaty stipulated that all settlers and traders of British nationality electing to remain in Michigan under American jurisdiction, could continue to enjoy their property, and the "nature and extent" of their interest in such property would be determined by the laws under which it was acquired. This meant that the older inhabitants could claim the protection of French and British laws. In deciding some early cases, Woodward had to recognize a 1793 statute of Upper Canada. Public discussion of this law in the course of the trial led many of the inhabitants to believe that all earlier laws remained in force.

If the Supreme Court was restricted to common law jurisdiction at the outset, the judges quickly increased their scope, and soon were hearing chancery, equity and admiralty cases. Altogether it was a busy court, alive not only to the requirements of a backwoods society, but also to the sovereign rights and dignity of the United States—as Judge Woodward soon had an opporunity to demonstrate.

2

In his varied juridical duties, Augustus Woodward sometimes found himself confronted with matters of international significance which, lacking firm but delicate handling, could have exploded into serious incidents. That they did not bears testimony to his ability to uphold the dignity of the United States, and at the same time tread gently where the sensitivity of other nationals was exposed. One such case, possibly more celebrated for the bizarre incidents which it produced than for any particularly profound principles it established, came before the Supreme Court late in 1806. It involved a question of American sovereignty and the recognition of its inviolability by British military authorities who were often prone, on the wilderness frontier, to treat American rights casually.

As an international barrier, the Detroit River imposed no serious difficulties for deserters from either the British or American armies who sought sanctuary on the other shore, as the case may have been. There were times when the commandants of Fort Detroit or Fort Malden, scanning their respective morning reports, must have concluded that the principal traffic across the boundary consisted of military fugitives. Having once gained the other side, they were reasonably safe. There was no agreement between the two countries for the apprehension and return of deserters.

Recruits for those distant garrisons were hard to get—and harder to hold on to. Exasperated officers, seeing their ranks depleted, pursued the fugitives without benefit of law, and there grew up an unofficial gentlemen's agreement that search parties from one side of the river would be assisted by officers of the garrison on the other. This practice was not approved of by the American civilian population. This was because the British had, on occasion, employed Indians to cover the trail between Detroit and the Maumee River over which the redcoat deserters sometimes tried to escape. These Indians were as likely to waylay an innocent farmer bound for market as to pick up a fleeing grenadier.

It was not Indians but a pair of His Majesty's officers, Captain Adam Muir and Ensign John Stowe Lundie who finally brought matters to a head and deposited the whole problem in the judicial lap of Judge Woodward. A soldier by the name of Morrison ran away from Fort Malden, the British post at the mouth of the Detroit River, and, it was suspected, escaped to the American shore. Captain Muir and Ensign Lundie, with a few members of the provost guard, set out in pursuit. While they were crossing the river, Thomas Nolan, a deputy United States marshal, was going by boat from Detroit to the mouth of the River Rouge, about six miles below the American fort. Just before reaching his destination, he was stopped by the British and, much to his annoyance, his boat was searched. After some purple language was exchanged on both sides, it was suggested that all hands go ashsore to a nearby tavern and settle their difficulties over a glass of something warming.

While the balm of hot grog was being applied to Nolan's wounded feelings, a British sentry posted outside sighted a canoe. Muir ordered his boat manned, the canoe was overtaken in American waters, and its passenger was discovered to be Morrison who was taken ashore. Nolan then collected a posse which forcibly took the prisoner away from his British captors. Nolan then escorted Morrison to Detroit and hid him in a private residence.

Muir and Lundie followed them, and told their story to sympathetic American officers who promised to assist them to recover their man. By evening, Morrison was found hidden in the house of Conrad Seek, a tailor. Muir and Lundie, accompanied by some American officers including Captain Henry Brevoort, Lieutenant Porter Hanks, Captain Abraham Hull, the governor's son, and Captain Tuttle, all "double charged with good Monongahela," went down into the town to take Morrison. What happened provided one of the liveliest Donnybrooks that Detroit ever witnessed. It can best be described by the colorful account later published in the Philadelphia *Aurora*.

"The besieged," the newspaper recounted, "was under the command of Lieutenant Seek [of the militia], an experienced officer who, having no other weapons of defense than his bodkin and Sheffield needles, did not hold out long against the impetuosity of such experienced veterans. A breach was soon effected, where the heroes of both nations entered, swords in hand. Lundi (sic) presented a loaded pistol to Seek's head, while Muir and Brevoort seized and dragged the vanquished Morrison into the street.

"'Murder! Fire! Indians!' was loudly vociferated from the throats of all the men, women and children that were in the house at the time; the same sounds were reverberated by the people of the neighborhood; a general terror prevailed and no wonder. The same day, in the forenoon, news was circulated in town that seven hundred Indians were lying in ambush fifteen miles back in the woods, ready to massacre all in this town and settlements. The people rushed from their houses, armed with swords, guns, shovels; others carrying buckets and barrels of water shouted 'Where are the Indians? Where is the fire?'

"Meanwhile the report of a pistol was heard, and in a few minutes another; which sounded in the terrified people's ears like great guns, and directed them to the scene of action. John Harvey, a baker, and next neighbor to Seek, was at his own door when the affray began. Seeing three or four men dragging one by the shoulders, and without knowing the cause of the custody, he ran, laid hold of Morrison's limbs, and detained him by main strength, in defiance of their threats to run him through and to blow out his brains. The old story was half realized of "Pull baker, pull devil.' 'Fire and be d__d, you ruffians!' was all the baker said till poor Morrison's clothes were all torn to atoms.

"Meanwhile Seek had been around the neighborhood spreading

the alarm, and returned amongst the first, and laid hold of Lundi. A struggle ensued, but Lundi, finding Seek had the command of his pistol arm, and perceiving an opening, fired it off towards the ground; and not with intention to kill Seek, as was erroneously stated . . . Captain Muir, seeing the people assembling, presented his pistol to Morrison's naked breast, swearing that since he could not take him alive, he would have him dead. Morrison, perceiving his intention, struck the pistol to one side, and instead of killing Morrison, the ball went through the calf of his own leg.

"The citizens by this time assembled in great numbers, and relieved Harvey from a very dangerous situation; surrounded the officers, and carried them in civic triumph to Smyth's Tavern, to get the wound dressed." They were then placed under arrest, turned over to the civil authority and "came under recognizance to stand trial at the next September term." [8]

While this affair was lightly treated in the press, it was no joking matter to the townspeople, or to the judges before whom the accused appeared for trial in September, 1806. Not only had British officers, in their official capacity, violated American rights by entering the United States for an illegal purpose, but they had been joined by United States army officers in forcibly entering a private dwelling without warrant or pretense of lawful authority, and making an arrest. That was something no American citizen could view with complacency.

Thus the trial at which Woodward presided had serious undertones. The formal charge was disturbing the peace. The trial was a fair one; Muir, Lundie and Brevoort were found guilty; Muir was sentenced to seventeen days imprisonment and fined $44.40; Lundie was given a six-months term and a fine of $8,888; Brevoort, $250 and seventy-five days.

These punishments, particularly Lundie's, were shockingly severe, but Woodward fully understood the necessity for making an example of the officers. Poor Lundie, hearing his sentence, was on the verge of collapse. He could hardly hope to pay such a fine on an ensign's pay and "hung down his head, and looked as any other man would do when condemned to pereptual imprisonment."

The citizens who had insisted that the offenders be taught a lesson now were appalled at the harshness of the sentences, and Woodward became the target of new criticism. Knowing what was involved, he shrugged it off.

It is hard to understand why Lundie's penalty was so severe. Perhaps Woodward believed the British government would be forced to pay it, thereby learning a salutary lesson concerning the rights of other nations. This suggestion seems to have some basis in the light of subsequent events. A few days after the trial, Major Alexander Campbell, commandant at Fort Malden, offered an official apology and a disavowal of his subordinates' conduct. Very likely this was what Woodward wanted, and he used Lundie's fine to force it from the British. At any rate, once the apology was received, the case was reopened. Judge Griffin who had not attended the first trial, called Woodward's attention to the fact that the officers had been sentenced under English common law, whereas the statutes of Indiana, in force in Michigan, limited the penalty for breach of the peace to a fine not to exceed one hundred dollars. Woodward conceded the point which he may have overlooked purposely in the first instance. The jail terms which had not been served were commuted, and the fines reduced to sixteen cents each.

While Woodward no doubt hoped that the Malden officers and the British government had been taught a lesson, he recognized that there might be other incidents in the future unless diplomatic measures were taken to prevent them. He introduced a bill in the next legislative board meeting which provided for the delivery both of deserters and escaped slaves. He also suggested to the secretary of state that a treaty be arranged with Britain "to obviate future interruptions of harmony." [9]

Neither the law nor the treaty was immediately enacted. And as Woodward feared, affairs of the Muir-Lundie type re-occurred, resulting in mounting tensions on both sides of the border. Not until 1815 when Governor Lewis Cass forced a showdown by vigorously prosecuting an offending British officer, and assuming an attitude of firm defiance that nearly led to an armed clash, were the border violations for all time ended.[10]

3

Slavery was a major social problem in Michigan under the early American regime. The Ordinance of 1787 prohibited it in the

Northwest Territory, but did not abolish it. The French and the British living in Michigan who had possessed slaves prior to the American occupation in 1796 continued to hold them. Legally they were within their rights under the provisions of the treaty of 1794 which allowed them to retain possession of all their property. The British, although they abolished slavery in their overseas dominions, conceded the right of residents of other nationalities to keep property held before British jurisdiction was established. As a result, many Frenchmen on the Canadian side of the border as well as in Michigan were slave owners. So were British subjects who had owned slaves before the emancipation law was adopted.

A British law of 1793 provided for gradual emancipation. Children of slaves owned by Canadians were to remain in servitude until they reached the age of twenty-five. Thereafter they were to be free.

The exact number of slaves in Michigan Territory in 1807 is not a matter of definite record, but compared to the total population it was substantial. Most of the well-to-do had one or more servants in bondage; they were used both as domestics and as laborers in the fur trade. William Macomb at one time owned twenty-six slaves; many other families had from one to five. These slaves were both Negroes and Indians. The former, for the most part, were descendants of Negroes kidnapped in Kentucky by raiding Indians during and after the Revolutionary War. The Indian slaves were captured by their own race in tribal wars. They were ransomed by the whites to save them from torture and death. These Indian slaves were called "pani," a corruption of Pawnee, a western tribe particularly despised by the Indians of the lake region. They were said to have made excellent house servants and were preferred to Negroes. In time the term "pani" became synonomous for slave and was applied to Negro and Indian alike.

Immediately following the American occupation, and before territorial organization, slavery existed "in a very mild form," according to Cooley, "and no glaring evils or abuses arrested public attention, or excited active hostility to the institution." That was because while slavery existed, the slave trade did not. It was not too difficult, apparently, for one held in bondage to obtain freedom; there were many free Negroes in Detroit by 1807.

By the time Woodward came to Detroit, there was a growing feeling against slavery. As far as can be determined, this was not the result of any sudden awakening of a social conscience. Rather, it was an expression of resentment on the part of those of American stock against some of the wealthier aliens who probably held the majority of the slaves.

The people of Detroit appeared incapable of detached consideration of any problem; without something to stir up tempers, life would have been pale and hum-drum on that frontier. Thus public excitement eventually made slavery a heated issue which finally came to a boil in Woodward's courtroom.

The first case to come before him was on a writ of habeas corpus, applied for by Attorney Harris Hickman, soon to become the son-in-law of Governor Hull. Hickman represented the Denison family—Lizette, James, Scipio and Peter, Jr. They were slaves owned by Catherine Tucker, a widowed British citizen, residing in the Huron District. Catherine's husband, William, had purchased the parents of these slaves in 1784. All the children except Peter, Jr., had been born prior to 1793. Notwithstanding that fact, they claimed that, having reached the age of twenty-five, they were entitled to their freedom under the Canadian law of 1793. The case was heard on September 23, 1807 with Woodward presiding. He gave the law as liberal an interpretation as possible.

"In this territory," he said, "Slavery is absolutely and peremptorily forbidden. Nothing can reflect higher honor on the american government than this interdiction. The Slave trade is unquestionably the greatest of the enormities which have been perpetrated by the human race. The existence at this day of an absolute & unqualified Slavery of the human Species in the United States of America is universally and justly considered their greatest and deepest reproach." [11]

This was a sharp indictment of "the peculiar institution," offered well in advance of general public opinion, even in the North. It was not made merely for popular consumption, but was a sincere expression of Woodward's abhorrence of the practice.

The prohibition of slavery in the Northwest, Woodward admitted, "ought to be considered as imposing a most serious and sacred duty." But eager as he was to uphold the interdict, a greater duty confronted him—that of upholding the law and the compact made with Great Britain in 1794 to protect the rights of settlers in their property.

"But," Hickman argued in effect, "'property' under the treaty was never intended to mean 'human property'."

Woodward disagreed. He pointed to a French ordinance of 1709 which permitted the people of New France to own slaves, thus acknowledging a property right which continued to exist under the British and which was confirmed by the British act of 1793 providing for gradual emancipation.

That was all true, Hickman contended. But the Treaty of Paris of 1783 ceded Michigan Territory to the United States. American laws, therefore, should apply retroactively to that date, even if the United States did not come into actual possession until 1796.

Once more Woodward differed. "Though this country was contracted to be ceded by the treaty of 1783, it was not ceded in fact . . . until the eleventh day of July, 1796," he declared. Up to that time, British law was in effect. This law recognized the right, under certain conditions, to own slaves, and the treaty of 1794 confirmed that right. The Constitution of the United States provided that "all treaties made, or which shall be made, under the authority of the United States shall be the supreme law of the land," Hence, said Woodward, "if a treaty duly ratified is in hostility with a local regulation previously made, the provision of the treaty is paramount and must prevail over the local regulation." [12]

Because the Denisons were the property of the Tucker family prior to 1793, they could not claim the benefit of the twenty-five year clause. The treaty of 1794 confirmed the Tuckers in their possession, the Ordinance of 1787 and all other acts notwithstanding.

Regretfully, Woodward dismissed the writ of habeas corpus and ordered the Denisons restored to their rightful owner.

The matter did not end there. What happened next was a sort of Denison case in reverse, involving the flight of some slaves owned by two Canadians to the United States where, through the instrument of Judge Woodward, they found sanctuary. As it happened, they did not gain their freedom until after Detroit had been thrown into a frenzied, riotous turmoil.

The slaves involved in this second case belonged to Richard Pattinson, a well-to-do merchant of Sandwich, and to Matthew Elliott, of Amherstburg. The latter, a native of Pennsylvania, had remained loyal to the British cause in the Revolution, and in company with the notorious Simon Girty and Alexander McKee, had fled to Detroit. As leaders of the Indians in raids against the American outposts, these three committed deeds which were recorded in indelible letters on the scroll of infamy by the American frontiersmen. After the war, Elliott remained in Detroit until the American occupation. Then, for his own safety, he moved across the river and settled on a large estate just below Fort Malden. He continued to serve the British government as Indian agent in the Great Lakes region, and his activities, past and present, made him unpopular on the American side of the border. When his slaves, a young boy and girl, escaped with Pattinson's, there was an almost universal conspiracy among Detroiters to make certain their masters did not recover them.

These slaves escaped less than a month after the Denison case was decided. Elliott's people found shelter in the establishment of Richard Smyth who served his fellow citizens as boniface, justice of the peace and hatter in his busy house on lower Woodward avenue.

Elijah Brush, who was retained by Elliott, applied to the Supreme Court for the surrender of the Negroes. A hearing took place before Woodward on October 15, 1807, and defying the wrath of the townspeople, Elliott came to Detroit to attend court and identify and prove ownership of his property.

The case was not concluded the first day. Leaving the courtroom, Elliott was menaced by a mob and ran to the fort for refuge. In the evening he proceeded by back streets to Brush's house, and there the mob, led by Squire Smyth, followed him. The intention, as Smyth later admitted, was to manhandle Elliott.

Brush tried to reason with the crowd, assuring them that Judge Woodward would see that justice was done. Smyth retorted "that if the judge should decide in favor of the application, he would be Served in the same manner," adding that they "were willing to Support the Constitution, but that if the Court decided the slaves of Mr. Elliott Should be restored, the Court Should be tarred and feathered."

That, Brush replied, "would produce a Sad dilemma," pointing out that "the Court were the Constitutional judges of the law, and that they ought not to medle with it."

"By God," shouted Smyth, "they would take upon themselves to judge in cases of that kind."

Despite the angry words, Brush's firmness turned the crowd away. The next day he and Elliott boldly walked through the streets unmolested. Later Smyth confided to Brush that the bad feeling toward Elliott was not an account of the slaves, but was the result of the Canadian's Indian activities.[13]

Four days later, with the case still pending, there was another flare-up. James Heward, an employe of Elliott, came to Detroit to testify. In the company of young James Dodemead, he decided to pay an evening visit to Smyth's tavern where the slaves were hidden. As he and Dodemead approached Smyth's, Heward suggested they stop in "and get a drink of grog." Dodemead advised against it, but Heward insisted. Inside they found several citizens who greeted Heward with an ominous silence. Among the company was William Dailey, a carpenter, and Peter Curry, a sailor.

Heward ordered a pint of brandy which he invited Curry to share with him. Dailey, who apparently had already imbibed freely, began an argument with Heward, called him a "British rascal and threatened to pull off his wig if he did not immediately sit down." This was an injunction not to be ignored. Heward sat.

Then, as if by prearrangement, several others walked into the tavern and began to badger Heward who by this time had absorbed courage from his pint of brandy. He became noisily aggressive. Austin Langdon, one of the new arrivals, pulled off his coat and offered to fight Heward. The latter announced his willingness, and despite the efforts of Dodemead to quiet him, declared loudly that all those in the room were "a damned rascally set of beggars." With that, he was escorted out the back door and given a liberal application of tar and feathers. While this ceremony was taking place, Doctor William McDowell Scott, Detroit's leading physician, stood in his doorway, watching the proceedings, and shouting "hurraw my boys!" Dodemead finally took Heward home with him, spent the night scraping off the tar and plucking his feathers. In the morning he went out to search for Heward's wig which he found nailed to a post on a street corner. He later testified it was his belief that the attack on Heward had been carefully planned in advance.

Meanwhile, Pattinson's petition for the extradition of his slaves came before the court. Because he was not the object of American hatred as was Elliott, his case attracted less public attention. But because the issues were exactly the same, the Pattinson decision controlled the Elliott case.

"Under the law of nations," Woodward ruled, "property of a subject or citizen of one country found within the territories of another country ought to be restored, but there is no obligation under such law to restore persons.

"As rights of property in persons cannot exist by the common law, but only by statute, the manner of protecting such rights must be regulated by statute . . . The Ordinance of 1787 prohibits Slavery, hence a right of property in a human being cannot exist in this Territory except (a) as to persons in the actual possession of British settlers within the Territory on July 11, 1796, and (b) as to fugitives from lawful labor in some other American state or territory.

"The principle which leads the American government to enforce the return of slaves from one part of the United States to another ought not to be extended to other countries in the absence of reciprocal provisions." [14]

There being no such agreement between Britain and the United States, neither Pattinson nor Elliott could claim their slaves, and the fugitives were entitled to their freedom in the United States.

Woodward's opinion was greeted with delight by the people of Michigan, and with general approval throughout the northern United States. It was published in the eastern journals, and Theodorus Bailey, postmaster of New York, reported that "the Decision very generally meets the approbation of the Bar." [15]

It had quick repercussions in Detroit. Noting the lack of reciprocity prevented the return of runaway slaves to their Canadian masters, the Denisons slipped quietly across the border and claimed sanctuary in Canada. With no legal machinery to force their return, Woodward's Pattinson opinion protected them as surely as if he had decided in their favor in the Tucker case. They remained several years in Canada, free. Years later they returned to Detroit and lived unmolested for the rest of their lives, completely emancipated for all practical purposes.

The decision of Woodward in the Pattinson case had a significance far beyond its immediate effect. It helped to solidify public opinion in Michigan against the institution of slavery. There was no sentiment in the Territory, as there was in Indiana and Illinois, to amend the Ordinance of 1787 respecting prohibition of slavery.

"The Ordinance," said Cooley, "was the beginning of the end of American slavery. It checked at the banks of the Ohio the advance of a system fruitful of countless evils, social and political."

If Cooley was correct—and who can doubt it?—Woodward helped strengthen the bulwark which Congress erected with the Ordinance. The attitude of the people of Michigan toward slavery in 1807 was passed on to their children and grandchildren. In the years to come, Detroit became an important terminus of the Underground Railway, and thousands of Negroes, fleeing from bondage in the South, followed the route of the Denisons across the Detroit River to freedom in Canada.

4

When Michigan was transferred to the United States in 1796, the powerful British capitalists lost control of the fur trade in the Territory. These merchants and traders with headquarters in Montreal, influenced the policy of the home government. They never lost the hope that eventually Michigan and the entire upper lakes region would be back in the Empire. Against that time, the British, aided by bribery, held the Indians, even those under American jurisdiction, to allegiance to the Union Jack. This state of affairs continued after the War of 1812 when such questions were supposed to have been settled for all time.

Woodward, like all the citizens of the Territory, was uncomfortably aware that the British lion crouched menacingly across the river from Detroit. The proximity of the watchful, waiting British influenced his official activities. He recognized the danger and sought a way by which it might be peaceably and permanently settled.

In 1818 he heard a civil suit, brought by James Grant, an employe of the Northwest Company, against Lord Selkirk, a rival trader who headed his own enterprise. Selkirk was a familiar figure in the Detroit-Sandwich area. Laird of St. Mary's Isle in Scotland, Selkirk conceived the scheme of planting a colony of Highlanders in Canada to raise sheep. He obtained a substantial grant of land on Lake St. Clair, stocked it with imported and domestic breeds of sheep, and brought over fifteen or more families of settlers, most of them from Mull.

The project was not a success. Selkirk lost heavily before the colony finally disbanded. Turning to the Red River district of what is now Manitoba, he sought to repair his fortune in the fur trade. It was in the course of this activity that the dispute arose between him and Grant. He accused the latter of poaching in his territory, had Grant seized and transported to Montreal. Grant claimed he had been taken within the boundaries of the United States and sued in the Michigan Supreme Court for fifty thousand dollars damages for false arrest.

Because of Selkirk's title and prominence the case attracted wide attention. As a matter of law, it was relatively unimportant. Selkirk sought dismissal of the suit, claiming he had been illegally served with a summons on Sunday. In a long opinion, Woodward upheld his lordship, citing authority which ranged from Leviticus in the Old Testament to the Acts of the Apostles in the New; from the Code of Justinian to the edicts of Charlemagne, and from Canute to Coke. The dismissal was accompanied by a sigh of relief from Woodward who confided that he actually believed the trespass might have occurred on the Canadian side of the border. He was happy to escape the necessity of determining that point of fact which he would have had to do if the case had gone to trial. It was, he felt, time for such geographical uncertainties to be settled once and for all. To Secretary of State John Quincy Adams, he wrote:

"I entertain the idea that it is the duty of the American administration to make a serious effort to obtain the whole of the British possessions on this continent, by negociation.

"Ordinary inducements would be inadequate, and some views were submitted to the present President [James Monroe], during the late war, which he may recollect; and which without compromitting the essential interest, or the honor, of the United States, would be powerful allurements to the opposite party . . . I would beg, however, that the mind of the President might be reawakened on this subject; and that I may be permitted to tender my personal services, in a secret mission, for this purpose.

"I do not entertain a belief that the first effort would succeed; but I am inclined to think that, on a principle of suspension of the execution of the stipulations for a limited number of years, with profound secrecy in the interval, and with a complete and liberal extinguishment of all private feelings and personal interests connected with the subject, a second exertion might be successful.

"The obstacles will multiply with every successive day; and the Russian interests, at present inconsiderable, may in no long time, assume a great consequence.

"The present era is, certainly, not unfavorable for a complete absorption of all foreign claims on our continent." [16]

This plan, it might be remarked, was offered more than four years before the Monroe Doctrine was enunciated by the same president and secretary of state to whom Woodward addressed his proposal. His scheme was not a sudden inspiration of 1818. As early as 1806 Woodward had recognized the problem and suggested that if the United States could definitely establish boundary rights in the North and far Northwest, it would have an important effect upon ultimate western expansion.

"I am convinced," he told the government in 1806, "a great deal of money will be saved by it, and the strength of our country greatly increased in a part by no means of subordinate importance. Of the three nations who are co-proprietors with us of North America, and whose settlements are all of them now growing into consequence, I mean the British, the Spanish and the Russians, I believe it requires nothing but a footing on the Pacific ocean, and our being beforehand in stretching the line of settlements across the continent from one ocean to the other to give us a marked superiority such as will continue as long as the world shall last." [17]

Just as there was no action on his proposal of 1806, neither was there in 1818. But nearly fifty years later Secretary of State William H. Seward would follow his plan in respect to the Russians.

Woodward proved again, even if the proof was belated, that

his mind worked half a century in advance of most of his countrymen.

5

The classic conception of Justice is a stately damsel, blindfolded, with a sword in one hand and a scales in the other, the symbols of her trade. There were occasions in early Detroit when she appeared more as a jade, cavorting in the streets and roistering in the taverns. She accomplished her ends, but often without dignity. Her ministers, the judges, were no gowned and periwigged dignitaries; they were Fellow Citizens whose regalia was sober homespun—not always too clean. Instead of the mace as the outward, visible sign of authority, a pitcher of good Monongahela whisky more often sat enticingly on the bench. Trying cases could be a dry business.

At first the Supreme Court sat where and when it could. It might convene in a private home or in the common room of a tavern. Sometimes the associate judges met in the chief justice's living quarters. They met in the morning, at noon, or at night—whenever the spirit appeared to move them. Attorneys complained that court was held on the spur of the moment without advance notice to counsel and witnesses.

The prevailing atmosphere when court was in session was one of easy-going, "republican" informality. Procedure and conduct were on the casual side. Some of the more serious minded lawyers and litigants professed to be shocked at the spectacle of judges, attaches and attorneys eating lunch and passing the bottle back and forth between bench and bar while a hearing was in progress. The attitude of the judges toward each other was not always edifying. There was no love lost between Woodward and Witherell who customarily sat with their backs toward each other. When bored by the dullness of arguments, Woodward might request the clerk to mark him absent; then he would tilt back in his chair and snooze until things livened up. Once a lawyer, pleading before the court, took the opportunity while Woodward napped to launch a spirited criticism of one of the chief justice's decisions.

The delighted Witherell nudged Woodward awake and mischievously whispered to him that he had been verbally attacked. Quickly aroused, Woodward berated the lawyer for his presumption and threatened him with contempt.

"You can't cite me," the barrister retorted, in effect, "You are not present in court. The record itself shows that you are absent."

"Mark me present," Woodward roared at the clerk. Then, having acquired legal presence, he turned his attention to the offending attorney and proceeded to give him a tongue lashing.

There was no such conflict between Woodward and Griffin as there was between Witherell and the chief justice. Griffin, concerned primarily with his ailments, and intent only upon being transferred elsewhere, was perfectly content to allow Woodward to do his thinking for him. So much was he under Woodward's domination that it became a standing joke. The following barbed notice appeared in the November 29, 1822 issue of the Detroit *Gazette:*

"A very singular question has arisen under the laws of this territory, exempting property taken on execution. This law exempts the *tools* necessary for the trade or profession of the party. Suppose now, that an execution were issued against the goods and chattels of his honor, Judge Woodward, would, or would not, his other honor, Judge Griffin, be exempt from seizure under this execution? (signed) Sciawassa."

"A learned counsellor," the following issue of the paper noted, "has given it as his professional opinion on this question, that judge Griffin must be *taken* because the law will not exempt tools used for purposes of fraud."

The judges could become lawmakers at will. The adequacy of a law, once being debated by the judges during the course of a hearing, they recessed court. Without moving from their seats, they resolved themselves into legislators and adopted an act that met all objections and clarified the issue. Court then reconvened, and the proceedings continued without further interruption. Many a later jurist must have wished he could settle troublesome legal problems with such ease.

Other situations arose which were more difficult to surmount. Language was one of them. French continued to be the tongue most commonly used; the habitants either knew no other or understood English imperfectly. Fortunately, Woodward spoke and wrote French easily, and many of his charges to the grand juries were delivered in that language.

Most of the court's work was in the civil division of the law.

Crimes of violence were relatively rare; misdemeanors and violations of local ordinances were handled by the justices of the peace. Occasionally, however, felonies, including murder cases, were brought before the Supreme Court. Usually these involved Indians who, instead of being tried according to tribal custom, were indicted under the laws of the United States or the Territory. More than one erring brave went to the gallows without the slightest understanding of how he came to be there.

In 1822, two Indians, one a Menominee, the other a Chippewa, were indicted for murder. Neither Indian spoke French or English. Most of the interpreters knew French but little English, and the regular interpreters, while familiar with the Chippewa tongue, could not speak Menominee. After much searching, a boy was finally found who could discourse in Menominee. He interpreted from that language into French; a man was employed to interpret from Chippewa into French, and a third citizen was called upon to turn the French into understandable English.

Woodward was as careful as possible, despite these handicaps, to explain to Indian defendants their rights under the law. To one Ketanka, accused of murder, he pointed out in simple language why he was on trial, that twelve men would decide if he was guilty, and that one man, the prosecutor, would speak against him. The chief justice then directed that this "one man" be pointed out to the defendant "that he may know him personally." Solomon Sibley and Charles Larned, acting as district attorneys, both objected violently to being identified as the Indian's prosecutors, and flatly refused to officiate if made to go through with this ceremony. They frankly admitted their fear of becoming objects of the Indian's resentment or revenge in the event he was acquitted, or if his relatives and friends decided to honor his memory with a blood feud if he was found guilty and executed. Woodward finally withdrew his order to the prosecutors to make themselves and their roles in the trial known to Ketanka. The Indian must have wondered what all the pow-wow in the Council House was about.

Punishments were generally mild—during Woodward's entire regime there is no record of any capital punishment being invoked against a white offender, and very few Indians were executed.

Whenever possible, Governor Hull preferred to pardon condemned Indians for the good will he believed such action created among the tribes toward the government. At one time, Detroit had a whipping post near the public market. The laws of the Northwest Territory provided that persons convicted of larceny might be lashed not exceeding thirty-one stripes. Despite this provision, the journal of the territorial Supreme Court reveals only one instance of a culprit being sentenced to be whipped. Even in this case, the sentence was reduced to a fine before the cat-o-nine-tails could be laid on. In 1806 a Chippewa, Wabouse, convicted of manslaughter, was branded in the hand "with a cold iron." Perhaps some offenders got off lightly because of a peculiar attitude on Woodward's part. In 1809 he ordered the quashing of an indictment for larceny under the territorial laws on the grounds that "the territory of Michigan possesses no sovereignty", and the action should have been brought as an offense against the United States.

Woodward relied strongly upon the grand jury. At the same time, he took precautions that it should not become an instrument of oppression, political or otherwise.

"If any man shall ever, here, unjustly die, or otherwise be unjustly punished, by the hand of power, and the banner of tyranny and oppression wave upon our land," he cautioned one grand jury; "if the laws against vice and crime shall cease to be efficacious, and a virtuous and pious community be plunged into depravity and irreligion; it is to you, gentlemen, that the responsibility for the melancholy results must attach."

Witherell did his share of the court's work; Griffin, as far as can be ascertained, never wrote or delivered an opinion in his entire sixteen years on the bench. On the other hand, an examination of the court's records reveals that Woodward was the most conscientious judge in the performance of his duty, and processed a far larger volume of business than his colleagues, either individually or, perhaps, collectively.

Despite the occasional storms of criticism which broke over his head, his relations with the bar were generally good. He was popular with most of the attorneys, and they respected him.

Some of Woodward's actions were politically inept and he gave the impression of purposely trying to make himself unpopular.

An instance of this occurred in 1822 when the clerkship of the court became vacant. He was urged to recommend the promotion of the deputy clerk, C. C. Trowbridge, a young man of ability who had the almost solid backing of the bar and the public. After giving Trowbridge to understand he would get the post, Woodward suddenly and inexplicably nominated his aged father, John Woodward, then close to his eightieth year. The old man still lived in the East and had never visited Michigan.

"Mr. John Woodward is a revolutionary character, of eminent zeal and much suffering; and is a man of information and integrity," the judge told his fellow members of the bench. Although this was a flagrant abuse of patronage, he was able to force the appointment. While journeying west to take the position, John Woodward died at Erie, Pennsylvania.[18]

With somewhat less justification, there was criticism of Judge Woodward for holding court alone in the absence of his associates. In so doing he acted with perfect propriety. Had he not presided when the others were not present, there would have been long periods when the court could not have functioned.

Despite such attacks on him, Woodward continued to perform his duties both as legislator and judge. As he conceived them, these were to foster sound Americanism and to encourage the spirit of nationalism which was not strong among the heterogeneous elements of the Michigan frontier. He made the court and particularly the grand jury a sounding board to further these ends. In carrying on this educational process, he rose, on occasion, to heights of impressive eloquence.

"It is the volition of a benevolent and equally powerful republic," he told one grand jury, "that her citizen shall enjoy unmolested, his home and fireside; his land, his vine, and his fig tree; that he may, in safety, walk abroad to inhale the breath of heaven; that peace shall be in his borders, and that there shall be none to make him afraid. Wherever he is, and wherever he goes, adhering firmly to his own integrity, the peace, the dignity and the power of his country cover him with a mantle. Guard, therefore, gentlemen, with a religious care, the personal inviolability of the citizen, the safety of his family and the security of his property, considering every offense against them an invasion of the peace and dignity of the United States of America, and in their name, the Territory of Michigan, and a high contempt of their power." [19]

That statement is a fair appraisal of Woodward's own ideals, a clear declaration of the privileges and obligations of a citizen in a free and civilized society.

CHAPTER VI

One Stayed Behind

1

AARON BURR's conspiracy was a fantastic, chimerical thing, but it threw the whole nation, and particularly the West, into a frenzy of excitement in 1806. Jefferson, who always expected the worst of Burr, issued a proclamation of national emergency. Ohio mobilized its militia, and Lewis Cass, then a fledgling Buckeye legislator, sponsored legislation that empowered Ohio's governor to seize Burr's boats and supplies, and arrest such conspirators as he could lay hands on.[1]

Michigan was remote from all this, but it shared the national hysteria. At the president's request, Governor Hull formed an active volunteer defense corps which was held in service for nearly a year. Secretary Griswold circulated the malicious rumor that Hull and Woodward were secretly in league with Burr. Nothing was further from the truth.

If Woodward really was in Michigan as a counter-irritant to Burr, he fulfilled all of his obligations. Following the president's emergency proclamation, he offered a resolution to the legislative board, calling for appointment of a committee "to enquire and report whether any, and, if any, what measures ought to be taken by this Government in relation to military expeditions in this territory against the United States or any foreign nation in amity with the United States." Woodward was appointed a committee of one to conduct the investigation, and he reported back promptly. "That from certain transactions which have taken place in the western parts of the United States, and from the notice which has been taken of them by the President of the United States, and by the Governments of some of the individual States, particularly the States of Kentucky and Ohio, it cannot be doubted that Serious causes of alarm exist on the Subject matter of the resolution referred." He had received a copy of the Cass resolution from Ohio, and presented it to the legislative board for adoption. Woodward also urged "that a respectfull address be Sent to the President of the United States, assuring him of the patriotism and fidelity of the officers of this Government, and of the people of this territory."

This action by the Michigan government in January, 1807, was anti-climactic. The Burr conspiracy had been smashed months before, but so slow was the news in reaching the outpost on the Detroit River that the excitement there remained at white heat long after it had cooled in other parts of the country. Nevertheless, the action was in accordance with Jefferson's desires, and it served notice to the world that treasonable enterprises would win no support in Michigan.

This incident is indicative of the nervousness prevailing in the Territory. Michigan citizens were firmly convinced that disaster was about to overwhelm them. There were older people who vividly recalled the narrow escape from extinction at the hands of Pontiac a generation or two before. The Pontiac story grew exaggerated with the telling over the years. Everyone lived in terror of attack by the Indians or British, either singly or in combination. Remote as they were from the mass of American population, with no means of being quickly reinforced or supplied, Michigan settlers of the early territorial period sometimes considered themselves abandoned by the Federal government. "The whole territory is a double frontier," Woodward once remarked. "The British are on one side. The savages on the other."

Michiganders believed any rumor, particularly if it was sinister. Hardly had the Burr affair quieted down when Woodward thought he had stumbled on another conspiracy, this time between the Indians and some of the French whom he suspected of plotting with Napoleon for the recovery of the entire Northwest by France. He warned Secretary of State Madison that an Indian chief had gone to Paris where Napoleon had received him, and had made arrangements for a delegation of Indians and French-Canadians to go to France for another conference with the emperor. This desperate cabal, Woodward warned, was unknown to Hull who, he said, lacked close contacts with the people of the Territory.[2]

There were many who shared Woodward's concern. Thomas B. Reed wrote him from Danville, Kentucky, in 1809 that "there is much expectation of the speedy rupture with Spain," with an attempt by the latter "to retake the territory of Louisiana." The prospect of war in that quarter was alluring to Kentuckians. "The merchant thinks it will give us money, and the farmer calculates that it will increase the price of his harvest," Reed declared.

If stories of this kind were distilled from fantasy, there was reality enough in the dangers from the Indians and, shortly, from the British. As early as 1807 and 1808 the war clouds were gathering, and the people of Michigan had the uneasy feeling that it would be on their heads that the storm eventually would break. Peter Audrain gave Woodward the picture of impending disaster in a letter dated March 9, 1808, in which he quoted Aaron Greeley, territorial surveyor, who had recently returned from a trip East.

"From the best information he could obtain at Washington, the general opinion was that war with England was inevitable. If that should turn out to be the case, we are in a miserable situation. Report says that there are now at Amherstburgh 300 Indian warriors without women and children; that 5 Indians arrived yesterday from York [Toronto] with dispatches to Col. Claus, Superintendent of the Indian Department." [3]

Hull lived in pathological fear of an Indian attack. His correspondence with Washington was full of alarms and rumors of hostile intentions. Three months after his arrival at Detroit in 1805, he was warning the secretary of war of a conspiracy of the Northwest tribes against the United States. In the spring of 1807, Captain Dunham reported on conditions at Mackinac where he commanded the garrison. His story was hardly guaranteed to reassure the nervous governor.

"Their (sic) appears," Dunham said, "to be an extensive movement among the Savages of this quarter, which seems to carry with it a good deal of the *dark* and *mysterious*. Belts of Wampum are rapidly circulating from one Tribe to another; and a Spirit is prevailing by no means pacific—What I have been able to learn through sources to be relied on, leaves little room for conjecture, as to the object of their hostile intentions. . ." A few weeks later

Dunham reported that "the Savages . . . have passed the Winter almost Wholly in the War dance. . ." [4]

After the Napoleonic plot dissolved, Woodward's fears of the Indians subsided. While Hull continued to listen to and pass on to the government every frightening item that dropped off the grapevine, Woodward remained determinedly cool and objective. He thought Hull was spending too much money for a stockade around Detroit, and for other defenses. Reports "alarming to the good people of the territory respecting an invasion upon them by a savage force," were totally unfounded, Woodward insisted.

In 1807, Hull frantically notified the War Department that "the Pottawatamies on the River Huron of Lake Erie, have very lately left their Villages, with their corn fields all standing, which is said to be an unusual circumstance at this season of the year." This band and others, he stated with authority, "are preparing to strike on some of our Posts and Settlements."

Woodward pooh-poohed this shrill alarm. "I met with a young man, an Indian, from these settlements," he said. "He stated that his village had all gone on a visit to the prophet at Greeneville, were pacific, would soon return."

The Prophet was the Shawnee leader, Tenskwatawa, brother of the war chief, Tecumseh. He was organizing a confederacy of western tribes, and trying to persuade the Indians to return to the habits and customs of their forefathers, forsaking all association with the whites, British as well as American. In the exchange of argument between Hull and Woodward, the latter's calmer attitude proved justified. In 1807, the Prophet was not yet ready to send his followers on the warpath.

The state of nerves in which Detroiters habitually existed sometimes had amazing results. The report that the Pottawatamies had left their village gave birth to a collateral rumor that seven hundred and fifty bloodthirsty braves were skulking in the adjoining woods, ready to attack Detroit. One night, the citizens were aroused from their uneasy sleep by a blood-curdling caterwauling in the lower part of the town. The alarm was sounded and, certain the savages were upon them, the men snatched up their weapons and mustered at their appointed posts, ready to do or die. But investigation turned up only anti-climax.

"An alarm, at break of day," Woodward related with ill-concealed relish, "[announced] that the Indians had actually come. The militia turned out, marched to the spot from which the disturbance came, and it appeared to be no more than a drunken quarrel between a frenchman and a german and two indian women." [5]

The disgusted militiamen marched back to their warm beds, and a few days later the grand jury, exasperated by this sounding of the tocsin, decided the Federal government should pay the expense involved, and presented a bill for $14.53 to cover all costs.[6]

2

By 1808, the intention of the British for war was so apparent that it no longer was possible to cling to the wishful belief that the border alarms were only imaginative exaggerations. It was all too obvious that the unrest of the Indians, being fomented by the Prophet and Tecumseh, was being secretly encouraged by British agents. The unfriendly acts of Britain toward the United States made war almost unavoidable. The ultimate fact of conflict became a certainty; the only question was: When?

Hull, amazed at the power the Prophet was acquiring, felt the Shawnee must be the tool of some other malign influence—possibly one in a red coat.

"The foundation of this business," he told Secretary of War Dearborn, "I am not able to develope—Some think he is a tool of Brants [Joseph Brant, the Mohawk chieftain of Revolutionary War fame who, in 1808, was living in Canada]. Others that he is moved by Spanish or French influence, and others that he derives all his influence from his own arrangements & enthusiasm—Let it be what source it may, it seems all directed against the U. States—in the event of a war with Great Britain, there can be little doubt, but every effort will be made to call in the aid of this League and the other Savages who have not joined it." [7]

Hull's view was concurred in by most people on the frontier. A meeting of citizens on July 25, 1807 resolved "that any attack from the Indians upon our settlements, shall be considered as actuated by the British Government and that we shall act accordingly." This Michigan ultimatum was prompted by news reaching Detroit of the attack on the U.S. frigate *Chesapeake* by the British cruiser *Leopard.*

"If we have a war," Woodward suggested to the War Department, "I cannot believe that our government will neglect to authorize us to take immediately the British side of this strait—from the lowest settlement to the River Thames or aux Trenches, an enterprize to which we are adequate and which puts down forever all further Indian apprehensions. A thousand militia from Kentucky or Ohio would be necessary to secure the acquisition. The people of Vermont will take care of the country from Niagara to the St. Lawrence."[8] A group of southerners and westerners in Congress, labeled the War Hawks, led by such fire-eaters as Clay and Calhoun, would very soon be talking the same way.

As war became more certain, only the national administration seemed to exist in a vacuum; fumbling, delaying, indecisive; hoping the catastrophe could be averted by refusing to recognize its imminence. Defense measures, despite the urgings from exposed frontiers like that of Michigan, were painfully slow in taking form. A committee of safety was organized in Michigan late in 1811. Its members were Woodward, Solomon Sibley, Harris H. Hickman, George McDougall and Richard Smyth. A report, written by Woodward, pointed out that besides the militia, the armed force of the United States within the Territory consisted of only one hundred and seventy-three regulars, about evenly divided between the two posts at Detroit and Mackinac. The civilians, it was stated, were practically defenseless.

"Every individual house is a frontier. No one farm is covered by another farm in the rear of it," Woodward wrote.

"It may therefore be at once conceived, what would be the situation of the people of the territory of Michigan, in a case of determined hostility against them, by the savages. The inhabitants are so dispersed, that to assemble one hundred men, upon any one spot, on a sudden nocturnal notice, is physically impossible, and how are even the one hundred to be induced, in the hour of danger, to relinquish the last pleasure this world can present them, that of dying along with their innocent and helpless families, and to abandon them to certain destruction, under the, perhaps, visionary hope of any where embodying in force adequate to meet an enemy? What shall reduce into concert the exertions of two distinct people, unacquainted with the languages of each other; and who have reason to be divided in the degree of their fear? Is there again a refuge for the helpless in flight? On the south the savages intercept them from their brethren of the States. On the west, on the north, they perfectly surround them. Shall they then lift an eye to the east, throw themselves on the mercy of the British, and will they, or can they, there, find mercy? Will reason sanction the idea, or have past events authorized the hope! And what, lastly, is to be expected from the military? They *can,* and *will,* defend themselves. But they will not march out of the walls of their garrison. They have not even men enough to man their works."

The conclusion was that the regular military force should be materially strengthened; that additional garrisons be established so that some degree of defense in depth could be achieved, and that strong militia detachments from Kentucky, Ohio and Pennsylvania be sent to Michigan.[9]

Governor Hull chose this crucial moment to apply for a leave of absence in order to spend the winter of 1811–12 in Massachusetts. But before his leave expired, he was summoned to Washington where he spent several months discussing defense arrangements. He was persuaded, against his wishes, to accept command of the Army of the Northwest which, based at Detroit, was to hold the line of the northwestern frontier.

Meanwhile other developments were taking place. Seeking to check the growing power of the Prophet and stop the Indian raids against the Indiana settlements, William Henry Harrison, led a mixed force of regulars and militia to the upper Wabash country. On November 7, 1811, the battle of Tippecanoe was fought and the Prophet's village was destroyed. With this act of war, Tecumseh discarded all pretense of friendliness to the United States and led his braves to Fort Malden and an open alliance with the British. The battle on the Tippecanoe was actually the first engagement of the War of 1812. It sealed the doom of Michigan Territory.

3

Governor Hull—now Brigadier General Hull—returned to Michigan Territory in July, 1812, as commander-in-chief of an army of two thousand men consisting of three regiments of Ohio volunteers and one regiment of regulars. War between the United States and Great Britain had been declared while Hull was marching north from Urbana, Ohio. What his force lacked in equipment and training, it made up for in its enthusiasm. The colonels of the three Ohio regiments—McArthur, Findlay and Lewis Cass—were aggressive, pugnacious young men, itching for glory. Upon their arrival at Detroit, they found the local militia, commanded by Elijah Brush and Judge Witherell, was fully mobilized and garrisoning the town. The army's objective was about what Woodward had previously suggested—an immediate invasion of Canada, the capture of Fort Malden, and the occupation of the country as far east as the Thames River, or possibly the Grand River; there to meet a force from Niagara. Hull's command was adequate for the task assigned it, outnumbering the enemy opposing him by about three to one. Fort Malden was weak and incapable of sustaining either a vigorous assault or a prolonged siege. Its garrison was prepared to evacuate. The Canadian militia exhibited no enthusiasm for joining the colors and, except for Tecumseh's band, the Indians were impressed by the American show of strength and, momentarily, remained neutral.

Thus in early July, the odds all seemed to favor a quick and easy American success. That it was not accomplished can be attributed largely to the hesitation and fears of Hull. His subordinates urged an immediate invasion of Canada. Hull delayed until he received specific orders from Washington, and not until July 12 did he move his army across the river. As if satisfied with this maneuver, he showed no inclination to do more. He sat at Sandwich and refused to attack Malden.

The arrival of the army at Detroit just about wrote the end to civil government in Michigan. Hull remained governor in legal name only. Having put on the sword, he regarded the rights of the civilian population as subordinate to military necessity. Judge Witherell also was in uniform, and Judge Griffin, at the first hint of trouble, decided that a vacation in the East would do wonders for his delicate health. This left Woodward practically alone as the representative of civil authority. Under the circumstances he was unable to carry out any legislative functions, and he exercised only limited judicial powers.

As might be expected, Woodward and Hull clashed almost immediately as the judge sought to protect the civil rights of the people against military encroachment. On occasion he even challenged measures which Hull considered necessary for the maintenance of army discipline.

Among the Ohio volunteers was Blackhall Stephens, a British subject who had deserted from the British army years before. When Hull ordered his troops into Canada, Stephens refused to go, fearing that, if captured, he would be treated as a deserter and not as a prisoner of war. He appealed to Woodward for advice. The judge, instead of making a legal test of the matter, tried to arrange a compromise. He got Stephens to agree to serve in any capacity in a unit remaining in the United States. This was agreeable to his immediate superiors, but not to Hull who threatened —or so Woodward reported—to punish the judge for interfering in what was strictly an army matter.

"I was the more inclined to credit the information from violence having before been resorted to by mister hull towards those who differed with him in opinion," Woodward said. He appealed to the secretary of war, asking for a definition of civilian rights under what had become, understandably and partly through necessity, a military dictatorship.

"I have thought it a duty to suggest to you whether an explicit instruction might be given that in no case whatever violence is to be offered to the civil authority. If there is an error or misconduct there are lawful ways and means by which to investigate and punish it; but what security has the citizen, on our government, if the military shall undertake to pronounce on the error, or resent the real or fancied consequences of it?" [10]

If Woodward ever received a reply from Washington, the settlement of the issue became wholly academic. Hull's campaign was fast approaching the point where future decisions would be dictated by the enemy. While Hull and his army were idle at Sandwich, the British were busy. Reinforcements were gathered. In the north, an enemy expedition composed of a few soldiers, sailors, trappers and Indians, took Mackinac by surprise on July 17. This disaster, coupled with Hull's hesitation, convinced the Indians they had nothing to fear from the Americans. Openly discarding the fiction of neutrality, they swarmed into the British camp. Hull respected the British; he actually feared the Indians. Without further ado, he ordered his troops, on August 8, to evacuate Canada. On the same day, his orders reached the small garrison at Fort Dearborn (Chicago) to evacuate that post. The soldiers and their families marched out of the fort, and before proceeding far were ambushed by the savages. Many were brutally massacred; most of the survivors were carried away as prisoners.

At this same time, Major General Isaac Brock, a man as energetic and aggressive as Hull was slothful and timid, took command at Fort Malden. Playing upon Hull's fears, he demanded Detroit's surrender, hinting he might have difficulty restraining the Indians. To back up his threat, he planted a battery opposite Detroit and began to bombard the town. Although damage to life and property was slight, Woodward had a narrow escape. Awakened by the cannonading, he jumped out of bed. As he did so, a shot came through the wall of his room, struck the bed beside which he was standing, and carried the pillow and bedclothes into the fireplace. The ball then rolled back harmlessly out on the floor.

Later that morning, August 16, Brock dressed his few militiamen in the uniforms of British regulars to make his force appear more martial. Then he transported them to the American side of the river, and with Tecumseh's braves howling around the stockade, marched toward the town. That was enough for Hull. To the mortification of his troops, he ran up the white flag, surrendering unconditionally without firing a shot in defense. Once again Detroit and all of Michigan Territory had become a British possession!

"As a military operation," Woodward observed of this shameful event, "this enterprize was conducted on the part of the British general, with a degree of genius, judgment, energy and courage, reflecting the highest lustre on his personal character; and presenting, in every point of view, a contrast the most complete to that of the American general."

That was not only Woodward's opinion; it was history's verdict. It was the end of Hull. Prisoners of war, he, Witherell, and the regulars were carried off to Montreal. The Ohio volunteers were sent home under parole. Before long Hull was exchanged; tried by court martial, convicted of cowardice and sentenced to death.

He was reprieved, at the last minute by President Madison, and finished out his days in Massachusetts, attempting to justify his conduct and regain his good name.

4

The day after Hull's ignominous capitulation, the victorious Brock returned to Canada, leaving a garrison of two hundred and fifty men under Colonel Henry Proctor in Detroit. Before he departed, he decreed that for the time being the American laws should remain in force.

This posed something of a problem for Proctor, a brutish, unimaginative man who possessed none of Brock's gallantry. He knew nothing of American law or of the laws of the Territory. Requiring someone to administer them for him, he issued a proclamation defining Brock's orders, and stating that "the civil officers, remaining in the country shall continue to exercise the respective functions appertaining to their offices . . ." and "Courts of Justice shall be held as usual." Woodward, being the only territorial official remaining, thus had imposed upon him by edict the choice of carrying on his regular duties, or risking the penalty of disobedience. Proctor then went a step further and appointed him secretary of the Territory—the British officer naming himself governor.

This appointment was apparently made without consulting Woodward, and placed him in a desperate dilemma. To accept service under the enemy in time of war would be regarded by his countrymen as an act of treason. Two alternatives suggested them selves. He could request to leave Michigan. Or he could remain, co-operating with Proctor short of accepting official status, and acting as the intermediary between the British and the American inhabitants who had no one else to look to as their advocate.

A sense of duty dictated the latter course, although there was the danger that his own government might misconstrue his motives and actions. But it was a risk he felt obligated to take. He informed Proctor that the Constitution of the United States prevented him from accepting office, honors or remuneration from a foreign country without permission of Congress. He suggested that he write Washington for instructions. Proctor agreed, and Woodward's letter, dated September 7, addressed to Secretary of the

Treasury Albert Gallatin, was sent through the lines. With it went copies of all communications between Proctor and himself. His letter was carefully worded so as not to offend the British.

"My being nominated Secretary, for the time being, must be considered as a compliment to my country and not to myself," he wrote. "The functions of lieutenant-governor, you will recollect, are attached to the office of Secretary; and as it was thought respectful and conciliatory that an American citizen should, in present circumstances, be selected for that purpose, and particularly one of the officers of the late government. Of these I was the only one left; and I conceived it of a nature demanding my acquiesence, until the pleasure and wishes of my own government should be made known . . . An explicit instruction, on this head, will be requisite; if the course of events should not be such as to supersede the necessity of it.

". . . I have no idea that the American government would wish to relinquish the hold upon any of their territories which circumstances permit, and my construction of those obligations, which a high sense of duty, and the most cordial affection to my country, impose, is: *That I am bound to stay, in the protection of her claims, in the maintenance of her power, and her laws, to the very last, and to abandon the hope of their being, eventually, effectually asserted, only at her own express command.* Besides this duty, which I consider simply as a *political one,* there is another, not less imposing, *commanded by philanthropy.* To intercede for my suffering countrymen; to save their lives, their persons, from the victorious and insulting savages; to preserve the remnants of their little properties from pillage; to aid, in the means of departing, those who will go to find the standard of their country where her power is yet readministered (sic), and her glory untarnished; and to uphold and comfort those whom stern necessity compels, or hardier resolution prompts, to bear the full fury of the storm, and see its last effects; are duties, in the exercise of which I have derived the most exquisite pleasure, a pleasure which even the severest *censure* of my country can never take away. I shall not cease however to believe that, in fulfilling them, I have consulted her inclinations not less than my own." [11]

"The severest censure of my country—!" Woodward knew what

to expect. He fully realized that his determination to remain would be misinterpreted and subject him to sharp criticism and even, possibly, punishment. His decision was not that of a traitor to his country, but the action, as Judge Campbell later expressed it, of "a brave and good man" who loved his countrymen.

Neither by act nor intent did Woodward merit that ugly appellation of a later day—"quisling". He did not serve the British government during the period of occupation; he received no remuneration from the crown; he performed no official acts as secretary of the Territory as far as can be ascertained, and he did not conduct a single session of court while the British remained in possession of Michigan.

While waiting a reply to his letter to Gallatin—a reply he did not receive—he lost no time in making himself useful to the inhabitants of the Territory. His first act was on behalf of the unfortunate survivors of the Fort Dearborn massacre who remained prisoners of the Indians. He urged Proctor to send messengers to the tribes to determine how many survived, where they were being held, and to ask that their lives be spared while ransom arrangements were made.

"I am not authorized by my Government to make the assurance, but I shall not doubt their cheerfully defraying such expense or ransom, or conveyance, as circumstances will justify, and private funds are also ready to be applied to the same purpose. I do not less doubt your willing and zealous assistance," Woodward told Proctor.[12]

Woodward did not wait for assistance, either from his own government or that of the enemy. Both in the cases of the Dearborn survivors and later captives, he formed his own relief organization. On more than one occasion, the hapless prisoners of the Indians were paraded through the streets of Detroit by warriors at whose belts hung fresh scalps of less fortunate victims. Their object was entirely mercenary; to obtain ransom. The prisoners whose freedom was not purchased were taken to remote Indian villages where they often were tortured to death. Although many humane British officers and civilians aided the Americans in redeeming these unfortunates, the official attitude was to keep hands off for fear of offending their red allies. As George Catlin stated: "When the Indians brought in prisoners to be sold for ransom, he [Woodward] was energetic in rounding up men of wealth who would pay ransom and contributed liberally of his own small means." Woodward and other Detroit citizens literally impoverished themselves in helping the survivors of Indian atrocities.

The humanitarian efforts of Woodward were not confined to the more dramatic rescues of Indian captives. He made himself useful to the Americans in a hundred ways. He provided necessities for sick prisoners who could not be moved from Malden. Fugitives from the backwoods farms and settlements outside Detroit flocked into town for safety. They appealed to Woodward for help in finding shelter, and he did not fail them. He acted as a buffer between the citizens and the military. James May, a justice of the peace, was instructed by Proctor to perform the duties of his office. Fearful that in doing so he might jeopardize himself as a turncoat with his own government, he appealed to Woodward for instructions for himself and others in a similar predicament. In some ways, these minor officials were in exactly the same position in which Woodward had been placed. May received the following advice from the judge:

"The man who stands firm upon his own integrity; and who, in his conduct to his country, acts with a pure heart, and with clean hands, is always safe; and constitutes a rock, upon which the billows of malignity may roll, but are repelled, and broken, in the contact." [13]

The "billows of malignity," as he foresaw, surged around his own head. There were, of course, those in Washington and elsewhere who denounced him as a traitor. Congressman Poindexter of Mississippi, declaring the chief justice "had accepted a commission under the British authority," proposed to Congress that the act establishing Michigan Territory be repealed and the territorial government abolished. There was some malice in Poindexter's resolution; he insisted that the judges were continuing to draw their salaries, neglecting to explain how Woodward was able to collect his.[14] When Woodward's letter stating his position reached Washington, Congress declined to act on Poindexter's resolution. Like a jackal, waiting to pick the bones of another's prey, Stanley Griswold, the deposed territorial secretary, thought he saw an opportunity to benefit himself.

"I see in the public newspapers, that Judge Woodward is said to have accepted an office under a foreign government . . ." he wrote the secretary of state. "If this be correct information, I presume our government will consider it sufficient cause for vacating his office as a Judge of that Territory. In this case I wish to be considered as a candidate to supply such vacancy." [15]

The people of the Territory understood better how Woodward, according to his lights, was serving his country. No matter what others, elsewhere, might say of him, they appreciated what he was doing for them. When, having received no reply to his request for instructions, he announced his intention of leaving the Territory, more than thirty citizens, American and French, expressed their gratitude in a memorial dated January 6, 1813, in which they stated:

"We feel it a duty incumbent on us to acknowledge, that your stay in the country since the Capitulation, together with your exertions in favour of its inhabitants, has contributed in an eminent degree towards the preservation of their lives, their liberty, and the property of perhaps every individual in the Territory." [16]

Among the signers of this document was his old antagonist, John Whipple.

This appeal abolished all thoughts of departure from Woodward's mind. To James Monroe, secretary of state, he sent a copy of the memorial, together with a brief account of conditions in the Territory, and informed him of his decision, lacking specific instructions to the contrary, to stay where he was. In conclusion, he begged that "if I should not survive the disasters with which I am surrounded," he might be permitted "to commit to you my good name. I am acting with a pure heart, and with clean hands; and my country will find it so."

5

Instead of the compliant tool he had expected Woodward to be, Proctor discovered that the angular, unkempt, garrulous judge was nothing but trouble to him. Woodward's conduct proved he had no intention of helping the British acquire a firmer grip on the subjugated Northwest.

Proctor's military situation was becoming uncomfortable. Arms and men were being collected by the Americans in Ohio, Kentucky and Indiana for the relief of Michigan. By early winter, William Henry Harrison was preparing for the retaliatory move against the British. It did not improve Proctor's temper and disposition to learn that the test was coming. He began to view the inhabitants of Detroit and its environs with distrust. With Woodward to speak for them, they refused to act like conquered people should. The British commandant feared the result if they should in any way link up with Harrison.

The fortunes of war meanwhile continued to play into British hands. In January, 1813, a division of Harrison's army composed of Kentuckians under the command of General Winchester advanced to the River Raisin for the purpose of re-establishing a foothold in Michigan from which offensive operations could be launched. Winchester was as inept a leader as Hull, and his errors were equally disastrous. On the night of January 21, Proctor surprised him at Frenchtown and, after a spirited fight, compelled him to surrender his entire force.

There followed one of the most shameful episodes in the annals of warfare. Proctor returned to Malden, leaving the wounded American prisoners behind in Frenchtown. Despite assurances they would be protected, the Indians got out of hand, and in an orgy of bloodletting, three hundred and ninety-seven Kentuckians were murdered, scalped or carried away into the forests. And while this horrible deed was being enacted, British officers stood by, making no move to prevent it!

The shocking event stunned Detroit; raising new fears of the Indians. Proctor, rewarded with a generalship for his victory, became an object of bitter, unconcealed hatred on the part of the American population. Throughout the entire United States, and particularly in the Northwest, there was grim determination that the Frenchtown massacre would be revenged. "Remember the Raisin!" became the West's new battle cry.

To aid the survivors and trace those whom the Indians had carried away became Woodward's first concern. Once more his relief committee went into action, raising money for ransom and providing for the prisoners' general comfort. Knowing that the families of men reported missing would be frantic with concern over their fate, Woodward sent them what information he could obtain. "These letters," he stated, "were all destined to Kentucky, and intended to relieve the connections of the prisoners from the heartrending anxiety necessarily attending an uncertainty with respect to their fate . . ."

He described his personal sense of responsibility to his countrymen in these words:

"To alleviate the calamities which were evidently impending over the inhabitants, to endeavor to restrain excesses and indiscretions which might prove fatal to them, to aid them in the means of repairing to where they might find the arm of their country still adequate to their effectual protection to ward off, to the latest possible period, the sanguinary disorders with which they were constantly threatened, and at length afflicted; in short, amidst a scene of general disaster, devastation and ruin, to sustain, as far as my humble powers would admit, the claims of my country, and the rights of my fellow-citizens; and to promote, as much as was practicable, in such arduous circumstances, a spirit of humanity, charity, and mercy; this was the task which I found myself, by considerations of irresistible cogency, and without reference to danger or obloquy compelled to undertake . . ."

Ensign Isaac L. Baker, of the 2nd Infantry, was one of those who, taken prisoner, owed his life to the efforts of Woodward and his associates.

"The extertions of these worthy people were directed, and point given to them, by our ever to be venerated countryman, Augustus B. Woodward, who with unwearied zeal exerted himself in our behalf at Detroit," Baker gratefully recorded. "He was the life and soul of the remaining Americans, the man to whom they all looked up for success in the hour of difficulty; for advice on every occasion. This, added to the influence he at first had with some of the British officers, enabled him to do wonders for us. This gentleman, whose exalted understanding entitles him to the first consideration for talents, appears to have no wish separate from the interests of his country; though eminently qualified to enjoy society, he gives up all its sweets to shield the unfortunate of his country from savage cruelty and British oppression." [17]

This tribute was echoed years later by Judge Campbell, not always an admirer of Woodward. "If the history of his time requires his foibles and his oddities to be recorded, let it also be recorded that before such qualities as he showed during those scenes of trial, his weaknesses, though magnified an hundredfold, were of very small account."

Gathering all available information on the Raisin disaster, Woodward reported to Secretary Monroe, citing military errors which Winchester had committed. He criticised the disposition of the American troops before the battle, and pointed out that Winchester had established his headquarters a mile and a half from his main body, and thus was not in contact with them when the British struck.

"The operations of the British Commander," he said, "are marked with the same minute correctness of judgment in this instance and the same boldness of conception and execution, which distinguished, in the former instance, his illustrious predecessor, General Brock. It is, in fine, a military movement of equal, and in fact of greater splendor."

But, he continued, all the glory Proctor might have gained from his success was tarnished by the massacre which, he predicted, would "plant a thorn in his heart."

The affair at the Raisin ended all pretense at amicable relations between Proctor and Woodward; the latter was openly scornful of the general's conduct.

The fear of being held accountable for not restraining the Indians at the Raisin seems to have caused Proctor to lose his head. Aware of the intense feeling against him, and fearful that it might flare into organized resistance, he decided to banish from the Territory those leading citizens whom he regarded as potential troublemakers. An order to that effect was published on January 20.

This edict was received with consternation and defiance. Twenty-nine Detroit citizens included in the order, met and adopted a series of resolutions accusing Proctor of violating the terms of Hull's capitulation of 1812. Warning him that they would resist any efforts to banish them, they offered Proctor a list of their own terms under which they would cooperate in maintaining order and an attitude of non-resistance. In return, the British were to guarantee protection of the lives and property of all.

Proctor angrily attributed the authorship of these resolutions to Woodward, denouncing him as "an artful, designing, & Ambitious Man, & his only objects have been to ingratiate himself, with his own Government, & to court popularity."

Woodward replied in spirited language, strongly indorsing the resolutions (which he unquestionably had written and certainly had transmitted). He accused the British commander of failing to observe the fundamental rules of international law. He presented a long list of incidents in which lives and property had been jeopardized by British failure to live up to the terms of the capitulation. This further defiance enraged Proctor, and although he temporarily refrained from enforcing his exile order, he suspended all operations of civil government and declared martial law.

During this clash with Proctor, Woodward was more than ever looked to by the people as the source of all their strength and hope. George McDougall who had never been friendly with Woodward, now hailed him as the "Champion of our Rights." The judge was instrumental in saving the life of his one-time assailant, Whitmore Knaggs. After the battle at the Raisin, Knaggs was arrested, charged with bearing arms in violation of the parole he gave at the time of Hull's surrender. In a lengthy communication, employing his best legal logic, Woodward came to Knaggs' defense.

"I stand here," he informed Proctor, "not to shield guilt and depravity, from proper punishment, but I regard it as my bounden duty to defend the innocent, and, even with respect to the guilty, to see that that guilt, viewed through a medium of prejudice and passion, should not be magnified beyond the bounds of reason." He described Knaggs as "an ignorant and a turbulent man," but denied there was any evidence he had borne arms against the British at Frenchtown. Knaggs had only carried a gun in his own doorway to protect his family against the carousing savages, he insisted. He produced affidavits from eye-witnesses and American officers, including the captive General Winchester, to support his claim of Knaggs' innocence.

Despite opportunities for such service to his friends and neighbors, Woodward realized that his usefulness to them, in the face of Proctor's animosity, was at an end. On February 6, he asked for his passport.

It was not immediately given to him. Still smarting from Woodward's accusations concerning his conduct in relation to the Frenchtown massacre, Proctor peremptorily summoned the judge to Sandwich where he demanded documented proof of his charges. Woodward went armed with sworn affidavits of participants and eye-witnesses, but for two weeks he was forced to cool his heels in Proctor's anteroom. Finally, he was granted a short interview with the general, but was not given an opportunity to present his evidence. A few days later, he was ordered to appear again. This time Woodward curtly refused to attend, stating he had no desire to expose himself to "an intemperance of demeanor . . . which . . . is as unbecoming in an officer of rank, as it is indecorous in the character of a gentleman." That was enough for Proctor. On February 19, Woodward was handed a pass, permitting him to go east by way of Fort George where he was escorted across the border.[18]

On March 16, he was in Albany and he reported by letter to Secretary of State Monroe. In this letter he expressed concern for official and public reaction to his activities under the enemy flag. He had, he repeated, executed no official judicial acts; he had declined a commission as secretary of the Territory under Proctor; he had accepted no remuneration from the British, and had given no parole.

"To expect," he concluded, "that in the *singular,* perhaps unexampled situation in which I was placed, unaided, alone, the counsel of my own government cut off, the course which I have pursued should meet with the *entire,* or, at least, the *immediate* approbation of every mind, might be to expect too much. It was a course liable to misconception; and, in which, some charity of construction might, in the first instance, be requisite. That it has been marked with *perfect purity of heart* I am abundantly confident. *I hope that I have done my duty; I hope that I have done my WHOLE duty; and I hope that I have done NOTHING MORE* than my duty. Desirous not only that my conduct should *be correct,* but that it should fully *appear* to be so; I, at the same time, derive, from the remembrance of it, a sweet satisfaction, which no malignity can touch, and which no worldly contingency can destroy."[19]

6

Upon arrival at Albany, Judge Woodward discovered he possessed a high propaganda value. The American people were dissatisfied with the way the war was being conducted. They were weary of defeats, and discouraged by disasters such as the surrender of Detroit and the River Raisin massacre. Public opinion was fermenting into righteous indignation.

A delegation of Albany citizens called upon Woodward on March 26, 1813, and requested that he turn over his official correspondence, particularly that relating to the Indian atrocities, for general publication. Woodward agreed to do this, admitting that nothing he might disclose was confidential. It could, with propriety, be given to the public. He explained to Monroe that he had acceded to the request, and that the Albany *Argus* would print his account of events in the Northwest after accepting his stipulation that it should not be accompanied by editorial comment, or used for partisan political purposes.

Woodward felt that the whole story should be given the people of the United States to arouse them to their dangers. His passport had been held up for two weeks by Proctor, and his departure from Michigan delayed because, he believed, the British were afraid he would reveal in all horrible detail what occurred on that frightful January 22 at Frenchtown.

"It was an apprehension, prevailing, very strongly, in the minds of the British officers at the time of my departure from the Territory, that my intention was to expose the subject of the massacre; so as to exacerbate and inflame the public mind in the United States, against them."

He had assured the British, he said, that he had no intention of misrepresenting or magnifying the facts. His object was not to inflame the American people. By placing a factual account of what had happened before the world, the result, he hoped, would be "that a similar massacre should not occur again."

The Albany *Argus* gave generous space to what Woodward had to say. For the most part, the articles consisted of affidavits he had obtained from French-Canadians who had witnessed the brutal deeds of the Indians. He published his letter of February 2 to Proctor in which he charged that following Winchester's surrender the prisoners had been tomahawked, shot and burned; and that some of the Frenchtown civilians had been shot and their houses pillaged and burned.

"The facts," Woodward declared in this communication, "evince that in some quarters, and in some department or other, either the moral or physical means of preventing a violation of your capitulation do not exist. The alarms of the inhabitants therefore, are the more highly excited by the expectation of another battle; and they feel, perhaps very justly, that their persons and property are not respected." [20]

Public reaction to his story and to his own role in the British occupation was all Woodward could have hoped for. The *Argus* articles were widely reprinted and favorably commented upon in the American press. A Georgetown newspaper, publishing at least part of his correspondence, editorialized approvingly.

"We cannot therefore but express our high approbation of the very correct course pursued by Judge Woodward . . . He determined to remain on the spot consoling his fellow citizens, assisting them, encouraging them, protecting them as far as practicable . . . No one will hesitate to approve and applaud his conduct, which was humane and intrepid. It is altogether doubtless, that his determination to remain with the people of Michigan, and his firmness in protecting them by his influence, address, and frequent intrepid opposition to the conduct of the Conquerors, saved their lives and property, and at the same time preserved their allegiance to the laws and government of the U. States." [21]

Leaving Albany, Woodward proceeded to Washington where he placed his correspondence in the hands of Congress. He conferred with President Madison and congressional leaders on conditions in the West and the conduct of the war. He made himself quite useful to the government, and learned that his reputation had not suffered in the least. About a year and a half was spent in the East, in New York, Philadelphia and Georgetown, pursuing his own interests and devoting himself principally to his personal affairs. This welcome interlude naturally provided occasion for visits to Monticello. Prior to one of these calls, he suggested that if Jefferson could assemble some scientific-minded cronies "at leisure to bestow an hour, for a few days, say from twelve to one p.m. each day or every other day . . . it would be gratifying."[22] He confided to Jefferson his intention of resigning his judgeship; he was heartily discouraged by the lack of progress made under Hull's administration, and he felt that the little that had been accomplished would be wiped out as a result of the war.

Mostly, however, he was not occupied with such gloomy thoughts. He proposed a plan to substitute a legal code for the common law in the District of Columbia, and he spent several weeks in Philadelphia studying the testimony in the case of Eugene Aram whose murder trial was a sensation of Eighteenth Century England.

While Woodward was enjoying a protracted breathing spell from his official duties and the personal involvements of war, the tide of conflict was turning in the West. In September, Oliver Hazard Perry's fleet sailed out of the harbor of Presque Ile (Erie), Pennsylvania, and decisively defeated the British squadron off Put-in-Bay Island. With the Great Lakes under American control, General Harrison re-took Detroit and invaded Canada. On the banks of the Thames River, he overtook and whipped the fleeing Proctor, and smashed the Indian confederation into complete impotency. Once more Michigan Territory and the Northwest were secure under the Stars and Stripes.

On October 29, 1913, President Madison appointed Lewis Cass to replace Hull as the new civil governor of Michigan. That appointment marked the beginning of a new era of peace, prosperity and advancement for the Territory. As soon as possible, Cass took steps to restore all civil processes. In the spring of 1814 he set the third Monday of the following August for the resumption of governmental operations, and notified the judges to be on hand for a meeting of the Governor and Judges. Woodward received his notice at Monticello.

With the other judges, Witherell and Griffin, he was back in Detroit on the appointed day. Only the secretary, Reuben Atwater, did not answer his summons and the President revoked his commission. In his place, Cass secured the appointment of his close friend William Woodbridge. On September 19, 1814, the Supreme Court held its first session in more than two years. The full machinery of government once more was turning—with unaccustomed smoothness.

The treaty of peace was signed on December 24, 1814, and was ratified by Congress on February 15, 1815. To make it official, Detroit celebrated the event on March 24 with illumination of the streets, a public banquet and a grand Pacification Ball at Ben Woodworth's Steamboat Hotel. British officers at Fort Malden were cordially invited to attend. It was a gala occasion and worthy of the best efforts of Judge Woodward who was a member of the committee on arrangements.

To the accompaniment of fiddles and clinking glasses, and assurances of perpetual amity, Michigan returned to postwar normalcy.

CHAPTER VII

A Man About Town

1

THE MICHIGAN to which Woodward returned in 1814 was a sorry place. War had laid a devastating hand on the entire Territory; Detroit and the settlements on the Rouge and Raisin were in desperate straits. For two years, commerce had been at a standstill. The fur trade had, of necessity, been suspended, and as a result no credits had been placed on the books of merchants and factors in New York or Montreal, to be drawn against in the form of such essential commodities as food and clothing. In a territory which was far from self-sustaining, cessation of the importation of many of life's necessities resulted in serious hardship. Local agriculture, never very far advanced, was in an equally deplorable state. With hostile Indians roaming the woods, the farmers did not dare venture into their fields. Barns had been burned. Livestock had been carried off by the Indians or commandeered by the British. The spectre of famine loomed threateningly in pasture and market place. Hungry people turned to the army in Detroit for assistance but got none. Even the soldiers were on short rations.

Aaron Greeley, the territorial surveyor, reported a story of personal ruin that was more or less typical. "I have been singularly unfortunate in the loss of my property by General Hull's Surrender of Detroit, the hard earnings of Six years work I have totally lost by that shameful transaction. I have nothing but my hands left me to support a helpless family."

During most of 1814 and the early months of 1815, Governor Cass was absent from the Territory, winding up his affairs in Ohio. Needing help, the people turned to Woodward who had never failed them in times of trouble or danger.

"The desolation of this Territory is beyond all conception," he reported to the secretary of war early in 1815. "No kind of flour or meal to be procured and nothing for the subsistence of cattle. No animals for slaughter and more than half the population destitute of any for domestic or agricultural purposes. The fencing of their farms entirely destroyed by the incursions of the enemy for fuel for the military. Their houses left without glass and in many instances even the flooring burnt. Their clothing plundered from them by the Indians.

"It is a literal fact, and it will scarcely be deemed permissible to shock the feelings of human nature so much as to state it, that the inhabitants of the River Raisin have been obliged to resort to chopp'd hay, boiled, for subsistence." [1]

Woodward appealed for supplies, including seed for spring planting. Father Richard and Cass, upon his return, added their voices. In reply, Washington sent relief, food for the people and livestock for the farms. The gratitude of the people to all three was boundless, and Woodward was regarded by the French, particularly those of the Raisin district, with an affection that was almost veneration.

By 1816, conditions had improved. The end of the war started a westward migratory movement into the Northwest, and while Michigan, at the outset, did not benefit from this influx of settlers to the same extent as Ohio, Indiana and Illinois, the tide soon turned in its favor. Things also were much different in the legislative board. Cass presided with more dignity and patience than Hull had shown; he was courteous, considerate, but also firm. Woodward and Griffin continued to dominate the court at the expense of Judge Witherell, and Woodward and Secretary Woodbridge were often at odds during the frequent occasions when the latter presided over the legislative board during Cass's absence from the seat of government. Nevertheless, there was much less friction generally. It has been stated that "Cass was a person not to be trifled with, as Hull had been, and he sought in every way to smooth over the difficulties and did not undertake to meet them face to face. He and Woodward seldom clashed."

Woodward and Cass treated each other with respect, but did not become intimate friends. Like many, Cass never came to understand the chief justice. "His very singular opinions of things generally would baffle any little sagacity . . ." the governor once remarked. With a semblance of unity among the Governor and Judges, more was accomplished in a year under Cass's regime than in seven years under Hull.

Between 1815 and 1820 Detroit's population increased from one thousand to approximately three thousand. In order that the interior of the country might be better known, the citizens were encouraged to set out on short exploratory expeditions, in groups of two or more, to wander about, more or less at random, observing the land characteristics, and locating favorable town and farm sites. Woodward traveled through the wilderness into southern Michigan and northern Ohio and Indiana, even to the Wabash district which he found "a most delightful country." As early as 1807 he was urging the national government to extinguish by treaty the Indian title to the interior, particularly the areas separating Detroit from Ohio, and around Saginaw Bay.

It remained for the more resourceful and energetic Cass to do what Woodward suggested. By 1819, a series of Indian treaties were negotiated which gave the United States title to practically the entire eastern half of Michigan's southern peninsula, and to large areas along the western margin of Lake Erie. Within a short time, enough of the public domain had been surveyed so it was possible to conduct the first land sale. In 1818 the *Walk-in-the-Water,* the first steamboat to cross Lake Erie, arrived at Detroit. Soon steamers were running on regular schedules, carrying an increasingly larger volume of traffic. The opening of the public lands and the development of steam navigation on the Great lakes combined to furnish the impetus which brought settlers from the East into Michigan in an engulfing flood. Before many years, John Farmer, Michigan's pioneer cartographer and gazetteer, would observe this migration and remark that a settler's wagon was leaving Detroit for the interior on an average of every five minutes.

In 1817, President Monroe journeyed west, soon after his inauguration. He visited Detroit where Woodward, who had known him in Washington and Virginia, was in the front rank of the reception committee. In that year, too, progress was sufficiently advanced so that Detroit's first regular newspaper, the *Gazette,* was established. In 1817, the first county, Monroe, was set off from the original Wayne County which, as an administrative unit, had been contiguous with the entire Territory. Roads began to appear; the Governor and Judges extended a home rule franchise to Detroit. By 1820, a new, American community was emerging in a pattern of small farms and villages.

In this period of Michigan's first real expansion, Detroit was a lively place. No longer the crude frontier settlement, it was becoming a cosmopolitan town with its Yankee, English, French, Scotch, and occasional Irish and German settler. New ideas were abroad; there was a push and drive in the business and commercial community which left the older French habitants shaking their heads in perplexity. Altogether it was a stimulating place for one of Woodward's interests and temperament.

Among the new buildings being erected there was, here and there, a bookstore, offering the latest imports from London and the eastern cities. The Detroit Book Store, quite an emporium in 1819, was featuring Thomas Moore's *Irish Melodies,* and a thriller titled *The Scottish Probationer,* a novel in two volumes. B. Stead's clothing store offered a wide enough selection of fashions for gentlemen so the bloods of Detroit could choose between being "dandies or dunkers." The Governor and Judges adopted an act "to incorporate Medical Societies, for the purpose of regulating the practice of Physic and Surgery in the Territory of Michigan." What really caused tongues to wag was the elephant being exhibited (admission twenty-five cents) at Whipple's hotel.

Barber Enos Banks proved himself enterprising by offering to shave his customers on a contract basis—twice a week for fifty cents a month, payable in advance. A new bank was organized—Woodward let it severely alone—and the *Gazette* was pirating the poems of S. T. Coleridge. Citizens were debating the need for a public water works; such discussions reached their liveliest pitch in the common room of "Uncle Ben" Woodworth's Steamboat Hotel, the acknowledged social center of the town. "Uncle Ben" was a useful citizen; not only was he Detroit's best known boniface, he also operated the ferry to Canada and, when occasion required, he could expand his talents and serve as the public hangman. Now and then he was visited by his brother Sam, who had earned lasting fame by composing the popular *Old Oaken Bucket.*

F. T. & J. Palmer were beginning to get rich as proprietors of a general store which advertised such fascinating items "newly arrived from Boston" as "Pearl, myrtle, gold and silver lustre, Egyptian brown and blue Tea Setts." And if their customers didn't care for tea, they had on hand "227 barrels of Ontario rectified whiskey."

A major topic of conversation was the expedition led by Governor Cass and Henry Rowe Schoolcraft into the far Northwest in search of the true source of the Mississippi River, but it lost precedence for a time to the duel fought by Captain John Farley, of the Corps of Artillery, and Lieutenant Otis Fisher, of the Fifth Infantry, in which the latter was killed. A. Edwards, having successfully operated a cooperage works, decided it was time to branch out, and opened a shoe factory.

A *Gazette* subscriber, signing himself "H. Phobia," protested against the number of dogs running the streets. He suggested they could be gotten rid of by adopting a licensing ordinance. Most of his neighbors, he said, "are so penurious they will kill their dogs before paying a tax." Maine had been admitted to the Union, and some Michiganders were wondering when it would be their turn. Joseph Hanchet raised a twenty-nine-and-a-half pound watermelon on his farm on the River Rouge in 1820, but he wasn't bragging about it much. The year before he had grown one weighing thirty-five pounds. Tailor Joseph Gooley was having trouble with his no-account apprentice, William Thorn, and when William ran away, Gooley offered a reward of one cent for his return. He wouldn't go any higher; he felt that was all William was worth.

Letters to friends and relatives and to the newspapers back East contained glowing accounts of opportunities in the new land, and Detroiters urged their former neighbors to join them and get in on the Michigan boom. Woodward was an early victim of this "Michigan fever." At a session of the grand jury some years before, he had urged the members to encourage domestic industry instead of relying on Canadian and British markets. "I have the honor," he pointed out, "to appear, now before you, clothed completely in the manufactures of our Country; trusting that even an humble example may not be without Some weight, or utility." He continued:

"The territory of Michigan, Gentlemen, may perhaps be justly

Considered as standing now in the same relation to the Atlantic board which those Settlements, when colonies, stood to the mother-country; and it is not unreasonable to encourage a similar reciprocity of benefits & intercourse. . .

"To what nature had done for us in providing an internal navigation, the most superb in the world, the attention of the liberal & enlightened State of New York is proposed to be united with that of the national rulers, in preparing artificial additions of the most important kind.

"I exhibit to your inspection the report of the Commissioners acting under the government of the State of New York, and the map of the canal by them proposed, as objects too interesting to this country not to excite a lively and general attention.

"The face of this fine region of our continent will soon be fairly expanded to the rays of American enterprize; and the day is not distant when we Shall behold the energy of its operation. Perhaps our own era may Witness the extension of our settlements to the pacific, and the standard of our republic reflected from the shores of another Ocean."

A little progress, obviously, whetted the taste for more!

2

Interest in an all water route between the Northwest and the Atlantic seaboard developed soon after the end of the Revolutionary War. Plans for a canal linking Lake Erie and the Hudson were under consideration in 1810 when a New York state commission was created to study a route and means of financing the project. The proposal aroused a good deal of interest in Michigan. The value of such a link was obvious. It would facilitate and encourage settlement, providing not only easy access to the West, but also furnishing an outlet for products of the hinterland, lack of which was one of the chief obstacles to Michigan's early development. Thus, when the New York canal commission sent its prospectus to the Governor and Judges of Michigan Territory, requesting their comments and proposing territorial participation in the financing, the subject received careful attention. The legislative board referred the matter to Woodward who, as a committee of one, was asked to prepare a reply.

The War of 1812 held up Woodward's report until April, 1814.

As he so often did, Woodward took the large view, going beyond the immediate practicalities of the moment. While he wholeheartedly indorsed the principle of the waterway, what he actually recommended came closer to the modern scheme for a St. Lawrence Seaway development than to the Erie Canal.

"The importance of this grand object to the territory of Michigan will be at once obvious," he wrote. "It remains only to consider the plan and route contemplated by the commissioners; and the means and supplies by which they propose to effect the object."

He expressed regret that the commissioners recommended bypassing Lake Ontario in favor of a western terminal on Lake Erie. This, he said, would mean "the productions of the western country will find a market in the city of New York, instead of the city of Montreal." Naturally, that is what the New York commission intended.

Woodward thought he foresaw the day when Canada would be part of the United States, and Montreal an American port. The New York route, he stated, "is predicated on the eternal adhesion of the Canadas to England." It was his suggestion that New York, at her own expense, build a canal between Albany and Oswego on Lake Ontario, and that a supplemental canal around Niagara, anticipating the Welland Canal, should be built as a federal undertaking. This would give the West a choice of outlets—New York or Montreal.

"Let an extensive city, from four to twelve miles square, be laid out at the mouth of the river Niagara," Woodward proposed. "Let a mound be made, at the head of Grand Isle, on the American arm of the river, with a sluice. Let a mound be made at the bottom of Grand Isle, without a sluice; solid, substantial and durable.—Let a canal be drawn from this last point, 60 feet wide, excepting immediately at the locks, twenty feet deep, with all the necessary lockage, whatever the size or expense, directly into the river Niagara, entering it between the city before mentioned and Lewiston.

"A canal at Niagara has been estimated at a million dollars. It is more than probable that, executed as it ought to be, it would cost five millions of dollars. Its productiveness, on the other hand, would be both immediate, certain and great. The present trade is of immense amount. It would double in very short periods. The whole western commerce, forever, whether destined to the St. Lawrence or to the Hudson, whether attracted to Montreal or to New York, must pass this canal. Once afloat on Lake Ontario, a canal around the rapids of the Oswego river, which, as will presently be shown, ought to be executed at the exclusive expense of the State of New York, at *whatever cost,* will present a fair competition between both markets. The commodity will reach that port where its price is highest.—This is the only fair and just rule. This alone is the interest of the *producer*. It is also eventually the interest of the *consumer*. It is a narrow and selfish policy to sacrifice these to the interests of the *mere carrier*." [2]

Woodward's scheme was elaborate, but not impractical as modern events have proved. Needless to say it found, at the time he presented it, no favor in the eyes of the State of New York. Under Governor DeWitt Clinton, one of the original commissioners, New York built the canal, completing it in 1825. From Michigan's standpoint it was the perfect complement to the availability of cheap land and steam navigation on the lakes. It provided the comfortable highway for thousands of westward-bound immigrants who used it, as the folk song of the period said, to "sail down the waters to Michigania."

3

In the winter, Michigan people stayed close to their own hearths. For long periods each year official business was limited to what could be transacted without going far abroad. These interludes were welcome to Woodward; they provided opportunity for reflection and study. In a room in which piles of books, soiled clothing, unwashed dishes and empty bottles contributed to the general confusion that grew progressively worse as the weeks passed, he lived in an atmosphere as closely approaching serenity as he ever achieved. By the light of pine knots sputtering in the fireplace, garbed in a long and none-too-clean dressing gown, his feet buried in a pile of straw, he kept bachelor quarters and let his mind roam on philosophical flights which were recorded, eventually, in books, pamphlets, letters and newspaper articles.

His thoughts were much on problems of government. Like Jefferson who helped him mature some of his theories, he was not at all satisfied that the constitutional formula presented governmental perfection. He found little fault with the workings of the legislative branch; he was too much the republican for that. But he felt that the executive system contained inherent dangers and evils, with the threat of too great a consolidation of power in the hands of one man.

These opinions were put in writing, probably in 1808, and published in 1809 as a discussion of the presidency, titled *Considerations on the Executive Government of the United States of America*. This pamphlet proposed reform of the executive office by a constitutional amendment which would have stated in part: "The executive power shall be vested in a Presidency of the United States. The Presidency shall be composed of a President of the United States, and four Councillors. The President, and, after the first election, the Councillors, shall hold their offices during the term of five years; and the office of one of them shall expire annually."

Under this plan, the office of vice president would be abolished; the Senate would choose its own presiding officer just as the House did. The president, who would preside over the executive council, and the councillors, would be established in line of precedence according to the number of votes cast for each. In the event of the vacancy of the office of president, through death or impeachment, his duties would be assumed by the first councillor. "It shall require the assent of the President and two Councillors to constitute an act of the Presidency."

This radical concept of the executive authority undoubtedly stemmed from the *Directoire* which was the nucleus of the government of France immediately after the French Revolution. It was also, in a modified way, similar to the privy council of the British monarchy.

The president, Woodward insisted, is invested with powers "almost too great to be exercised, with undeviating correctness, by any individual mind; however energetic, and however enlightened."

The council system would not only limit presidential power, it would give continuity to an administration, inasmuch as the councillors' terms would be staggered, and prevent the excitement of elections by which "the nation is agitated to its remotest fibre." Obviously he did not anticipate the party system as it has evolved, or realize that his plan might saddle the nation with a self-perpetuating dynasty. Instead, he was concerned chiefly with the fate of the country at the hands of a corrupt or incompetent man in the executive office, a situation which, he felt, "must unavoidably occur," with the result that "the labors of preceding generations may be prostrated in dust."

His proposition may have been weak, but it was presented with a vigor of expression that was sometimes epigrammatic.

"He who acts alone is often exposed to error; and is not seldom liable to caprice," he declared. "In the administration of public affairs the will of a single individual ought not, perhaps, to prevail, even where it is right . . . The differences of residence, of society, and of education, in a great nation, still add to the differences of individual character, and attainment. It is difficult, perhaps it is impossible, to eradicate local prejudices and attachments. The more extensive the country, the more is that difficulty enhanced; and it is impossible, whatever single character the choice of the nation may select, for the administration of its affairs, perfectly to divest his mind of local sensibilities, and attachments . . . In the single administrator of executive power, local partiality may often be manifested, where it cannot be corrected; and will, still more often, be suspected, where it does not exist . . .

"A certain degree of publicity must attend the transactions of every political body," Woodward declared in another place. "There is no stronger fortification to the frail virtue of man, than the certainty that his conduct is truly before the world."

He concluded with the warning that an ailing or aged president might become the captive of his intimates or close advisers. "Gradually, as he bends beneath the infirmities attached to increasing age; his family connections may acquire an improper ascendancy over his mind; or his confidential servants may assume the unlicensed direction of the public affairs." [3]

The first copy of the *Executive* went to Jefferson with a note of elaboration.

"In every constitution formed in America, during the era of the revolution," he wrote, "a council was attached to the executive.

It is even a part of the British constitution. The federal constitution is the first without it. It is certainly of less importance in the state governments than in that of the union. You are yourself aware, Sir, of the extreme severity of the executive duties. To lessen that severity, without abandoning the advantages of a single executive magistrate, would be desirable. The difficulty of constituting a republican executive, of energy and vigor, without a resort to the monarchical principle of a supremacy in one individual, qualified however by the executive right, limitations of period, and a veto in the one branch of the legislative body, has deterred from the attempt. I do not flatter myself that I have been so happy as to have attained the correct medium in the proposition I have made; but I am certain, Sir, that the clearest refutation of all the principles I have advanced is to be found in your example." [4]

Jefferson found the pamphlet interesting enough to ask the author for additional copies. He contributed some comments of his own.

"I had formerly looked with great interest," Jefferson told Woodward, "to the experiment which was going on in France of an executive Directory, while that of a single executive was under trial here. I thought the issue of them might fairly decide the question between the two modes, but the untimely fate of that establishment cut short the experiment. I have not however been satified whether the dissensions of that Directory (and which I fear are incident to a plurality) were not the most effective causes of the successful usurpations which overthrew them. It is certainly one of the most interesting questions to a republican." [5]

Many Americans shared Woodward's doubts about the office of the presidency. His ideas were favorably received and widely discussed. His pamphlet was reprinted by newspapers, including the Philadelphia *Aurora,* a Republican Party organ, thereby giving it the semblance, at least, of official approval.

There were other subjects related to the conduct of public affairs upon which Woodward expressed himself. He conducted a correspondence with James Madison on a standard of weights and measures. That was a topic in which Jefferson was intensely interested. He also urged Congress for tariff relief on books and scientific apparatus. "Americans are not injured by the information in books in foreign languages," he pointed out. "On the contrary they are benefited, for to multiply readers by extending information to all classes of a community, and to multiply writers by the extension of their discussion to subjects which are agitated in those countries, is certainly to increase the demand for articles of this manufacture in our own language and country."

Woodward early became convinced, just as Jefferson did, that America's ultimate destiny lay to the west, and it was with some alarm that he observed Russian settlements planted upon the Pacific coast. Long before most of his countrymen, Woodward became fearful of "the bear that walks like a man." On a gala Fourth of July celebration he offered as his toast: "The Emperor of Russia—May experience convince him that the sagacious moderation and impregnable firmness of American policy are too strong for all exorbitant pretensions." To check Russian progress in North America, he urged a strong Pacific policy for the United States, based upon the establishment of diplomatic relations with China, and the development of oriental trade.

But it was the internal structure of the United States government which interested him the most, and produced his best literary efforts. In 1825 he published another pamphlet, *The Presidency of the United States,* in which he used a scatter-gun on the general organization of the executive branch. Although filled with specific recommendations, it lacked the penetration and cohesion of thought that marked his *Considerations on the Executive.* He discussed in some detail the development of the cabinet and the party system. He criticised the method of selecting the president's successor, pointing out that the choice usually was from the cabinet, thus permitting the president to name the man who would follow him, and giving a candidate from the cabinet a strong political advantage. He thought little of the vice president as a successor. "The Vice President selected was, in no instance, the person whom the nation wished to become, eventually, the President," he declared.

He warned that, although the legislative branch should be distinct and independent of the executive, it "is liable to influence from the executive by appointments to offices of trust, dignity, or emolument." Such appointments should not be made during a legislator's term of office—either for himself, his friends or relatives. There should be, he suggested, a permanent "commission for investigation" to inquire into governmental abuses and recommend remedies. And, with some foresight, he proposed a rotation of the office of president so the honor could be shared by each part of the country. Otherwise, if the presidents consistently came from one particular section, others might be tempted to withdraw from the Union.

Coming back to the cabinet, he suggested that department heads should be required to meet qualifications; he urged establishment of a Department for Interior and Domestic Concerns a full quarter of a century before one was created. His Interior Department actually included the functions of a number of future departments; his would have had bureaus for education, agriculture and commerce. He recommended a complete reorganization of the Department of State with separate bureaus created, each supervised by undersecretaries, to conduct relations with other nations according to ethnic or geographic classification. His system was not much different from that now followed by the Department of State.[6]

Henry B. Learned, in his *The President's Cabinet,* says that Woodward's *Executive* "was the first deliberate presentment of an intelligent account of the development of the Cabinet." Woodward had a true appreciation, he added, of the vice president in the national organization and commented with exceptional insight on phases of it.

This entire study was based upon careful examination, not only of the federal Constitution, but those of the original states. It led to correspondence by which he sought to determine the authorship of the Virginia constitution which he called the "first modern constitution." At first he was inclined to attribute it to Jefferson, but Madison informed him it was the work of George Mason. James Monroe thought Mason only made the first draft, but when Woodward showed him Madison's letter and refreshed his memory, he "wavers somewhat from his first sentiments." Jefferson, however, freely admitted that Mason was the author, both of the Virginia constitution and the bill of rights, although he said that he, Jefferson, wrote the preamble at the same time he was writing the *Declaration of Independence.* Both documents, he said, had the same object: "justifying our separation from Great Britain."

"Written constitutions," Woodward concluded, "are great moral levers. Those of America, produced the revolution of France . . . are emancipating the southern continent of the western hemisphere," and with an eye on events in Greece, "are even pervading the domains of ancient liberty."

Like that of the United States, he decided, constitutions might be imperfect, but "they will eventually change the whole aspect of human affairs upon this globe." [7]

4

After the early problem of land titles had been settled, Woodward began to acquire property in Michigan. He has been called a speculator and land grabber with all of the disagreeable connotations attached to those terms. Actually, purchase of land represented the only ready investment for any surplus funds he was able to accumulate; the federal law required that the governor and the judges of a territory own property. If Woodward purchased land in the hope that the settlement and development of the Territory would enhance its value, he was only doing what most other citizens did. He never benefited appreciably from his investments, but the fact that he liquidated some of his Washington real estate and applied the proceeds to Michigan lands, indicates a strong confidence in the Territory's future.

Soon after the fire of 1805, the enterprising James May gathered up the rubble of the chimneys of the ruined houses and used them to build the only all-stone structure in the town. It was a large, rambling place, located on what is now Detroit's West Jefferson avenue. Known as the Mansion House, it was purchased by Woodward. He leased it, in turn, for use as a hotel, keeping quarters for his personal use. It was a story and a half high, covering five lots with a frontage of two hundred and twenty feet, and containing sixteen apartments. There were commodious cellars, an ice house and stables. As an inn, it was called the "Sign of General Washington." It is believed Woodward paid about $7,500 for the structure, but when his estate was inventoried after his death, it was valued at only $7,000.

In 1807, he bought four hundred and ninety-eight acres at

Frenchtown from Samuel and George Egnew for $600. The property either had a cabin on it, or one was soon erected, and this estate, which Woodward named Monticello, became his favorite retreat. He sold this property in 1815 for an undisclosed sum.

Like many another pioneer, Woodward dreamed of becoming the proprietor of a new town. He obtained a twelve hundred and eighty acre tract, five miles north of the town of Detroit, in the Ten Thousand Acre Tract. He paid $1,780 for it. Here he platted a model village which he named Woodwardville. He had no success in attracting lot buyers, and the locality did not develop until a century later when it became part of Detroit's suburban Highland Park.

Another such enterprise was attempted in what is now Washtenaw County, with somewhat better results. On the then navigable Huron River, thirty miles west of Detroit, on the main turnpike between Detroit and Chicago, he acquired seven hundred acres. In conjunction with two partners, a town was laid out, starting with a mill and a tavern. Seeking a suitable name for the place, Woodward suggested it be called after two current heroes, the Ypsilanti brothers—Alexandre and Demetrios. They were Greek patriots leading the revolt of their countrymen against Turkish rule. The Greek struggle for independence aroused popular sympathy in the United States, and in the early 1820s public meetings and rallies on behalf of the Greek patriots were common affairs in Detroit. Woodward was a flaming partisan of their cause. "The emancipation of Greece is pregnant with consequences dear to the human race—peculiarly dear to America," he declared. "Our Mediterranean commerce will become highly interesting to us, as soon as the nation environing that sea shall have come to a state of repose." [8]

In 1825 he sold most of his Ypsilanti holdings to Lucius Lyon, future United States senator from Michigan, for $2,300, retaining only the mill site which he valued at $1,000. Although the land passed into other hands, the town prospered and retained the name which has puzzled many as to its meaning and origin.

In addition to these various parcels, Woodward also owned several other lots, at least one of them improved, in Detroit; eighteen small farms, and an interest in some property in the town of

Pontiac. At the time of his death, his equity in all this was about $15,000. A few more years and it would have been worth hundreds of thousands of dollars. He never had clear title to any of this land; it was all heavily encumbered. At one time he borrowed money from Amos Lawrence, the Massachusetts capitalist, giving him a mortgage. Eventually his taxes became heavy; foreclosure suits were begun from time to time. Woodward was definitely "land poor."

Perhaps the chief justice would have been more of a financial success if he had married and acquired the responsibilities of family life. Instead, he remained a bachelor, although it may be suspected, not entirely from choice. Certainly there were occasions when the love light gleamed in his eye, and he looked with hopeful interest on the fair sex. The vivacious, dark-haired daughters of the French habitants were especially attractive to him, and as he pursued them, his Detroit neighbors and associates were interested spectators of the bizarre turns his romances sometimes took.

Older residents of the town recalled that he once was smitten by a Detroit lady whose name they neglected to record. He courted her by taking her for rides in what was described as his carriage, but which was actually a gig. His procedure of such occasions was to dispatch his "carriage" to the lady's door, with instructions to his coachman to stand there. The arrival of the vehicle was supposed to be a signal to the fair object of his attentions, and she was expected to come out and get into the conveyance. Then the coachman, with his passenger, would go back, pick up Woodward, and off they would go for a ride in the country. At last, however, the lady tired of this routine, understandably enough. The carriage arrived at her door one day, but she made no appearance. The coachman waited an hour, and presumably Woodward did, too, chafing all the while. Finally the driver gave up; the empty gig was driven away and came there no more.

Judge Griffin, also a bachelor, watched over his associate's romances with an interested and, maybe, an envious eye. Once when Woodward was on one of his frequent trips to Washington, Griffin wrote him, expressing the hope that he was passing his time agreeably and condoling with him "for the loss of the all-heavenly (for surely such a composition could not be of earth and water) Miss

Duane." She could have been no other than the daughter of William Duane, publisher of the *Aurora,* and just how she became lost to Woodward is not clear.

Apparently Woodward was not greatly disturbed at losing the "all-heavenly" Miss Duane. Soon he was back at his cabin on the Raisin, taking part in the gay holiday festivities of the French, and flirting with the girls. "I wish that the calendar contained a larger number of Saints (both male and female) as St. Catherine and St. Nicholas, since the celebration of all the fetes furnishes you so much amusement," Peter Audrain wrote him from Detroit.

It was while he was spending one of these gay seasons in Frenchtown that he cast himself in the role of a Miles Standish, commissioning James McCloskey as his John Alden. McCloskey visited him, and was instructed on his return to Detroit to conduct a proxy courtship with Mlle. Victoire Maisonville, or Monique Navarre; either would do. Both were belles of Detroit; each could have brought him a handsome dot. Monique belonged to the high-born and influential Navarre family which claimed descent from the kings of France.

McCloskey, it would appear, was a conscientious man who did his best for Woodward, although he found that the course of even second-hand love does not always run a smooth course. He sent Woodward a detailed report of his progress—and difficulties.

"I have likewise attended to the courting of Miss Maisonville for you . . . The prospect is fair for you. When I mentioned your name, the Beautiful Smiles flowed from her Lovely Cheeks, in abundance, that in my calculation (what little I know about Love business) is *Quantum Suficit* for any man to proceed on in his courtship, and there shall be nothing wanting on my part to raise her smiles in your behalf.

"As for Miss Navarre I am not able to say anything about her. I have made several attempts to get into conversation with her but all to know (sic) purpose. Should your affection lay with Miss Navarre you must make the attempt yourself. I cannot be of any service to you in a courtship there . . . The courtship would be a courtship commenced running for I am told when a gentleman goes to pay his address to Miss Navarre; Monicke jumps out of the back window. Now if you can suggest any other mode of courting her, without jumping out of windows after her, I am willing to assist you. However I hope you will not despair. You have two strings to your bough—Victoire and Monick—and I am certain one will play very well, and was I in your place I should be for drawing my bough as near as possible to the Musicle (sic) part of the instrument. For further instructions I shall await your answer." [9]

Whether Woodward found the prospect of pursuing the fair Monique out the back window too strenuous can only be surmised. Or perhaps he found her sister (or cousin) Marianne Navarre of a less athletic nature and more to his taste. At any rate he switched his attentions to her. A note in her hand, found among his papers, states: "Mademoiselle Marianne Navarre accepts the invitation of Judge Woodward to promenade *en caleche*." That suggests she may have been the lady of the carriage. Perhaps there is a story herein of blighted romance for both parties, because Marianne never married, but devoted her long life to good works as a teacher, nurse and dispenser of charity.

5

The years between 1815 and 1820 were probably the happiest of Woodward's life. The animosities of Hull's regime had disappeared; his war time services to the older inhabitants of the Territory had earned him a warm and permanent place in their affections. Some of the newcomers may have regarded him with some astonishment, but that secretly delighted him, no doubt. At least he enjoyed congenial company and established some pleasant friendships.

Woodward and Father Richard were particularly close. The two men had much in common. The priest was a scholar whose attainments have only recently been recognized. In many of their endeavors, the pair worked hand in hand. When Richard went to Washington in 1809 to seek government assistance in establishing schools for the Indian youth of the Territory, it was Woodward who opened official doors for him with letters of introduction to important people, including President Jefferson to whom the priest was presented as "a worthy and respected clergyman, a native of France, and at present head of the Catholic religion in Michigan." [10]

Woodward had friends everywhere. Among them were the prominent political figures of the period, and such moguls of commerce and industry as John Jacob Astor with whom he dined when he was in New York. At home he listed among his intimates most of the leading attorneys of the Territory, and in general, the doors of Detroit's society were open to him.

There were times when he appeared to be something of a social lion. But one suspects this was less because of his graces than his peculiarities which made him a local curiosity. John Farmer says that he once called at the home of General Alexander Macomb, the hero of Plattsburg, and was invited to remain for tea. He at first declined, but on being urged, he seated himself and consumed sixteen cupfuls. He was fond of the company of ladies and accepted many invitations to dine out, or attend their afternoon parties. Deciding it was time to repay these social obligations, the first ladies of Detroit were invited to a tea at his hotel. All accepted and appeared in their best bib and tucker. The conversation was gay and delightful, but when it came time for the refreshments to be passed, each guest was handed a plate upon which was one almond, one raisin, one small bit of candy and one tiny cake. If this soiree was not a gastronomical success, it can be believed that it furnished a topic of lively conversation.

Not all of Judge Woodward's efforts to entertain turned out so well. In the late summer of 1816, he planned a dinner which did not come off at all satisfactorily. Among the invited was George McDougall who at first accepted. But he and Woodward had a falling out before the affair was held and McDougall changed his mind about attending. He duly informed his would-be host of his decision in a note which established a new mark in formality.

"Mr. McDougall is no longer doubtful of Mr. Woodward's unrelenting Enmity and that he would maliciously strip him to the last shirt, if in his power. Under these impressions & feelings, Mr. D would consider himself no better than Judas by dining tomorrow with Mr. W. He therefore hopes to be allowed the Honor of withdrawing his promise to that effect, made the other day."

Just what went wrong between the two is not clear, but apparently Mr. D's feelings toward the chief justice were violently outraged. Another note followed—an ominous one—in which "Mr. McDougall has the Honor to solicit a short interview with Judge Woodward, out of Doors, on matters of Public utility." A third note suggested that the meeting be held anywhere except the premises of Judge Woodward. Such a meeting would be "the most likely to terminate their differences in an Honorable way." If this was a challenge—duels were fairly common in Detroit at that time—there is no record of Woodward's reply, and no meeting on the field of honor occurred.

Matthew Elliott of Amherstburg, also invited to that dinner, found it necessary to decline; his excuse being that he had a crowd of Indians to entertain.

A footnote to this affair was a note from Robert Forsyth, stating that Woodward's servant, Conrad, had taken several of his ducks, and Forsyth demanded they be returned immediately. One can only speculate upon what Judge Woodward planned to serve his guests at that dinner.[11]

Woodward was a member of several Detroit social organizations including Zion Lodge, the oldest Masonic lodge west of the Alleghenies. Being considered an authority on constitutional law, he was often called upon to draft the constitutions and by-laws for local societies. He wrote that of the Mechanics Society of the City of Detroit, and was rewarded by being made an honorary member. He did the same thing for the French Moral and Benevolent Society of Detroit, which he served as its first secretary. But he achieved really magnificent heights of constitution writing when he drew up one for the Ladies Society, Detroit's first charity group. In it he included a clause which stated that "No lady who is a member of this institution shall be at variance with any other lady who is a member, and whenever any difficulties may arise, it shall be the duty of every member to bring the matter before the society, who shall adjust the same, and reconcile the parties."

His most notable contribution was in the organization of the Detroit Lyceum in 1818. Its constitution provided that there be kept "lists of all the productions of American literature about to emanate from the American press . . . a library, a museum, a mineralogical cabinet, and an Athenaeum." In addition, the Lyceum was to maintain "a philosophical apparatus, an observatory, and laboratory erected, a botanic and an agricultural garden instituted, conducted and maintained; and any other enterprise undertaken which may be for the benefit of science, to learning, to humanity, or to public interest." He was made the Lyceum's first president, and as such he delivered the first annual address which was approvingly described as "elegant, appropriate and original." The same year in which he founded the Lyceum, he took an active part in a movement to promote agricultural societies in the Territory.

Thus he played an important (although little recognized) role in promoting the intellectual and cultural life of the Territory.

"The fact was," William L. Jenks, the historian, pointed out, "that in many ways he was the most interested in purely intellectual pursuits of any man at that time in Michigan, and found few to sympathize or appreciate him or his endeavors."

CHAPTER VIII

A Lamp in the Wilderness

1

AUGUSTUS WOODWARD was a precocious youth. While still a student at Columbia, his mind was directed into channels of scientific thought, and throughout his lifetime he never ceased to explore them. The unknown and the speculative fascinated him. But, being no idle dreamer, he sought to achieve broader human comprehension through his investigations.

There were many questions he asked himself concerning natural phenomena. Like most schoolboys, he wondered what the sun consisted of; what were the properties, the manifestations and the application of light and heat, of electricity and magnetism. During his undergraduate days he searched in books for the answers and, no doubt, conducted elementary experiments. None of the explanations he found completely satisfied him and he looked beyond them for the truth. To that extent, he displayed a truly scientific approach to the solution of the problems which interested him.[1]

After careful study, he finally was ready to present his own conclusions. In 1801, at the age of twenty-seven, he published a curious little booklet which he titled *Considerations on the Substance of the Sun*. This was the first of a series of contemplated reports on other natural phenomena. As it turned out, however, it was the only one he completed.

"A knowledge of the true substance of the Sun," he stated, "would probably tend more to enlarge our acquaintance with the real Constitution of the Universe, than any other discovery, relating to matter alone, could possibly do." In other words, to understand the source and nature of energy, the place to seek the key was in the sun from which, he felt, all life and natural phenomena were derived.

What conclusions, he asked, had others reached? For the answer, he turned back into furthest antiquity. Beginning with Thales of Iona, who in the seventh century before Christ proclaimed that the stars consisted of an earthy substance which was continually red hot, he came down through the ages to Bacon, Newton, Franklin and Erasmus Darwin. Altogether, he weighed the theories of fifty-eight savants, covering a span of twenty-five hundred years. This is indicative of the careful preparation with which he approached his task.

Of the evidence presented by the "authorities," he retained only that which impressed him as sound and which he could himself utilize in developing his own conclusions. In so doing, he again demonstrated an open-mindedness and selectivity which were scientifically correct.

If none of his predecessors gave him convincing answers, it was necessary for him to provide his own. Beginning as he did with an unknown quantity, he had first to supply his own "x." Nothing in existing terminology met his requirement, so he boldly devised his own nomenclature.

"It is in vain that the easy and indolent mind inveighs against all innovation in language," he explained in justification of this initial step. "In order to arrest innovation in language, it is first necessary to arrest innovation in knowledge; and this, if ever desirable, would be a measure highly to be regretted in the present barbarous and incomplete state of human science." [2]

The term he settled upon was electron, and with his "x" thus supplied, he was prepared to state his hypothesis which, he declared, "is that the substance of the Sun is electron." Electron, he elaborated, would designate the matter itself; the term electricity would apply to its manifestation.[3] With his hypothesis based on a speculative premise, he proceeded to his conclusion through speculation rather than by demonstrable proof. Existence of electricity, the effect produced by the presence of electron, had been established, he claimed, by the successful experiments of Benjamin Franklin. A Russian scientist, Richman, was killed repeating those experiments. His assistant, Solokow, observed that the bolt which struck Richman down was "a globe of blue fire, as large as his fist." From this incident, he decided, "a mass of electron . . . exhibits the appearance of a globe of blue fire."

Having thus, to his satisfaction, offered visual evidence of the substance, based upon its known manifestation, he was prepared to offer the application of his own conclusion.

"It remains to suggest," he stated, "the means by which the hypothesis advanced in this work may be subjected to actual experiment.

"When the eye of man shall behold a sphere of electron revolving on its own axis, and surrounded by spheres of other matter, which revolve both on their own axes, and round the central sphere; and when to such primary bodies satellitary ones are added, which revolving also on their own axes, and round their primaries, are with them carried round the common centre; then will full conviction be produced on the mind. Such an orrery, thus apparently animated with the same *vital energy* which seems to be infused through its prototype, will present incontrovertible evidence of our having attained the true solution of the phenomena of the solar system . . ." [4]

"If then," he continued, "electron composes the substance of our Sun, it also composes the substances of all the Fixed Stars; and if it composes a principal part of all the planetary and cometary bodies of our system, it also composes a principal part of all the planetary and cometary bodies of the systems belonging to those Stars. Thus we shall find electron, long unknown, and its importance long unappreciated, the greatest, the most energetic *material* agent, in the Constitution of the Universe. Thus shall we see, that if *attraction* pervades the Universe; so does *repulsion* also. Thus shall we see why one system does not rush into another; and why all the matter of the Universe does not consolidate into one chaotic mass. If to these ideas of the material Universe, contemplating it as a whole, and not with regard to the arrangement of its particular parts, we add those of *infinity* and *eternity,* we shall have attained the most sublime conception of it we can form; and that the most consonant to all the qualities we are disposed to ascribe *to that great mental agent,* in whose incomprehensible power is sought the solution of all our difficulties, respecting the production and sustention of this great frame of nature." [5]

Was this conclusion based upon true scientific exploration, or was it a wild flight of imagination—the reflection of a mind that had absorbed more information than it could logically apply? Perhaps it was a mixture of both. If Woodward's theories do not stand up in the light of modern scientific techniques, neither can they be casually dismissed as fanciful meanderings. By the standards of his own day, his procedures not only were acceptable, but advanced. He exhibits, says one modern scientist, "a pedantry worthy of the period, and a fertile imagination rarely surpassed in any century of the History of Science." [6]

William W. Bishop, a scholar of distinction, goes even further in his critique of *Considerations on the Substance of the Sun.*

"Remember," he suggests, "that this was printed in an age before the spectroscope and before most modern solar studies, when pure speculation was almost completely divorced from observation, whether original or recorded. The little book is a curiosity, but it well illustrates the eager and curious mind of the author and is far removed from the modern works of wholly 'crankish' character, which occasionally appear in our own day . . . Woodward really summed up what was known in his day about the sun and then indulged in speculation as to the source of its tremendous energy and power. We cannot imagine his writing it today, but in 1801 it was a permissible exercise of an informed imagination." [7]

2

Woodward never intended that his *Considerations on the Substance of the Sun* was to be his *opus magnus.* His great contribution to science was to be a much grander project and, in his opinion, a more useful one.

From his boyhood studies, Woodward was struck by the apparent lack of an adequate classification of the various branches of knowledge, and particularly of the sciences. There was, he discovered, a heterogeneous mass of accumulated information, constantly being augmented by new experiments, researches and studies of scientists and philosophers. Some of this impinged upon other fields; the borders were too flexible and the result was confusion. What was needed was a comprehensive system of classification which would catalog and assign proper place and order to the separate departments of knowledge. Even more important, he saw the need for a new nomenclature to be applied to the divisions and subdivisions of science which would be permanently and universally acceptable.

He was acquainted with the classification of the Swedish naturalist Linnaeus who systematized the three kingdoms of nature, and who first enunciated a set of rules for defining genera and species. And of course, any serious student of Woodward's time was familiar with the works of the philosopher John Locke, and his classification of knowledge.

In 1788, when he was only fourteen years old, Woodward conceived the idea of classifying the sciences himself, and by 1795 he had even begun an outline of the course he intended to follow. The next few years were devoted to constant study and consultation. The comparative isolation of his residence in Michigan gave him the welcome opportunity to press this undertaking toward its completion. Jefferson was one of those with whom he discussed his work. Jefferson, too, was interested in a system of classification—for the practical purpose of cataloging his library. It is possible Woodward even contributed some ideas which the president adopted, and he expressed the hope that this effort in which they were pioneering would eventually lead to the establishment of an American National Institute. That both men were thinking along constructive lines is indicated by the fact that Jefferson's classification employed in cataloging his library was used by the Library of Congress until 1899.[8]

In a letter to Jefferson in 1813, Woodward expressed the need, as he saw it, for a proper scientific classification.

"The general feelings of mankind revolt, at once," he stated, against any classification which shall bring together objects so diversified, as the horse, the cat, the ape, the whale, and man. Reason imperiously requires that the inhabitants of the water, the earth and the air, so widely separated in nature, should also be separated in science."

He defined his own concept as "an exact classification and correct nomenclature of all human science." This, he added, should be done in America by an American, because only in this country could there be sufficient freedom of mind and inquiry to produce satisfactory results.

"In science," he said, "the world is literally a republic. The mind, intuitively rejects control; and will universally, assert its freedom. Truth and reason, virtue and impartiality, are the pillars which sustain scientific decisions. Science acknowledges no tyrant, and accredits no party." [9]

Woodward developed his ideas during his numerous eastern trips while he was a territorial judge. All of his time on such occasions was not devoted exclusively to official business. He visited libraries in New York, Philadelphia and Princeton. He discussed his plans with several eminent scholars including Dr. Ashbel Green, president of Princeton, and the members of his faculty. He read the works of Bacon, D'Alembert, Diderot, Descartes, Hobbes, DeLaschache, Comemus, Legrand, Dr. Samuel Johnson, the American savant, and Chambers' *Universal Dictionary of Arts and Sciences.* It was no shallow background with which he provided himself; he undoubtedly possessed a knowledge of scientific thought as extensive as that of anyone then living in the United States. One author remarks that Woodward's interest indicated that he "recognized the coming of a scientific age."

His big opportunity came in 1813 when he temporarily left Michigan because of the war. During the period of nearly three years that followed, he had the chance to concentrate on his grand enterprise. He settled down to serious writing, and by 1815 his task was largely completed. In 1816, after another journey East, a syndicate of Philadelphia printers published his *A System of Universal Science.*

The premise of this remarkable work was that "all human knowledge must have relation to matter, or to matter in union with mind, or to mind." [10] The purpose and advantage of such a system of classification and nomenclature, as he explained, was "to display its relation to an intelligent and enquiring people, with respect to the diffusion of knowledge, the future advancement of science, and the improvement of the arts; to explain its application to education, and to national and state institutions for the propagation of literature, to encyclopedias and scientific periodical publications, to the establishment and arrangement of libraries, the collection and republication of the classics, and even to the manner of writing, and the form and size of books; and lastly, to investigate the principles on which a great national institution, ought to be constructed, embodying in one concurrent channel, all the learning and talents, all the erudition and genius, in the United States of America, for the honor of our particular nation, and for the general benefit of the human race." [11]

Speaking more specifically of the need for a scientific system of classification, he declared:

"The power of intellect appears inadequate to grasp the mighty mass; and a correct and satisfactory division of the knowledge at present in the possession of the human race, or an elegant and appropriate classification and nomenclature, of the sciences, have not yet been effected." [12]

To meet this need, he proposed "to ascertain, upon correct principles, the general departments, or provinces, to which all human knowledge ought to be assigned; to divide those respective general departments, or provinces, into their appropriate classes; to subdivide the several classes into distinct orders; to dilate every order into specific and individual sciences; and to apply to the whole a definite, and a classical nomenclature;—these are the objects of the present enterprize."

He then proceeded to catalog the various branches of science as he and the world generally understood them. As he had done in his *Considerations on the Substance of the Sun,* he ranged the whole historic field of science, exhibiting an impressive familiarity with the history, culture and philosophy of the Greeks, Romans, Arabs, Chinese, Persians, Hindus, Hebrews, and the more modern or contemporary European civilizations.

The core of his plan was the nomenclature. This, as the title of the book suggested, had to be universal. The best—the only—way to achieve this desired end was by invention. Terms had to be exact; therefore terms then in use, subject to the nuances of interpretation, were not acceptable.

Dr. Egbert Isbell comments that "he wished to insure that the precision achieved by his system should be preserved, whatever the language into which it might be introduced." [13]

In devising his own terminology, Woodward drew on Greek roots. To begin, he required a general designation that would apply to all knowledge. He decided on "encathol epistemia" or, literally, "universal science." This, in turn, was broken into three classifications which he labelled "the eparchia," which consisted of "hetaerica" (matter); "aesthetica" (matter in union with mind), and "ennoeica" (mind). The general grouping of the eparchia was further subdivided into the "synoeica"; these were broken down into still another category called "diorisimia," and these, in turn, were still further subdivided into sixty-three specific sciences which he called "the epistemia." It was from these basic, or fundamental, branches of learning that his whole method of classification took its general designation of the Epistemic System. Because he desired that his nomenclature should remain exact and not be subjected to the shadings of custom or interpretation, the term "epistemia" was the only one he was willing to have accepted as colloquial.[14]

Here, perhaps, he was on his weakest ground. If his nomenclature should not be universally accepted, his system of classification would obviously fail by having no chance of practical application. As a matter of fact, it did fail. His book, certainly, was not designed for popular consumption. As he conceived it, the work was a technical production with appeal to a limited audience. Unfortunately for his hopes, the field was too limited. There was not enough scientific investigation being conducted in the United States, and foreign savants, if they were aware of his ideas at all, would hardly be expected to become enthusiastic about them.

It is a coincidence that in the same year Woodward published his book, Jeremy Bentham undertook a similar work. His received more attention, but Woodward's was more complete and exhaustive.

Unfortunately critics and reviewers leaped upon his nomenclature with at best a vague understanding of his true purpose. When the book appeared, and for more than a hundred years afterward, it was dismissed lightly and generally ridiculed as pedantic.

There were some exceptions. Dr. Ezra Stiles Ely, writing in the *Analectic Review* for February, 1817, said: "Though it cannot claim the praise of perfection, it is justly entitled to that of being more complete than any other extant."

As if anticipating the generally unfavorable reception, Woodward defended himself in the introduction to his book.

"In nothing are there more tastes to gratify, more diversities of opinion to reconcile, more hostilities to avert, and more antipathies to conciliate than in nomenclature. To one, that will be pedantry, which to another, is substantial learning. Gravity must preside in one department; while from another, fancy must not be absent. One taste will relish that which displeases another; and sometimes, that will be deemed superfluous and over nice, which to a palate more fastidious, will not appear nice and refined enough. This wants polish, and that possesses an excessive brilliancy. Elevation is the fault of one side, of the other depression. One ear recognizes softness and melody where another acknowledges only harshness and dissonance. Here utility is sacrificed to beauty; and there a mere coarse and homely utility preferred to ease, and grace, and elegance.

"A good nomenclature may sometimes help a bad system; but even a good system can never aid a bad nomenclature." [15]

"'Pedantic,'" remarks Dr. Bishop, "has frequently been the mildest of the adjectives fastened by later writers on his unusual terminology. What most of them do not at all realize is that [it was] no chance product of a hasty consultation of a Greek dictionary by a confirmed pedant bent on exercising his somewhat rusty knowledge, but on the contrary the fruit of many years' study and reflection." [16]

For some unexplained reason, copies of the *System* were not distributed by Woodward to his friends for several years after publication. And when they did receive them, it may be believed they were baffled by the contents. John Adams wrote that "the formidable invasion of my ninetieth year, must be my apology for neglecting, and so improperly, your valuable and worthy present . . . but the loss of my eyesight prevents my making the use of it as I wish. It is a work of great labor and research and must be useful to those who wish to enquire into that subject." [17] Jefferson, who probably understood it better than most, called it "a monument of learning of the author and of the analyzing powers of his mind." [18]

What the people of Michigan thought of it is not on record. Few of them could have seen it, fewer could have understood or appreciated it. If it was read at all in the Territory, it was probably to the accompaniment of a tapping of fingers to foreheads, implying additional evidence that no one could completely fathom the strange mind of the chief justice.

3

Having expounded his Epistemic System, Woodward looked for a way to prove it practical. Its application to an educational system suggested itself.

The time was ripe for such an undertaking in Michigan. The complete absence of any publicly-supported education in the Territory distressed Woodward, as it did other enlightened citizens. In the more than one hundred years since its French settlement, Michigan had had no regular schools. The British, during their occupancy, had not filled the lack. Nor, at the outset, had the American community. What schools there were, had been conducted mostly by itinerant schoolmasters and were of the private variety. The well-to-do traders and officers sent their sons East to be educated. Father Richard had dreamed of establishing a seminary, and founding common and vocational schools for both Indian and white children. He had even undertaken, on his own initiative, to start such schools, but they had not flourished. Time after time, he memorialized Congress, the president and the Governor and Judges, begging financial support for public schools. Unfortunately, the French habitants were not interested and failed to support him.

In 1805, a legislative act was adopted calling for the "encouragement of literature and the improvement of the city of detroit." A lottery was authorized to raise funds to carry out an unspecified program. But because of its vagueness and because no provision was made for spending the lottery proceeds, the law never became operative.

As a close friend of Father Richard, Woodward assisted him in preparing and presenting his pleas to Washington. He was entirely aware, from the very beginning, of Michigan's need and was in complete sympathy with the priest's ambitions. As early as December 31, 1806, Woodward had written a resolution which he presented to the legislative board, in which he stated:

"Whereas, The means of information, both with respect to the present and rising generation, are deplorably deficient in this Territory, and,

"Whereas, it is one of the permanent articles of compact between the original states and the people of this Territory, that 'religion, morality, and knowledge being necessary to good government, and the happiness of mankind, schools, and the means of education, shall forever be encouraged,' therefore

"Resolved, That it is expedient to provide by law for the establishment of one or more seminaries of learning in the Territory of Michigan."

This resolution was enthusiastically received by the board. Nothing, it replied, could be more laudable or more useful than a public school system. "It will advance the future prosperity of the country and the happiness of millions yet unborn. To effectuate so important a measure, every means in our power ought to be exerted; our labors ought never to cease until the object is accomplished."

Soon thereafter a new act was adopted which provided for the maintenance of public schools wherever a sufficient number of children warranted. With that gesture, however, the board's labors immediately ceased, and nothing more was done. Only Father Richard continued to struggle along as best he could.

After the War of 1812, the public attitude began to show a gradual change. Among the progressive ideas which the new Yankee settlers brought with them was the conviction that education was a public responsibility. Governor Cass, himself a New Englander, concurred wholeheartedly. But for the moment there was little even he could do. The French, still in the majority, could not be shaken out of their apathy.

Soon Cass, Richard, Woodward and Secretary Woodbridge found a new ally in the Reverend John Montieth. A native of Pennsylvania, he attended Princeton where he prepared for the ministry and also for a teaching career which he hoped would be his real vocation. He came to Detroit in 1816 at the call of a committee of Detroit citizens to conduct non-denominational Protestant services which, up to that time, had never been regularly held in Detroit. While the requirement was not stressed, it was hoped he would also keep school.

Montieth and Father Richard discovered each other to be kindred spirits and a firm friendship was established. Their interest in education forged a strong bond, and this pair, along with Woodward and the others, soon comprised a single-minded group whose determined enthusiasm promised results.

Through their efforts the subject of a territorial school system was agitated. Most of the people undoubtedly thought in terms of an elementary school or academy. Woodward and Richard had a much bigger idea. Back in 1808, the priest had urged the Governor and Judges to establish an academy in the Territory "for the Encouragement of Literature, Scientific Knowledge and the Useful Arts." Just when the university idea evolved is not clear, but it had an ardent supporter in Woodward. Montieth noted in his diary that on June 20, 1817, "Judge Woodward invites me to an interview on the sub[ject] of a University."

Apparently Cass also became converted to the university, and while the plan does not seem to have been widely discussed, it has been stated that the ensuing legislation "did not spring up without antecedant facts in the public mind to give rise to it." [19]

Subtle, gentle pressure was applied to public opinion. The people gradually became conditioned to the acceptance of what they probably assumed to be a modest program, tailored to the limited requirements of a small and still somewhat primitive community. Even the French began to show interest. Undoubtedly inspired by Father Richard, this notice appeared in the August 8, 1817 issue of the Detroit *Gazette:*

> "Frenchmen of the Territory of Michigan! You ought to begin immediately to given an education to your children. In a little time there will be in the Territory as many *Yankees* as French, and if you do not have your children educated, the situations will all be given to the *Yankees*. No man is capable of serving as a civil and military officer unless he can at least read and write. There are many young people, of from eighteen to twenty years, who have not yet learned to read, but they are not too old to learn. I have known those who have learned to read at the age of forty years."

About mid-August, Governor Cass left Detroit to attend to official business. He was gone until late September. Secretary Woodbridge took over as acting governor in his absence. But it is clear that before Cass's departure, an understanding was reached and arrangements were made for some important legislation to establish a university in Michigan Territory. A call was issued for a meeting of the legislative board to be held August 26. Woodward, in recognition of his erudition and legal training, was assigned the task of drafting the law.

It was a welcome assignment and it found him well prepared. We can picture him, a few days before August 26, seated at a table in his littered room. Piled up high in front of him were the compiled statutes of the various states. They would furnish the form which his law must have. Also, within easy reach, was a copy of his *System of Universal Science*. That would provide the substance. Thus well armed, we can visualize him, sharpening a pen, and then, a sheet of foolscap before him, beginning to write slowly across the top of the clean page:

"An act to establish the catholepistemiad, or university of Michigania."

4

When Acting Governor Woodbridge and Judges Woodward and Griffin put their signatures to the university act of August 26, 1817, they created a piece of legislation which undoubtedly stirred more controversial discussion than any law adopted in Michigan before or since.

But they did more than that. They presented to the pioneer community of Michigan a framework for an educational system which, in its broad concepts, was far ahead of anything then existing in the United States. In fact, it would be difficult, if not impossible, to find anything comparable to it anywhere, at any time. As James B. Angell, president of the University of Michigan pointed out nearly three quarters of a century after the act of 1817 was adopted: "In the development of our strictly university work, we have yet hardly been able to realize the ideal of the eccentric but gifted man who framed the project of the Catholepistemiad, or University of Michigania."

The act itself was a curious collection of verbiage, but beneath what Woodward conceived as the new universal language of science was a solid, well-devised structure. It set up, first of all, the form and functional processes of the Catholepistemiad, including the vast range of instruction which it would offer. Thirteen departments were provided. These were to be known, individually, as didaxia. Drawn directly from the encatholepistemia of Woodward's *System of Universal Science,* the didaxiim encompassed just about all human knowledge.

The remainder of the act designated the university's organization and the means of its financial support. The governing body was to be the didactors, or professors, and the president who also was to be a didactor. Their authority was broad; they were actually an administrative body with power to name faculty members, and, in general, to carry out all of the executive functions of the university. For the support of the institution, general taxes were to be increased fifteen per cent and four lotteries (two of which were actually drawn) were to provide immediate funds. An appeal also was made for private contributions, to which the citizens of Detroit generously responded by raising three thousand dollars.

The scope of the Catholepistemiad had almost no limitations. As Wilfred Shaw, in his *The University of Michigan,* makes clear, Woodward's act contemplated a complete educational system. The university was to be the nucleus, and subordinate to it were to be colleges, academies, schools, libraries, museums, athenaeums, botanical gardens and "other useful literary and scientific Institutions consonant with the laws of the United States and of Michigan." [20] At the head of these various subdivisions were to be whatever directors, visitors, curators, librarians, instructors and "instructrixes" the president and didactors might find necessary. Use of the term "instructrixes" implies that Woodward intended the Catholepistemiad was to be coeducational. Fees for each course of lectures were fixed at fifteen dollars; classical instruction was to cost ten dollars per quarter, and ordinary instruction six dollars. The remuneration of the faculty was not lavish; each didactor was to receive twelve dollars and fifty cents for each subject he taught.

By far the most interesting and provocative feature of the Catholepistemiad was the curriculum which Woodward spelled out in considerable detail. Thirteen didaxiim were specified. Today, these would be colleges or departments. At the head of the list was a chair of catholepistemia, or universal science. The special concern of its didactor would be "the interrelation and correlated development of all the departments of learning." This man was to be president of the University. Of the twelve remaining didaxiim, Woodward provided designations drawn from his *Universal Sci-*

ence. Ten of them were broad classifications covering several divisions of related knowledge. The other two were narrower in scope—specifics or simple epistemia.

Briefly, the didaxiim, other than catholepistemia were:

1. Anthropoglossica, or literature, including all subjects relating to speech, composition and grammar.
2. Mathematica, or mathematics in all its branches.
3. Physiognostica, or natural history and science.
4. Physiosophica, or natural philosophy.
5. Astronomia, or astronomy.
6. Chymia, or chemistry.
7. Iatrica, or medicine and its related sciences.
8. Oeconomica, which included agriculture, manual and fine arts, education and political economy.
9. Ethica, or philosophy, law and political science.
10. Polemitactica, or military science.
11. Diegetica, or historical sciences.
12. Ennoeica, or intellectual sciences "relative to the minds of animals, to the human mind, to spiritual existences, to the Diety and to Religion." The occupant of this chair was to be the University's vice president.

Almost immediately following adoption of the act creating the Catholepistemiad, Montieth was appointed president and given seven of the didaxiim; Father Richard was made vice president with six didaxiim. It had been agreed before the act was passed that the two men would accept these posts, thus providing proof that both of them, as well as all others immediately concerned with the legislation were fully aware of what Woodward intended to write into the law. And while the commissions of Montieth and Richard bore the signature of Woodbridge, it is quite certain that he issued them with the prior approval of Governor Cass. The actual appointments were designated by Woodward.

On September 24, Woodward presided at ceremonies for laying the cornerstone of a university building. This two-story frame structure stood on Bates street, around the corner from St. Anne's Church, and a short distance from the old Council House. It remained in use as a school building until 1858 when it was torn down.

There is no evidence that the Catholepistemiad ever functioned as a university, at least as Woodward planned it. Instead, the two didactors applied themselves to furnishing the community with much more urgently needed lower education. They established at once a primary school and a classical academy. The former continued for a few years, supported by tuition fees alone. The classical school, to which Governor Cass and other local dignitaries sent their children, received public support until about 1827 when it, too, became dependent upon fees.

Public dissatisfaction with Woodward's tongue-twisting terminology, the meaning of which few Michigan people understood, led to a revision of the original act on April 30, 1821, when its management was placed in the hands of a twenty-one man board of trustees, and it was given the more functional title of the University of Michigan. This, in turn, was succeeded by new legislation in 1837 which established the present University at Ann Arbor. Nevertheless, the Catholepistemiad of 1817 has been recognized by the Michigan State Supreme Court, and by the modern institution itself, as the direct ancestor of the University of Michigan. If the Catholepistemiad filled no other practical purpose, it familiarized the people of Michigan, as Professor Hinsdale says, "with the conception of a state system of public instruction conducted on a scale co-extensive with its territory and with the needs of society." [21]

Just as *A System of Universal Science* suffered from its strange terminology, so did the Catholepistemiad. For several generations, the act of 1817 was ridiculed as outlandish, pedantic gibberish, the product of a mind which wandered far from the practicalities of everyday life. The people of Michigan Territory rejected the plan for the Catholepistemiad largely because they could not understand the wording by which it was framed. Nor could they comprehend Woodward's great concept. Fearful of how the act would be received, the Governor and Judges did not publish it until seventeen months after it was adopted. When the public was permitted to read it, along with Woodward's "translation" of its meaning, it was greeted with shouts of derision.

The practical-minded Cass was no exception. Years later, he described it as having "a pedantic and uncouth name." Isaac P. Christiancy, one of Michigan's political leaders of the mid-Nineteenth Century, thought the name Catholepistemiad was "unchristian." Justice Campbell refers to it as "neither Greek, Latin nor English . . . a piece of language run mad."

The wags of Detroit regarded it as hilariously funny and their ridicule was heavy-handed. Members of the Lyceum indulged in what they considered sharp satire in a broadside printed in the *Gazette*.

Pigtailania Society

The Members of the old Pig-Tail Club are respectfully informed, that the new name of the institution has been altered, agreeably to the New Nomenclature, to that of the "Pigtailania Society of Michigania." The annual meeting of the society, for the choice of officers and the admission of new members, will be holden at Gruntania Place, near Woodward Avenue, on Monday evening next, at 6 o'clock. Gentlemen desirous of joining the society, and learning the polite accomplishment of squealing scientifically, must make application to the head Squealer on or before Monday noon—Tails on the table at 10 o'clock—grunting to commence at 11, and the whole to conclude with a grand squeal by the officers elect.

Given at Gruntania Place, this seventh of the month of Tails, and third year of the society.—

By direction of the Big Hog,
GRUNT BRISSELL, *head squealer.*

As Dr. Isbell suggests, the democratic-minded people of that time saw only pretension and snobbishness in such terminology as Woodward employed. What they overlooked, and what most critics of the act have overlooked ever since, was that when Woodward listed the didaxiim, he set down in understandable English in a parallel column an explanation of what each one meant.

Past experience must have warned Woodward of the risk he was taking. Why, then, did he do it? A belief in his system of classifying knowledge, and pride in what he considered an advanced and useful nomenclature, would justify, in his mind, their application to a university prospectus. But how could there be justification for such an elaborate educational structure, to be superimposed on a frontier community; a structure so elaborate that "the combined curricula of the great University which today stands as its monument would have to be expanded to meet its requirements?" [22]

Woodward may have been a visionary eccentric, but he was no fool. He knew that a community of less than nine thousand souls, thinly spread over a vast area of thousands of square miles, was not prepared for an institution of higher learning which offered about seventy advanced courses. He could not have convinced himself that complementary academies would be built in the unsettled backwoods, or that libraries, botanical gardens and laboratories would sprout beside beaver ponds or in the heart of almost impenetrable forests.

The inescapable conclusion is that Woodward, looking to the future, presented a magnificent program that could be made to function on a small scale, and which was capable of gradual expansion as the Territory developed. He sought, in advance, to assuage the growing pains that would be unavoidable after the Territory was settled. He foresaw the need, not so much for a university, as for a complete, coordinated educational system. The didactors, and later the trustees under the act of 1821 were, as Professor Hinsdale recognized, "a Territorial Board of Education clothed with ample political powers as a University Faculty." [23] If that can be accepted, then, as his true objective, he did not fail, and Michigan's splendid achievements in the field of public education on all levels, stand today as his enduring monument.

An early historian of the University of Michigan has said of Woodward and the Catholepistemiad: "We are not allowed to think that this act was other than the product of his serious, sober deliberation and judgment." [24]

Even if the Catholepistemiad is accepted as an elaboration of his Epistemic System, the genesis of his plan still is not entirely explained. One group of authorities traces Woodward's idea to the influence of French thought on contemporary American life, reflecting "the pseudo-classic mania that broke out in the United States and France, at the beginning of the Revolutionary period."

"Students of educational history know very well where to find the original of the Catholepistemiad of Michigania," says Professor Hinsdale. "That original is the Imperial University that the first Napoleon gave to France in 1806–1808, which was not, in fact, a University at all, but rather a highly centralized organization of state instruction, having its center in Paris."

Dr. Ten Brook expands this theory. "When the catholepistemiad was founded, the great Napoleon was only in the second year of his exile. His marvelous career was still fresh in the minds of admiring Americans, whose warm and wondering regard for the great man was much enhanced by certain recollections of our own war with Great Britain, then just closed . . . Governor Cass and Judge Woodward, as public men, and contemporary with the exciting revolutionary movement at the head of which Napoleon had placed himself, and doubtless in deepest sympathy with it, must have understood the system organized under the name of the University of France, and certainly this act looks very much like an attempt to copy it in Michigan. It makes the university include in itself all the primary and higher schools, and gives all legislative and executive control over them into the hands of its president and professors." [25]

Woodward was influenced by the classic revival in this, no doubt, as he was in other matters. Moreover, he was the disciple of Jefferson, the foremost exponent of the classic revival movement in the United States. When Dr. Isbell declares the Catholepistemiad "was the product of the minds of a number of the outstanding thinkers and political leaders of the nation," he certainly had Jefferson in mind.

Both Jefferson and Woodward had hoped for the establishment of a national university, and in the Catholepistemiad Woodward came as close to attaining that ideal as circumstances allowed. Isbell suggests that the germ of the Michigan plan grew out of a discussion between the two men during a visit by Woodward to Monticello in 1814. Jefferson, at that time, was maturing his own scheme for the University of Virginia, the founding of which followed the Catholepistemiad by two years. Therefore the question arises: Did Jefferson influence Woodward, and did the latter, in turn, influence Jefferson?

No satisfactory answer is available, but it is a reasonable assumption that an affinity exists between the University of Michigan and the University of Virginia, as well as the University of Kentucky for which Jefferson supplied a prospectus. The similarity between the Catholepistemiad and Jefferson's broad educational concept appears in the Virginian's own words. In 1800 he wrote: "About twenty years ago, I drew a bill for our legislature, which proposed to lay off every county into hundreds, or townships of five or six miles square. In the center of each was to be a free

English school. The whole State was further laid off into ten districts, in each of which was to be a college for teaching the languages, geography, and surveying, and other useful things of that grade, and then a single university for the sciences . . ." [26]

It has been said that a copy of Woodward's act of 1817 was sent to Jefferson. We can be assured the Virginian studied it with interest, but he did not adapt it to his own university. While there are points of similarity between the plans, Jefferson's was the more practical and his curriculum was more utilitarian.

Woodward's curriculum for the Catholepistemiad was all-inclusive, writes Isbell. "No subject that had ever engaged the mind of man was omitted; nor any subject likely to appear in the future. To Woodward a university was a place for the conservation and the advancement of all human knowledge. A broader concept than his would be humanly impossible." [27]

If the actual result fell short of the ideal, one may still admire the vision and intellectual power behind it, and say with the poet,

> "Ah, but a man's reach should exceed his grasp,
> Or what's a heaven for?"

CHAPTER IX

A Prophet in His Own Country

1

In 1818, Governor Cass took stock of his administration. The five years since 1813 when he took office had seen many changes; they offered a preview of a good future for the Territory. There had been important social gains. The Yankee immigration, just beginning, foretold economic progress. It was time, Cass felt, for a forward political step.

This sentiment only reflected the desires of the growing American community. The Yankees, with their experience in self-rule in their towns and townships in the eastern states, saw little merit in the Governor and Judges system of government which deprived them of the franchise. Late in 1817, one hundred and forty-five freeholders, most of them newcomers to Michigan, petitioned Cass that the Territory be permitted to advance to the second stage of government by abolishing the Governor and Judges and substituting for it a popularly elected legislature.

Cass favored the idea, but not just because it would be a milestone in the Territory's democratic development. More important to him was that his second step would permit theTerritory to have delegate representation in Congress. Such a functionary would be most useful. Territorial officials spent too much of their time traveling to and from Washington to transact public business. Cass was at the national capital for months at a time, to the neglect, he believed, of affairs at home. Often he had to appeal to representatives of the states to look after Michigan's business. Writing to Congressman Henry Baldwin, of Pennsylvania, on December 5, 1817, he apologized for "troubling you on subjects connected with the interests of this Territory, as we have no representative in Congress." [1]

Woodward heartily indorsed the idea of political advancement. His early views on territorial organization had not changed; he continued to feel the system was at variance with true republicanism. Back in 1809 he had accepted the chairmanship of a committee which resolved "that it was expedient to alter the present form of government." Representation by a delegate was also suggested at that time.

Encouraged by such support, Cass decided it was time to act. Early in 1818, he designated the third Monday of February for Michigan's first popular election—a referendum "to ascertain whether it is the wish of a majority of the freeholders" that a general assembly should be established.[2]

The election was held on February 16, but when the returns were all in, Cass's pet project was soundly beaten. The French in all districts had voted against governmental reorganization almost to the man. The habitants were satisfied with things as they were. Home rule, they suspected, would only mean higher taxes. They preferred to remain wards of the Federal government, letting the latter pay for defense and public improvements, and provide public relief when it was needed.

Cass and his party, dissatisfied with the election's outcome, had no intention of accepting the decision as final. In July, 1818, the legislative board authorized either Woodward or Woodbridge to go to Washington "to procure . . . the passage of an act of Congress allowing the people of this Territory the privilege of electing a delegate to Congress." [3] Woodbridge made the trip, Woodward remaining at home writing memorials to support the secretary's personal arguments. Their voices were heard more clearly in Washington than the objections of the French. On February 16, 1819, Congress passed the permissive legislation, and once more Governor Cass ordered the polls opened so the people of the Territory might choose a man to represent them in Washington.

This was a position Woodward felt was made to his order. Who knew better than he the needs of the Territory and its people? Who had a better understanding of the territorial government than the man who, as legislator and judge, had helped create it? Had anyone a greater claim on the affections and the gratitude of the people? And besides, how agreeable it would be once more to live among old friends, and experience the almost forgotten delights of capital society! In July, 1819, two months before the election, he announced his candidacy for the office of delegate.

He was opposed by Woodbridge, the handpicked candidate of Governor Cass. The governor may have believed in free elections, but he had decided opinions about whom the delegate should be. He preferred a man who had worked closely, almost intimately, with him and upon whom he could rely to carry out his policies. Woodbridge, he believed, had every qualification. Cass assured him if he would run he could retain his offices of secretary of the Territory and collector of customs.

The issues between Woodward and Woodbridge were rather thin. Woodward appealed to the electorate in a couple of flowery broadsides in which he assumed the role of a man answering a call to duty, although he was honest enough to admit that he hankered after the office.[4]

"To represent my country, on the great floor of its national councils, if only for once in my course of existence among mankind, I deem too high an honor to be relinquished for any light considerations of whatever nature they may be," he said.

He promised, if elected, to resign his judgeship. This was a challenge to Woodbridge whom he hoped would be forced to agree to resign his territorial offices if elected. Woodward was certain that before making any such sacrifice, his opponent would withdraw from the race. But the secretary refused to accept the bait.

Woodbridge and his friends, on the other hand, suggested it would be unwise to entrust affairs of the territory to one as eccentric as Woodward.

"It is said I am eccentric," Woodward replied, almost plaintively. "This is a fault, and it is a small one. I must diligently labor to correct it. But what is not a little remarkable, there are many persons in the community who are supposed to be as much so as myself, and he who is reputed to be the author of this anonymous detraction stands himself at the head of the list."

This was a feeble attack and counter-attack. Woodward's eccentricity was an accepted characteristic—like a wart on the nose. Calling attention to it would change no votes.

But Woodbridge did resort to a more effective strategy.

Throughout the back districts his supporters circulated voting lists containing the names of most of the citizens. These, they told the Frenchmen, unpracticed in the arts of American electioneering, were pledges of support of the secretary, proving that Wayne, Monroe and Macomb counties were unanimously on record in favor of Woodbridge. Backed by these pledges, they declared, the secretary was as good as elected. Transparent as this trick was, it worked. Woodward was able to counteract the effects in Macomb and Monroe counties, but it was too late for him to do so in Michilimackinac.

The election was held September 2, and when the returns were counted Woodward discovered just how influential Cass and his circle were. He recived strong support from his former neighbors around Frenchtown. Elsewhere Woodbridge was the favorite, although not an overwhelming one.

The new delegate, his election duly certified, took his seat in the House of Representatives on December 10, but only after Woodward had protested to the president against the propriety of his successful rival holding three remunerative offices at the same time. Cass defended his protege, however, and Woodward's remonstrance went unheeded.[5]

Thus he lost the first skirmish of what was to be a bitter campaign in which, eventually, he suffered a complete political defeat.

2

One session of Congress was enough for Woodbridge. He preferred to be home with his family, supervising his farm and attending to his territorial offices. Within six months after he had been elected, he wrote Cass, announcing his determination to resign before his term was completed. "I pray you to make all necessary provisional arrangements for requiring a new Election." Although disappointed at losing Woodbridge's services at the capital, Cass had no course except to comply with the secretary's wishes. He called a special election for September 21, 1820, to fill the vacancy.

Once again Woodward declared himself a candidate, and prepared to wage a more energetic campaign. Three others opposed him. One was James McCloskey, the man who once had been Woodward's romantic emissary, but was now an implacable political enemy. Another was John R. Williams, a successful Detroit merchant and the town's first mayor, allied to some of the region's most influential French families. Finally, there was Solomon Sibley who had represented the Detroit district in the legislature of the old Northwest Territory years before. Sibley had the support of the "new men"—the Cass party—who had carried the previous election for Woodbridge.

There was a certain urgency in the way Woodward sought office. He realized that the days of the original territorial organization were numbered and his appointive office would soon be abolished. A return to private law practice at middle age held no attraction. Having tasted the fruits of office holding, he found them to his liking.

So, when he was defeated for the second time, his disappointment must have been keen. Sibley received an almost solid Yankee vote. The French still supported Woodward as they did in 1819. In Wayne County (Detroit), Sibley polled 108 votes; McCloskey 84, Williams seven, and Woodward 55. In Monroe County it was a different story. There Woodward had 151 to Sibley's 32, with only one for McCloskey. In neither Michilimackinac nor Oakland (there were no French in the latter county) did Woodward receive any votes, all but four going to Sibley. The grand totals stood: Sibley 213; Woodward 206; McCloskey 89; Williams seven. So Woodward lost again, by seven votes out of a total of five hundred and fifteen cast.

Woodward challenged the Michilimackinac result, demanding that the tallies there be voided because the election was supervised by only three inspectors instead of five as the law required. The matter was decided by Woodbridge and Attorney General Charles Larned. They admitted the election was improperly and illegally conducted, but they permitted it to stand. By ruling otherwise, they said, "the rights of a whole community shall be sacrificed."

The margin of defeat was so narrow that Woodward resolved to be a candidate again in the regular election of 1821. Sibley watched him warily, and wrote a friend:

"Griffin has not been at the legislative board this month, but Woodward has taken his place for the purpose of electioneering for himself against next year.—Every movement he makes has a bearing & Reference to the next Election, and many undertake to prophesy that he *must* succeed."[6]

Woodward and his friends campaigned hard during the summer of 1821. On August 27, "a very numerous and respectable meeting of the Canadians and American democratic citizens of the county of Wayne" was held at the house of Johnsy McCarthy, and a committee of seven was appointed to further Woodward's cause. A handbill was circulated, urging "that Augustus B. Woodward be supported at the approaching election, as possessing the most splendid talents; being also well known as a firm patriot, who evinced his capacity as such by the protection afforded to the Canadian population of this Territory from British and savage tyranny and usurpation, 'at a time which tried men's souls.'"

The committee worked diligently, answering every criticism aimed at Woodward by Sibley who sought re-election.

"The only objection that has as yet been offered . . . against Mr. Woodward is, that he is a man of too conspicuous talents to represent us; that he, if sent to Washington, might reach beyond the wishes of his constituents, by an overflow of his extensive knowledge, or from a free exercise of his superior mental faculties," his friends declared. "His opponents have represented his virtues as crimes, but every man that for a moment views the matter with an impartial eye, will see the motive that influenced those ambitious men, and must acknowledge that he is the man to whom we are to look for a redress of those grievances under which we labor from the mal-administration of our present form of government. He is well acquainted with every transaction of that administration, and will lay them before Congress, and urge the necessity of an inquiry into the conduct of the public officers here."

The chief grievance to which the committee referred was the delay of Congress in allowing compensation to the inhabitants, particularly those of Frenchtown, for losses and damages to their property at the hands of the British and Indians during the war.

The Territory's population was growing rapidly at this period. As a result, the 1821 election produced a vote which was nearly double that cast in 1820. But Woodward did not benefit by the increase which represented Yankee settlers who adhered to the party behind Sibley. The static French population which remained loyal to Woodward was shrinking in proportion to the whole.

Accordingly, when the votes were tabulated this time, Woodward was badly beaten. Sibley was well out in front with 514; Woodward trailed with only 309. The judge failed to carry a single county, Sibley nosing him out even in his previous stronghold of Monroe which also was gradually becoming Yankee-fied. Only in Wayne was his strength impressive. There he got 153 votes to Sibley's 167.

Surveying these results, Woodward realized his last hope of getting to Washington as a delegate had faded. He belonged to an old order; his services to the Territory meant nothing to the newcomers. New factions were arising, but he had no claim on their loyalties. With the accelerated change in the composition of the Territory, it was evident that his usefulness was nearly at an end.

3

Agitation for government reform did not lesson after Michigan had seated a delegate in Congress. On the contrary, the demand for a popular legislature became more insistent. The leading spirits in this campaign were a group of young men, of New England or New York origin; well educated, aggressive, and ambitious. Cass used them as their particular talents permitted. In return, he rewarded them with preferment when he could. As steps of governmental advancement were reached, creating new offices, usually it was from among the Cass disciples that they were filled. Men trained in the Cass school of public affairs exerted a powerful influence on the development of the Territory, the state of Michigan and the new West for forty years.

The demand for reform was at first aimed at the Supreme Court and the administration of justice. Lacking local or circuit courts of jurisdiction above the justices of the peace, inhabitants of the Territory had to go to Detroit to have their causes heard. For the people of the more remote districts especially, this imposed serious hardships. The situation was well summed up in 1821 in a memorial to Congress from the northern counties.

"The supreme court holds only one term yearly, at the city of Detroit," the northerners complained. "It commences in the third Monday of September, and continues four weeks. It is the only term held by that court. How is it possible for suitors and witnesses to attend the sessions of this court from these remote counties, without ruining themselves? If they reside at Prairie du Chien, they must leave their homes about the first of August. After the term has closed they will very seldom find an opportunity of returning by water; for about that time the navigation of the lakes ceases. They must either then remain at Detroit during the winter, at a very great expense, or return by land. The latter expedient none but a hardy, robust man could resort to; and certain it is there are very few who would undertake a journey of so many fatigues and perils. If they remain then until spring, they will perhaps get back to their country by the first of July, when they will probably be ready to commence the same voyage again, if the suit in which they appear shall have been continued."[7]

Several plans were suggested to correct this situation. A regular circuit court was proposed. So was the appointment of a fourth member of the Supreme Court to devote all his time and attention to the northern counties. The loudest clamor for an independent northern court came from James Duane Doty, one of the Cass proteges. Not only did he recognize the need for such a court, he also hoped for the appointment to it. His campaign for reform, then, was brightly tinted with self-interest. Cass even went so far as to recommend that Doty be appointed in the event Congress created a separate court or additional judgeship.[8]

Meanwhile the movement to abolish the Governor and Judges gathered momentum. Petitions originating in all quarters of the Territory, poured in upon Congress. The system established by the Ordinance of 1787 was held to be "abhorrent" to the free spirit of the American people.

Other citizens complained that the legislative board "do not meet to do business at the time fixed by their own statute for that purpose and they have no known place of Meeting and when they do meet no public notice of the time or place is given–And when that can be ascertained by enquiry, they are found sometimes at a Tavern–sometimes at private Rooms or offices where none have a right, and few except those immediately interested in the passage of Laws have the assurance to intrude themselves or can find room or seats if they should.–"

The intent of the Ordinance, the same declaration stated, "has been in our opinion continually violated by the Governor and

Judges in the *making* Laws instead of Adopting them from the Statute Book of the original states." [9]

Even the grand jury had its say. The January, 1820 panel pointed out that "the Grand Jurys are aware that nothing but a Legislature constituted by the people, can be a radical cure for the evils complained of." [10]

Not everyone, of course, concurred in these sentiments. The conservative element, the French particularly, refused to be stampeded out of the status quo. They answered petition with petition.

"It is but justice to the members of the government, to state, that in every instance where the public will has been expressed, they have manifested a great willingness to gratify the people. . .

"A partial change at the present time, would only subject us to great expences and public burthens, and to the evils inseperable from frequent changes in all governments. . .

"Your memorialists also beg leave to represent, that they Consider the permanency of the Judiciary, as one of the noblest features in the science of Government, and a mirror in the Constitution of The United States, which reflects with the brightest refulgence, on the Liberties of our Republic; Therefore, that to render the situation of the judges less independent, by appointing them for any other period, instead of during good behaviour, would be an innovation, which in its bearings, would probably be replete with mischievous consequences. . ." [11]

Another group claimed the Territory was not yet economically advanced to creep out from under the protecting Federal wing. It wasn't the rank and file of the people who demanded change; "those who now apply for reform, being principally Lawyers and Office men," it was stated with sharp insight.

Thus assailed from both sides, Congress showed a disposition to temporize. Doty and his friends, becoming impatient, devised a new form of attack. If Congress's pedestrian pace could not be quickened by a calm, orderly presentation of the shortcomings of the territorial judiciary, there was another way to arouse its interest. That was to bring the whole matter down to the common denominator of personality. Backstairs gossip would be listened to where cold logic was ignored.

A cunningly conceived and effectively executed campaign of propaganda was unleashed. Griffin and Woodward, the latter particularly, were made the scapegoats. Everything that was wrong with the courts and the general government was translated into terms of Woodward's personal characteristics, his weaknesses and his failures. Where these did not validly exist, they were invented. His past conduct, his official acts were re-examined and distorted into every possible kind of misfeasance. Woodward was presented to the public as a social monster, a corrupt, incompetent official, a venal judge and a traitor to his country.

The keynote for this campaign was sounded by Doty in a letter to his friend Henry R. Schoolcraft. In it he revealed the nature of the plot.

"The good work has commenced here. Woodward & Griffin are likely to have something happen to them. If you take the *Detroit Gazette* you will perceive their conduct for years past is presented to them for their inspection—A petition will probably be presented to Congress for a repeal of the Ordinance under which they hold their offices. This is a modest way of turning a man out of office." [12]

Month after month the attacks continued. Woodward's proceedings against John Whipple and Whitmore Knaggs, and the case involving Muir and Lundie were revived and presented in newspaper columns in a manner notable for their bias. These were intended to prove Woodward's judicial incapacity. Every minor quarrel with Judge Witherell was dressed up as incontrovertible proof of Woodward's dictatorial turn of mind. One writer, presumably Doty, sneeringly suggested that Woodward resign in order to save the government the cost of impeaching him. He openly dared the chief justice to cite him for libel.

The lowest blow of all was the accusation that during the War of 1812, Woodward had betrayed his country by accepting office under the enemy. This produced a shocked denial and protest to the secretary of state. By remaining in Detroit during the occupation, Woodward insisted, he had been able to prevent a massacre of the civilian population. He denied having been on free and easy terms with enemy officers stationed in Detroit. He had only been civil to them out of necessity. During the Revolution, he recalled,

Jefferson had entertained captured British officers at Monticello.

"In like manner," he said, "the hospitalities of my house were offered, after the battle. In the former case they were prisoners. In the latter, I was."

The *Detroit Gazette* refused to publish Woodward's replies to the attacks on him. So he sought the columns of friendly eastern papers to present his defense. This led the *Gazette* to observe hypocritically that "he appeared more desirous of being thought clean at Washington than in Michigan."

From the vantage point of the House of Representatives, Sibley kept hammering away for reform. The propaganda and pressure gradually wore down congressional resistance. On January 30, 1823, a bill was passed providing for the oppointment of a fourth judge for the northern district of the Territory, with the same jurisdiction as the Supreme Court, and subject to the latter's appellate jurisdiction only on writs of error. On February 17, Doty received his commission as the new judge from President Monroe.

Then, on March 3, Congress passed another bill to permit Michigan to enter the second stage of territorial government by replacing the Governor and Judges with an elected legislature. It fixed February 1, 1824 for the expiration of the judges' terms. On that date a new bench was to be named, each of its members to serve a four year term.

Cass received news of this victory for the "new men" on March 27 in a letter from Sibley. That night Detroit celebrated with a civic banquet at Smyth's tavern, the buildings were illuminated, and the garrison artillery fired a salute.

Augustus Woodward, needless to say, took no part in the festivities.

4

Achievement of government reform did not end the attacks on Woodward. Instead they were intensified as members of the Detroit bar joined the hue and cry. Nothing would satisfy except his complete ruin.

The motives behind all this were obvious. They were intended to prevent his reappointment to the new tribunal on February 1, 1824. Every man in the Territory with a certificate to practice law yearned to become a judge. There were many more aspirants than available places, so it became necessary to discredit Woodward and Griffin so completely that President Monroe would not reappoint them.

There was no objection to Judge Witherell. As a veteran of the Revolution he was safe from political attack. The venom was all reserved for his two colleagues. Toward the end of 1823, as the time for naming the new appointees drew near, the Detroit bar fired a broadside.

"We feel it our solemn duty not only as professional men, but as citizens of the Territory to remonstrate against the reappointment of Judges Woodward and Griffin.—Whilst the former has afforded too many demonstrations of his entire want of practical knowledge coupled with habits unbecoming his station, the other has uniformly exhibited an imbecility of character which has rendered him worse than useless as a Judge." [13] Among the signers of this letter were the nephew of Woodbridge and the son of Witherell.

Another memorial went even further, accusing Woodward of intemperance, and of being "destitute of honor, probity and respect for established law." His reappointment, it was claimed, would be "a public calamity." This unique document was drafted by James McCloskey, who had become cashier of the newly organized Bank of Michigan, and would soon be exposed as an embezzler.

Realizing he had small chance of winning a reappointment, and not caring much anyway, Griffin decided he had taken all the abuse he could stand. He quietly resigned a few weeks before his term expired. The opposition then concentrated on Woodward.

None of these accusations made a very deep impression, apparently, on President Monroe who was wise to the ways of office seekers. And for every calumniator, there was someone ready to come to Woodward's defense. William Brookfield, a Detroit schoolmaster and surveyor, declared the judge was a man "whose disposition is mild, manners affable, and erudition profound." John McKenney commented on his "gentlemanly deportment, secluded and studious life, undeviating rectitude and great judicial knowledge," and expressed the hope that he "would long live to trumph over the malice of his enemies." James May recalled his services to his fellow citizens during the war when the people "justly styled you their 'rock of defence' . . . As a public officer, no person could act, with more independence,—with more dignity than yourself, and none—could do it with more honour to himself."

Unfortunately, these and other expressions favorable to Woodward were inexplicably delayed in transmission to Washington. Before the president and secretary of state could see them, his enemies were able to deliver the coup de grace.

In August, 1823, there was a mild epidemic of typhus fever in Detroit and many citizens were stricken, although few died. Woodward became ill just before the opening of court in September. His sickness, he thought, was not serious enough to prevent his attendance. His doctor prescribed liberal draughts of "aether, wine, brandy, spirits, opium and mercury." Well saturated with these concoctions, Woodward started for the Council House in his gig. Too weak to walk, he had to be assisted to the bench and there, publicly, he dosed himself again.

This was all his foes needed. Letters, accompanied by affidavits, were speeded to Washington, charging that the chief justice had been seen reeling drunkenly into court, and while on the bench had continued to imbide to the scandal of all good citizens and to the disgrace of Justice.

It did not matter that his friends and disinterested spectators expressed admiration at his fortitude in going to court at all. Colonel Rufus Hatch "believed the Judge never would recover from his sickness." But the damage was done.

On January 20, 1824, President Monroe completed his list of appointments to the Michigan court. It included Woodward's name, along with Sibley, Witherell and Doty, the latter as the "additional judge." These names were to go to the Senate for confirmation the following day. Then the charges of intemperance arrived at the White House. Monroe, who would tolerate almost any human weakness except drunkenness in an office holder, made a hurried, last minute revision. Woodward's name was stricken from the list and that of John Hunt was substituted. It was more than a coincidence that Hunt traveled all the way to Washington to present the charges in person. The Senate gave swift approval to the president's revised nominations.

When news of what had happened reached Detroit two weeks

later, Woodward was flabbergasted. "I indulge in no recriminations; but shall endeavor to conduct myself in an honorable and upright manner," he told Father Richard who, meanwhile, had been elected territorial delegate. His hope lay in clearing his name and regaining Monroe's confidence. If this could be done, he believed, the president might be persuaded to find other employment for him.

He began to dispose of his property and pack his belongings. "My farm is already broken up; and I am selling all my utensils, furniture, and library." Then he added, rather pathetically: "This is the second time that my establishments have been broken down, in this country, first, by the war, and now, by the late event."

Watching these preparations for departure, Detroit suddenly had an attack of conscience. The people remembered he was the first American judge appointed to the Territory. It was nearly nineteen years since he had come to this new country, a pioneer among pioneers. Of all the officials who had been sent out to govern them, he had succeeded in getting closer to the people than any other with the possible exception of Governor Cass. When the connection to the national government seemed remote, he had preached a doctrine of sound Americanism; he had lifted a corner of the curtain and offered a glimpse of the future. His idiosyncrasies had amused them. But when an enemy had gripped them in an iron fist of tyranny, injustice and danger, he alone had remained steadfast, protecting the weak, succoring the defeated and helpless.

His reward had been scorn and the reviling abuse of ambitious men. He was being turned out now, a shabby, discouraged and wronged man, without fortune, without employment and worst of all, without the gratitude of a people or a government to whose service he had been sincerely devoted.

"Never, in my opinion was a man more shamefully treated," declared Brookfield. "But his enemies, 'deceitful above all things, and most desperately wicked,' have not left anything undone to accomplish their ends!"

Others began to feel the same sentiments of shame and indignation. The reaction set in, and suddenly, full blown, there was a community-wide movement to pay him belated honor.

On the evening of Saturday, February 14, the townspeople

gathered at Ben Woodworth's hotel—"a numerous and respectable Meeting." John McDonnell, presiding, explained that the purpose was "to take into consideration the Public Services of the Hon. Augustus B. Woodward." Then, some of the leading citizens stepped forward, one by one, and paid him lavish tribute. Among them were a few who had most bitterly opposed him. Now they were contrite, eager to make what amends they could.

Be it resolved, they said, "that the extensive legal information, incorruptible integrity, splendid talents, correct and gentlemanly deportment, tried patriotism and great literary acquirements of the Hon. Augustus B. Woodward, eminently entitle him to the respect of every American."

Be it further resolved, they continued, "that the intrepid course pursued by him during the prevalence of the power of the enemy in this country, and his zeal in the protection of our unfortunate citizens and prisoners, have lastingly endeared him to us; and that we shall ever cherish the most grateful recollections of his fortitude and active philanthropy."

It was very flowery; some of it was a little maudlin, as such things are apt to be, but it all came from their hearts. "We have beheld you presiding on the Bench of the Supreme Court . . . and with what dignity—strict integrity—and true independence of character! . . . It is unquestionable that you possess no common share of legal as well as scientific knowledge . . . Your strict attention and unwearied exertions in whatever conduced to the public prosperity, could not be surpassed in any country or in any age . . . Intrepid Patriot!

"If foul play has been used—If impure feelings have prevailed, the actors in such unholy transactions, will learn that in a land of freedom, merit cannot be depressed. . . After times will do you justice. . . It is a melancholy reflection that the virtuous citizen often finds no shelter from the storm of calumny. . ."

Woodward responded quietly and with dignity.

"Be pleased to accept, Gentlemen, for yourselves and for your fellow Citizens, my sincere thanks for the respect and politeness with which the communication of your sentiments has been accompanied; and believe me your welfare and prosperity are objects which will ever be dear to my heart."

A few days later he announced his intention of going to Washington where, "as I suppose, I shall have to resume the practice of Law." He promised to satisfy all his creditors, and asked them to call upon him and submit their accounts.

March came, and he left Detroit. Navigation opened late in 1824; he rode south to Ohio, and following the long overland route, he retraced the steps which nearly two decades before had taken him to Michigan Territory.

5

Woodward arrived in Washington, less intent upon resuming the practice of law than upon re-establishing himself in the good graces of the president and winning new preference. While he occupied himself selling his Washington property in order to pay his debts in Detroit, his friends were busy in his behalf. From them he received more tangible support than high-sounding resolutions. Most active in his cause, and most influential, was Father Richard. The Kentuckians in Congress, not forgetting his efforts in behalf of the unhappy victims of the River Raisin massacre, also backed him. Kentucky's Senator Richard Johnson did all he could.

Father Richard went directly to Monroe and protested the injustice that had been done.

"The President answered me that he was not hostile to you," Richard informed Woodward, "and that he will give you some other appointment, provided you clear yourself of the accusation of habitual intemperance by the testimony of some respectable Gentlemen in Detroit and its vicinity, especially the Governor whose name he mentioned repeatedly, as the best testimony you could give to justify yourself." [14]

An appeal was sent to Cass who responded promptly. "At the request of Judge Woodward," he wrote Richard, "I take the liberty of stating to you, that I have been officially connected with him in the transaction of publick business almost ten years. During that time I have never seen him intoxicated, nor have I in fact ever observed the slightest appearance of intemperance. I have frequently met him at private parties, and allthough like most other gentlemen he takes his glass, Yet I never discovered, that it produced the least effect upon him." [15]

There was a sheaf of substantiating affidavits. Richard submitted them to Monroe and his secretary of state, John Quincy Adams, and amends were soon made. Scanning his patronage list, the President found a place for which he thought Woodward would be admirably suited. There was a vacancy in the Federal court for the middle district of the Territory of Florida. With his long background in territorial government and his judicial experience, Monroe felt, no doubt, that by appointing Woodward he would be bringing together in perfect union the man and the post. In Florida, Woodward would be only a judge; there were no legislative duties to lead him into trouble as there had been in Michigan.

When the offer was made, Woodward was doubtful. Florida was a long way off. It was sparsely settled, offering few of the inducements of comfortable civilization. In many respects it was the Michigan of 1805 all over again. It is said Woodward asked, instead, for a diplomatic post in Latin-America, but there was none open. It was Florida or nothing, so Woodward accepted. On August 26, 1824 he was given an interim appointment which the Senate confirmed the following February by a vote of thirty-seven to five.

Without waiting for Senate action, Woodward set out for Florida, arriving in Tallahassee, the territorial capital and the seat of his court, on October 4, 1824. Three days later he appointed Cary Nicholas of Pensacola as his clerk and, according to evidence, made a quick investment in Florida real estate which was then enjoying a speculative boom.

The Florida newspapers were cordial, and the mixed society of southern planters, Yankee traders and the French and Spanish elements greeted him enthusiastically. It was all very heart- warming and encouraging, and Woodward's self-esteem was easily healed of its Michigan bruises. Early in 1825 he returned to Washington, then journeyed to Detroit where he spent several weeks winding up his affairs. In mid-July he left, this time never to return. His departure, unlike that of the year before, was accompanied by the universal good wishes of the people of the town upon which he had set an ineradicable mark.

His course was now set for his new post, and the nineteen years of his Michigan experience were behind him.

6

Woodward was welcomed to Florida by a friendly but cautiously worded item in the *Pensacola Gazette*. "Judge Woodward is said to be an amiable and learned man, and eminently calculated to be useful in the station he holds. His selection of a clerk of his court is a judicious one and we hope that his usefulness may be commensurate with his inclination and ability to serve us."

Florida was purchased by the United States in 1821; its territorial structure was as new as Michigan's had been when he went there in 1805. Florida Territory was given a civil government in 1822. As created, it was in advance of that under which Michigan started. The executive authority was the governor, appointed by the president. There was a popular legislative council of thirteen which regulated territorial, county and municipal affairs, subject to final approval of Congress.

In 1824, Congress reorganized the Florida judiciary by creating three districts, divided by the Apalachicola and Suwanee Rivers, with one judge for each district. The seat of the eastern district was St. Augustine; that of the middle district was Tallahassee; that of the western district Pensacola. Jurisdiction extended to both Federal and territorial matters, with appellate jurisdiction over local courts. The district courts held two sessions each year; in addition the three judges sat en banc at Tallahassee in January as a court of appeals.

Woodward's middle district extended southward from the Georgia border, between the Suwanee and Apalachicola. It was raw, undeveloped country in 1825 and, prior to 1824, almost uninhabited. Tallahassee was created out of nothing to become the territorial capital as a geographical compromise of the claims of Pensacola and St. Augustine for that honor. In April, 1824, the first settlers arrived at Tallahassee and within two days the first cabin was erected. By September, 1825, about the time Woodward took up permanent residence there, the town was described as having "more than fifty houses, many of which are occupied by quite large families; there is now one house for public worship, one schoolhouse, two very commodious Hotels, seven stores, and one Apothecary's shop; the mechanics shops are, one Printing office, two shoe-makers, two blacksmiths, three carpenters, one tailor, three brickyards, etc."[16] No courthouse had been provided, and Woodward held court in the residence of Charles Pindar.

Ralph Waldo Emerson, visiting there at that time, found Tallahassee to be "a grotesque place . . . rapidly settled by public officers, land speculators and desperadoes." He thought there was "magic" in the way it had sprung out of the wilderness.

If the village was crude, so was the adjacent countryside which Richard K. Call, the territorial delegate, described as a "tangled mass of vines and a labyrinth of undergrowth."[17] But it, too, was beginning to develop. Large plantations were being established by planters from Georgia, South Carolina and Virginia. These people brought their slaves; they built fine houses, and gave root to a typical southern culture. Near Tallahassee was the large plantation of General Lafayette. It was an entire township, the gift of the American people. On the other side of the picture were the small farms and holdings of the backwoods settlers, living in their log cabins and struggling desperately to scratch a living from the earth.

This was the society of which Woodward became a member. He found the people, the social and economic conditions much different from those he had known in Michigan. But many of the basic problems of a new, struggling community, seeking to get on its feet politically, were almost identical in the two territories.

Woodward made friends quickly and soon was on terms of intimacy with the leading public figures. Among his early associates was Governor William Pope DuVal, a Virginian who had spent most of his early life in Kentucky. He was a shrewd lawyer and an adept politician, thoroughly familiar with the frontier mind. Also in this circle was James Gadsden of South Carolina, who became one of Florida's wealthiest men.

Woodward's closest friend was the fabulous Achille Murat, prince of Naples, nephew of Napoleon, and son of the Emperor's distinguished marshal who had been rewarded for his services with the hand of a Bonaparte sister, Caroline, and the crown of the Kingdom of Naples.

With the decline of the Bonaparte fortunes, Achille emigrated to the United States, married a niece of George Washington, and embraced democracy with flaming enthusiasm. One of Tallahassee's first settlers, Murat could match Woodward, idiosyncrasy for idiosyncrasy, although Woodward appears to have presented a somewhat more subdued set of characteristics to the view of Floridans. Murat was as notoriously untidy as Woodward; he possessed as avid a curiosity; he was as incorrigible a land speculator (and no more successful). He possessed literary talents and wrote extensively and with fair success in the field of political science. His effort to interpret the United States and its system of government to the people of Europe has been compared favorably to that of his better known countryman, Alexis de Tocqueville.

Both having arrived in Tallahassee about the same time—Murat from St. Augustine where he owned a plantation—the two men discovered a mutuality of interests, and got along together famously.

In Florida, Woodward was not beset by petty enmities; there was none of the bickering and factionalism that had made life so unpleasant at times in Michigan. Secure in his judgeship, he was no longer the target of political jealousy. His accomplishments in science and literature, together with his long career of public service, gave him a satisfying distinction. He was respected by all classes of society, and he did nothing to lessen this regard.

His duties were not arduous, and he found plenty of opportunity to indulge his other interests. He found companionship with the members of the Masonic lodge, Andrew Jackson No. 1, with which he became associated, but did not join. He pursued his scientific investigations, proposing a botanical classification according to the principles of the epistemic system. In April, 1826, he wrote the aged and failing Jefferson for the last time, explaining Jeremy Bentham's Chrestomathic system of classification, and enclosing a dozen seeds of "the indigenous orange of Florida." Within six weeks Jefferson was dead.

Much of Woodward's attention seems to have centered on promoting and improving agriculture in the new territory. He was one of the organizers of the Florida Institute of Agriculture, Antiquities and Science, and served as its president as long as he lived. He also was the organizer and president of the Agricultural Society of Middle Florida.

In deference to his standing in the community, he was made

chairman in 1826 of a committee to arrange a grand observance of the Fourth of July—the fiftieth anniversary of the signing of the Declaration of Independence. The occasion was an important one, far more so than the ordinary holiday celebration. The joy of the day, however, soon turned to sorrow with news of the deaths on July 4, 1826 of Thomas Jefferson and John Adams. More than most men, Woodward grieved over the loss of a close personal friend and patron whom he all but idolized.

There has been considerable speculation about Woodward's career, particularly in his official capacity, in Florida. It was not as eventful as his life had been in Michigan, and the reason is easily explained. Altogether he spent less than two years in Tallahassee. Most of that time was taken up with routine judicial work. He had less opportunity, as a district judge, for spectacular or controversial performance than as chief justice of Michigan's Supreme Court and member of its legislative board.

The decisions of the early Florida territorial courts have not been published, and the archives of the state contain few references to Woodward's activities. That is not surprising when it is realized that he presided over not more than four sessions of the district court and may not have attended more than one or two sessions of the court of appeals.

During his brief visit to Tallahassee in the autumn of 1824, while waiting Senate confirmation, he was requested by the legislative council to conduct a special session to iron out a point of controversy which had arisen under the organic law. At the first meeting of the legislature, charters had been issued to state banks. Governor DuVal vetoed these, whereupon the council passed them over his veto by a vote of six to three, only nine members being present. It was argued that a two-thirds majority of those in attendance was all that was required to over-ride a veto. The territorial secretary refused to certify the council's action, insisting that a two-thirds vote of the entire membership was necessary. Woodward upheld the secretary and governor with the result, so it is said, that establishment of banks in the Territory was delayed several years. Recalling, perhaps, an earlier unhappy experience with banks, Woodward proved he had learned a lesson and took the conservative side. This ruling is the only one of his Florida decisions which found its way into the local history books. Yet, in spite of his brief and rather colorless record, R. H. Rerick, in his *Memoirs of Florida,* calls Woodward "one of the most interesting characters associated with the Territory." [18]

One might almost conclude that Augustus Brevoort Woodward's zest for life had diminished. The painful end of his Michigan career was a blow from which he never completely recovered. The injustice done him by those from whom he had reason to expect more consideration left him saddened and dispirited. His ego was his most tender spot, and it was there he was most grievously wounded. To withhold from him the high regard and approval of the world was to deprive him of the essence of life. Looking back, he must have felt himself a failure without really understanding why.

He was, despite his friends and his interests, essentially a lonely man. To him Florida was a strange country. The people, the customs and the institutions with which he was most familiar were no longer part of his life. The only remaining family connection was a brother, John Woodward, who lived in New York and with whom he had little or no intercourse. The death of Jefferson had left a gap which no other could fill.

Woodward died in Tallahassee on June 12, 1827, at the age of fifty-two years and eight months. The cause is not known. Apparently he was in ill-health for at least two months prior to his death, because his last official act was on April 2, 1827 when he appointed Edward R. Downing as crier, and admitted Edgar Macon to practice. His last court appearance was on April 14.

He was buried June 13, from the residence of George Fisher, with the rites of the Masonic order. If his grave was marked, its location has long since been forgotten. Belief has been expressed that he may have been buried near his friend Achille Murat. But Murat did not die until 1847, twenty years later. Murat was visiting in Philadelphia at the time Woodward died, and did not return to Tallahassee for several months.

His death was announced in court on the morning of the thirteenth, and the same day the members of the bar met and adopted the appropriate resolutions, "testifying their respect for the memory of the deceased, and their sense of the loss the profession has sustained." The newspapers noted his passing briefly but respectfully. The *National Intelligencer* reprinted an obituary from the *Florida Advocate,* stating "the deceased possessed many virtues, and was distinguished as an enlightened and profound jurist—he enjoyed the esteem of all who knew him, and the highest compliment that can be paid his memory is, that he died without an enemy."

Just that, and nothing more. The curtain was drawn on a turbulent career. Only a few men who knew and respected him may have paused a moment in tribute, and then hurried on about their affairs.

That is the habit of the living, and the way of the world.

CHAPTER X

Epitaph for an Unmarked Grave

IT IS INCREDIBLE that the name of Augustus Brevoort Woodward is nowhere to be found on the map of Michigan. In Detroit his name adorns no school, park or public building. The great university which he conceived has no hall dedicated to his memory. More than his name is lost; he must have sat more than once for itinerant painters, but no known portrait of him exists.

The only physical reminder that Judge Woodward once loomed great on the Detroit scene is an accident of his own modesty. When he was planning Detroit, he intended the main street to honor his idol, Jefferson, and assigned to it his name. In a rare moment of self-effacement he designated what he thought would be a secondary avenue for himself. He could not foresee the effect of time and the city's growth. Woodward avenue became Detroit's main street; Jefferson avenue, although still a major thoroughfare, is of secondary importance.

Today, Woodward avenue is a street of sharp contrasts. It is lined with noble edifices, and bordered by slum decay. It is a street of rich stores, and honky-tonk dance halls, shooting galleries and all night movies; of cathedrals and garish saloon fronts; of magnificent museums and hamburger stands. It is a street of contradictions, and that is appropriate because Augustus Woodward was a living conglomeration of contradictions.

He went to Michigan, if not under protest, at least without enthusiasm. He accepted service there out of consideration for President Jefferson. But through the years he became sincerely attached to the Territory; he labored zealously for it and for its people. Then he left it, unwillingly; discarded by the community to which he had dedicated himself.

A thorough-going Jeffersonian, Woodward's mind rebelled at

the undemocratic form of government of which he was made a part. He rejected its essential federalism as incompatible with the then current American ideology that man was a free spirit, master of his own political destiny. He was the first who sought to produce a change, to light the hearth fires of democracy in that wilderness. He was ambitious to promote the Territory's political advancement, but circumstances made him the champion of the reactionary and conservative element, bitterly opposed to the progressives who worked toward the same ideal he had proclaimed earlier. When the change eventually did come, enabling Michigan to move forward along the road of self-determination toward statehood, it was effected by making him the sacrificial offering. That, in itself, should be something of a distinction.

Augustus Woodward, despite many inherent qualities of greatness, fell short of achieving greatness. He deliberately cloaked splendid attributes of intellect and character with a clown's costume of eccentricity—perhaps to hide from himself and the world the doubts, the sense of inadequacy, the insecurity and loneliness which are often the hallmarks of genius. It is ironical that the tangible qualities which could have given him, and did give him, stature are all but forgotten. In popular recollection only the facade of personal peculiarity remains.

As a frontier judge, Woodward was occasionally unorthodox, sometimes high-handed. Before he went to Detroit, the Territory had been ruled by the army. Local courts were held from time to time, with eminent lawyers of the Old Northwest attending. But usually it was necessary for litigants and witnesses to travel to Chillicothe or Vincennes. Only the wealthy could afford that, and justice was for the rich. The result was that the poor man's justice was informal; more often than not wilderness disputants took matters into their own hands.

It was Woodward who brought Michigan Territory its first real law, and it was necessary from the beginning for him to instill into the people a respect for the legal processes, to teach a largely alien people that the American system was a government of laws, with equal justice for all. This required firmness, patience and understanding of human nature. He was a teacher as much as he was a judge.

In the latter role, he was particularly effective. He managed without serious disruption of public tranquillity to purge the community of the ancient customs and codes of the French and British, and substitute for them a new body of American law, some of which he evolved, some of which he appropriated from the older states. He made it all square with the emerging pattern of a new kind of government in the Northwest. While his acts made him the target of violent controversy, it is indisputable that he provided the Territory with a sound, stable legal base upon which it was able to develop and mature, economically and socially.

Perhaps his most cruel treatment was at the hands of those who accused him of infidelity to his country in time of war. Unfounded and unfair, the slander has persisted as part of Michigan's folklore to this day.

No other man in American history was ever placed in exactly his position, or had to make the kind of fateful decisions that he was forced to make. Detroit is the only continental American city to have been occupied in time of war by a foreign power. Like most of the people of the United States, Woodward did not expect General Hull and his army to fail so miserably. Yet after the abject surrender, Woodward was confident the town would speedily be retaken. What, then, should he have done that he did not do? Should he have abandoned the people as he was free to do, leaving them without a single American official to act as intermediary with the enemy? To remain called for courage and involved personal risk. Still, he chose to stay with his people. It was good diplomacy to ingratiate himself with the unpredictable General Proctor. To have defied British authority while in its power would have availed him or the populace nothing. Apparently he avoided intimacy with the British leaders; his attitude toward them was respectful but firm. His deportment proved to be correct because it enabled him to acquire a certain influence with the enemy which he used to save the lives and property of American civilians, and succor the distressed prisoners of war. Woodward honestly believed that his insistence that the British restrain the Indians and respect the articles of capitulation averted a massacre of civilians. He may have been right. Certainly he was convinced that his conduct was correct; when his influence waned and he could no longer be useful to his subjugated countrymen, he left the Territory. The surprising thing is that Proctor permitted him to go. Had Woodward elected to turn his coat, he undoubtedly could have had preferment from the British; had he adopted their cause, he could have claimed their protection and found safety when the Territory was recovered simply by crossing a river less than a mile wide.

Augustus Woodward was a thoughtful, studious man, of keen intellectual powers which he assiduously cultivated. He possessed a limitless curiosity. By any set of standards he was widely read. This did not necessarily give him intellectual depth, as his excursions into literature and science suggest. Yet even in those fields he was no dilettante. His scientific methods were imperfect by modern standards, but in his own day his accomplishments won him some recognition. At least he was probing an unexplored realm that was closed to most Americans of the period. And more important, he was able to produce a practical application from his theories. This was the system of higher education which evolved from his laudable efforts to classify knowledge. The University of Michigan, first of the great western state universities, is his enduring monument.

While not a great man, Woodward was an able one, and when placed together in the scales, his contributions to the Americanization and development of an important sector of the western frontier heavily out-weigh the faults of his nature and personality. That being the case, why have his solid achievements been overlooked or forgotten? Why, when he is remembered at all, is it as a semi-comic character whoses foibles have become local legend?

The answer is plain. He was discredited by men who, later becoming persons of the first influence in the community, were able to exert powerful pressure upon public opinion. After them, their children and grandchildren continued to keep alive the fiction of Woodward's inadequacies. To a large degree, it was necessary to their own dignity and prestige to perpetuate the myth that Woodward was a charlatan and a fool. To admit the contrary would be a diminution of their own stature and standing as "founding fathers," and a confession that they had been unscrupulous in their treatment of him.

Let it not be thought that Woodward, both in his own lifetime and as a figure of history, lacked friends. The few modern scholars who have taken the trouble to investigate have acclaimed his talents and his contributions to the development and progress of the Northwest.

His enemies and detractors were potent, but they were relatively few. While he lived, he was respected by men of high station; he was loved and revered by the vast majority of the humble people among whom he lived and worked.

Once in the heat of controversy when he was being attacked, his friends came to his support. To assure him of their loyalty and esteem, one of them addressed him in these words:

"Be assured, Sir, that when the little bickerings and prejudices of the transient hour are buried in the vale of oblivion—when the pulse of the calumniator shall have ceased to beat—when his organ of detraction will no longer furnish a banquet to the worm, and when he himself is sunk in forgetfulness, a generation yet unborn will do justice to the man in whom were united the Philosopher, the Patroit, the Judge and the Philanthropist.—In that day the cultivation of the sciences will add an additional ray to the light which will shine around your name, and a grateful posterity will venerate the memory of him whose labours have enlarged the boundaries of their knowledge."

Augustus Woodward would have wanted no other epitaph!

Notes

Chapter I

[1] Moore, Charles: in *Columbia Historical Society Records, Washington,* 1901; Vol. IV, pp. 118–119.

[2] William Hull to James Madison, August 3, 1805; Michigan Territorial Papers, State Department Records, National Archives.

[3] Bald, F. Clever: *Detroit's First American Decade;* University of Michigan Press, Ann Arbor, 1948; p. 240.

[4] Dilhet, Jean: *Etat de l'Eglise Catholique ou Du Diocese des Etats-Unis de l'Amerique Septentrionale;* typescript in Burton Historical Collection, Detroit Public Library.

[5] Robert Munro to William Henry Harrison, Detroit June 14, 1805; in *National Intelligencer,* August 7, 1805 and September 6, 1805.

[6] *Michigan Pioneer and Historical Collections,* Vol. I, p. 347.

[7] Secretary of War to Governor Hull, July 23, 1805; in *The Territorial Papers of the United States* (Clarence Carter, ed.), Government Printing Office, Washington, 1942; Vol. X, p. 24.

[8] Cooley, Thomas M.: *Michigan, A History of Governments;* Houghton, Mifflin and Company, Boston, 1885; p. 127.

[9] A. B. Woodward to Legislative Board, Detroit, Nov. 5, 1806; in Michigan Territorial Papers, State Department Records National Archives.

[10] Jenks, W. L.: Legislation by Governor and Judges; *Michigan History Magazine,* Vol. III (1919), pp. 202, 212, 215.

[11] Documents Relating to the Erection of Wayne County and Michigan Territory, 1922–1923; edited by Burton Historical Collection, Detroit Public Library, p. 34.

[12] Blume, William W.: *Transactions of the Supreme Court of the Territory of Michigan,* University of Michigan Press, Ann Arbor, 1940; Vol. IV, p. xxi.

[13] Governor Hull to Secretary of War, Detroit, March 4, 1807; in *MPHC,* Vol. XL, pp. 103–106.

[14] Cooley, Thomas M.: op. cit., p. 525.

[15] Bald, F. Clever: op. cit., p. 76n.

[16] Report of the Governor and Judges of Michigan Territory to Congress, October 10, 1805; original in Burton Historical Collection.

[17] A. B. Woodward to James Madison, River Raisin, March 8, 1808; Woodward Papers, Burton Historical Collection.

Chapter II

[1] Burton, C. M.: *Sketch of the Life of Augustus Brevoort Woodward,* (MSS) in Burton Historical Collection.

[2] A. B. Woodward: Notebook, in Woodward Papers, Burton Historical Collection.

[3] A. B. Woodward to Thomas Jefferson, New York, June 3, 1809; Jefferson Papers (microfilm), Alderman Library, University of Virginia.

[4] Notebook, Woodward Papers, Burton Historical Collection.

[5] Farmer, Silas: *History of Detroit and Michigan;* Silas Farmer & Co., Detroit, 1884; p. 26.

[6] Bryan, Wilhelmus Bogart: *A History of the National Capital,* Macmillan Company, New York, 1914; Vol. I, p. 414n.

[7] *Detroit Gazette,* Nov. 15, 1822.

[8] Burton, C. M.: in *MPHC,* Vol. XXIX, p. 639.

[9] Cooley, Thomas M.: *Michigan,* p. 149.

[10] Campbell, James V.: *Outlines of the Political History of Michigan,* Schober & Co., Detroit, 1876; pp. 238, 250, 253.

[11] Woodward, A. B.: *Epaminondus on the Government of the Territory of Columbia,* No. V; Green and English, George Town, 1801.

[12] Woodward, A. B.: *Considerations on the Government of the Territory of Columbia,* No. VII; S. Snowden & Co., Alexandria, 1802.

[13] Bryan, Wilhelmus Bogart: *A History of the National Capital;* The Macmillan Company, New York, 1914; Vol. II, p. 463.

[14] *National Intelligencer,* Washington, June 14, 1802.

[15] Notebook, Woodward Papers, Burton Historical Collection.

[16] Moore, Charles: *Governor, Judge and Priest;* DeVinne Press, New York, 1891, p. 8.

[17] A. B. Woodward to Jefferson, Washington, August 16, 1802; Jefferson Papers (microfilm) Alderman Library.

[18] Bryan, Wilhelmus Bogart: op. cit., p. 551.

[19] James, James A.: *Oliver Pollock, The Life and Times of an Unknown Patriot;* D. Appleton-Century Company, Inc., New York, 1937; p. 20.

[20] Woodward, A. B.: *A Representation of the Case of Oliver Pollock;* Samuel Harrison Smith, Washington, 1803.

[21] Woodward, A. B.: *Supplement to the Representation of the Case of Oliver Pollock;* William Duane & Son, Washington, 1803.

Chapter III

[1] A. B. Woodward to the President and Secretary of War, Washington, March 5, 1806; Woodward Papers, Burton Historical Collection.

[2] Governor Hull to Secretary of State Madison, Detroit, August 3, 1805; Letters and Papers from the Territory of Michigan, 1805–1815; *Michigan Pioneer and Historical Collections,* Vol. XXXI, p. 523.

[3] Pickens, Buford L.: Early City Plans for Detroit, A Projected American Metropolis; in *The Art Quarterly,* Winter, 1943.

[4] Notebook, Woodward Papers, Burton Historical Collection.

[5] A. B. Woodward to the Citizens, December, 1806; Woodward Papers, Burton Historical Collection.

[6] A. B. Woodward to President and Secretary of War; Washington, March 5, 1806; Woodward Papers, Burton Historical Collection.

[7] Pickens, Buford L.: op. cit.

[8] Ibid.

[9] Olmsted, F. L. Jr.; and Robinson, C. M.: *Report to the Detroit Board of Commerce—Improvement of the City of Detroit,* 1905.

[10] Petition from inhabitants of the Territory; in *Territorial Papers of the United States,* (C. E. Carter, ed.), Vol. X, p. 116.

[11] Report of the Governor and Judges of Michigan Territory to Congress, Detroit, October 10, 1805; in Burton Historical Collection.

[12] Governor Hull to Secretary Madison, Albany, April 30, 1806, in Michigan Pioneer and Historical Collections, Vol. XXXI, p. 559.

[13] Petition from inhabitants of the Territory, 1807; in *Pittsburgh Commonwealth,* December 9, 1807.

[14] Memorial to Congress by Judge Woodward and Others; December 1806, in *Territorial Papers of the United States* (C. E. Carter, ed.), Vol. X, p. 69.

[15] Frederick Bates to A. B. Woodward, St Louis, June 18, 1807; Woodward Papers, Burton Historical Collection.

[16] A. B. Woodward to James Madison, Detroit, March 14, 1807; *MPHC,* Vol. XXXVI, pp. 193–4.

[17] *MPHC,* Vol. XII, p. 474.

[18] A. B. Woodward: Protest Against the Sale of Certain Lands in Detroit, June 1, 1818; Woodward Papers, Burton Historical Collection.

Chapter IV

[1] Governor Hull: General Order No. 27, Headquarters, Detroit, September 27, 1805; Burton Historical Collection.

[2] *Michigan Pioneer and Historical Collections,* Vol. XXXI, p. 519.

[3] William Hull to A. B. Woodward, Boston, April 1, 1806; Senate Documents, First Session, Ninth Congress, National Archives.

[4] Woodward, A. B.: Considerations on the Affairs of the Territory of Michigan, No. IV; La Riviere aux Raisins, Jan. 12, 1808; Woodward Papers, Burton Historical Collection.

[5] William Hull to James Madison, Detroit, May 26, 1807; State Department Records, National Archives.

[6] Thomas Jefferson to William Duane, Washington, February 7, 1808; Jefferson Papers, Library of Congress.

[7] Governor and Judges to President Jefferson, January 31, 1807; Jefferson Papers, Library of Congress.

[8] Governor Hull to Secretary Madison, Detroit, August 3, 1805; *MPHC,* Vol. XXXI, p. 225.

[9] Governor Hull to Secretary of War, Detroit, November 24, 1809; Secretary of War Files, War Department Records, National Archives.

[10] Moore, Charles: *Governor, Judge and Priest;* DeVinne Press, New York, 1891, p. 22.

[11] Secretary Griswold to Secretary Madison, Detroit, November 27, 1806; in *MPHC,* Vol. XXXI, p. 571.

[12] A. B. Woodward to James Madison, Detroit, July 18, 1807; Woodward Papers, Burton Historical Collection.

[13] Governor Hull to President Jefferson, Detroit, March 12, 1808; Jefferson Papers, Library of Congress.

[14] A. B. Woodward, unaddressed, River Raisin, March 8, 1808; *MPHC,* Vol. XII, p. 510.

[15] A. B. Woodward to Governor Hull, LaRiviere aux Raisins, May 2, 1808; *MPHC,* Vol. XXXVI, pp. 213–217.

[16] A. B. Woodward to John Griffin, Washington, January 15, 1809; Woodward Papers, Burton Historical Collection.

[17] Carter, C. E. (ed.): *Territorial Papers of the United States,* Vol. X, p. 251.

[18] Frederick Bates to A. B. Woodward, St. Louis, February 23, 1808; Woodward Papers, Burton Historical Collection.

[19] Peter Audrain to A. B. Woodward, Detroit, January 19, 1808 and April 8, 1808; in *MPHC,* Vol. XXXVI, pp. 206, 218.

[20] Blume, William W.: *Transactions;* Vol. I, pp. xxi–xxiii.

[21] A. B. Woodward to Legislative Board, Detroit, November 5, 1806; *MPHC,* Vol. XXXI, p. 567.

[22] Blume, William W.: op. cit., pp. 124–125; 323.

[23] William Hull to Secretary of War, Detroit, December 23, 1809; Secretary of War Files, War Department Records, National Archives.

[24] Deposition of George Ewing Wilson, July 22, 1811; Woodward Papers, Burton Historical Collection.

[25] Blume, William W.: op. cit., p. 225.

[26] Ibid, p. 330.

[27] *MPHC,* Vol. XXXVI, p. 249.

[28] A. B. Woodward to Ephraim Pentland, La Riviere aux Raisins, January 12, 1808; Woodward Papers, Burton Historical Collection.

[29] Dated February 13, 1808; Woodward Papers, Burton Historical Collection.

[30] The President to William Duane, Washington, February 7, 1808; Jefferson Papers, Library of Congress.

[31] Frederick Bates to A. B. Woodward, St. Louis, March 26, 1808; Bates Papers, Burton Historical Collection.

[32] Lewis Bond to Aaron Greeley, Miami of the Lakes, December 26, 1811; Bond Papers, Burton Historical Collection.

[33] Blume, William W.: op. cit., Vol. I, introduction.

Chapter V

[1] Burton, C. M.: *Sketch of the Life of Augustus Brevoort Woodward* (MSS), Burton Historical Collection.

[2] Ibid.

[3] Blume, William W.: *Transactions,* Vol. I, p. liv.

[4] Potter, Justice William W.: The Michigan Judiciary Since 1805; in *Michigan History Magazine,* Vol. XXVII (Winter 1943), p. 645.

[5] Andrew G. Whitney to Solomon Sibley, March 21, 1822; Sibley Papers, Burton Historical Collection.

[6] Blume, William W.: op. cit., p. xxxii.

[7] *MPHC,* Vol. VIII, p. 611.

[8] *Aurora,* Philadelphia; in Farmer, Silas: *History of Detroit and Michigan,* p 183.

[9] *MPHC,* Vol. XII, p. 650.

[10] Woodford, Frank B.: *Lewis Cass—The Last Jeffersonian;* Rutgers University Press, New Brunswick, 1950; pp. 103–106.

[11] Woodward, A. B.: The Denison Decision, in Woodward Papers, Burton Historical Collection.

[12] Ibid.

[13] Blume, William W.: op. cit., Vol, II, pp. 215–16.

[14] Woodward, A. B.: The Pattinson Decision, in Woodward Papers, Burton Historical Collection.

[15] Theodorus Bailey to A. B. Woodward, New York, January 12, 1808; Woodward Papers, Burton Historical Collection.

[16] A. B. Woodward to John Quincy Adams, Detroit, December 5, 1818; State Department Records, National Archives.

[17] A. B. Woodward to Secretary of War, Washington, January 31, 1806; Woodward Papers, Burton Historical Collection.

[18] A. B. Woodward to the Honorable Judges of the Supreme Court of the Territory of Michigan; Woodward Papers, Burton Historical Collection.

[19] *MPHC,* Vol. XII, p. 524.

Chapter VI

[1] Woodford, Frank B.: *Lewis Cass,* p. 38ff.

[2] A. B. Woodward to Secretary Madison, River Raisin, March 8, 1808; Woodward Papers, Burton Historical Collection.

[3] Peter Audrain to A. B. Woodward, Detroit, March 19, 1808; Woodward Papers, Burton Historical Collection.

[4] Captain J. Dunham to William Hull, Fort Michilimackinac, May 20, 1807; *MPHC,* Vol. XL, p. 124; same, June 12, 1807; p. 135.

[5] A. B. Woodward to Secretary of War, Detroit, August 12, 1807; Woodward Papers, Burton Historical Collection.

[6] Grand Jury Presentment, September 23, 1807; Woodward Papers, Burton Historical Collection.

[7] Governor Hull to Henry Dearborn, Detroit, July 25, 1807; *MPHC,* Vol. XL, p. 160.

[8] A. B. Woodward to Secretary of War, Detroit, August 12, 1807; Woodward Papers, Burton Historical Collection.

[9] Memorial to Congress by Citizens of Michigan; in *MPHC,* Vol. XL, p. 346.

[10] A. B. Woodward to Secretary of War, July 28, 1812; War Department Records, National Archives.

[11] A. B. Woodward to Albert Gallatin, Michigan, September 7, 1812; Michigan Territorial Papers, State Department Records, National Archives.

[12] Helm, Lieutenant Linai T.: *The Fort Dearborn Massacre* (edited by Nelly Kinzie Gordon), Rand McNally & Co., Chicago-New York, 1912.

[13] *MPHC,* Vol. XXXVI, p. 270.

[14] *Annals of Congress,* 1812–13; p. 195.

[15] Carter, Clarence E. (ed.): *The Territorial Papers of the United States;* Vol. X, p. 416.

[16] Memorial of the Citizens, January 6, 1813; Woodward Papers, Burton Historical Collection.

[17] *Niles Register,* April 10, 1813.

[18] For correspondence and official papers, January 28 to February 19, 1813, see *MPHC,* Vol. XXXVI, pp. 227–301.

[19] A. B. Woodward to James Monroe, Albany, March 22, 1813; supra.

[20] *Albany Argus,* March 23, 1813.

[21] *Spirit of 'Seventy-Six,* Georgetown, D. C., September 14, 1813.

[22] A. B. Woodward to Thomas Jefferson, Washington, April 21, 1814; Jefferson Papers (microfilm), Alderman Library, University of Virginia.

Chapter VII

[1] A. B. Woodward to the Acting Secretary of War, Detroit, March 5, 1815; War Department Records, National Archives.

[2] *Niles Register,* April 30, 1814.

[3] Woodward, A. B.: *Considerations on the Executive Government of the United States of America;* Isaac Riley, Flatbush, N.Y., 1809.

[4] A. B. Woodward to Thomas Jefferson, Philadelphia, April 25, 1809; Jefferson Papers (microfilm), Alderman Library, University of Virginia.

[5] Thomas Jefferson to A. B. Woodward, Monticello, May 27, 1809; supra.

[6] Woodward, A. B.; *The Presidency of the United States;* Derick Van Veghten, Washington, 1825.

[7] James Madison to A. B. Woodward, Montpelier, Va., September 11, 1824; A. B. Woodward to Thomas Jefferson, Washington, March 25, 1825; Thomas Jefferson to A. B. Woodward, Monticello, April 3, 1825; all in Jefferson Papers (microfilm), Alderman Library, University of Virginia.

[8] Lagondakis, Charilaos: Greece and Michigan, in *Michigan History Magazine,* Vol. XIV, p. 19.

[9] James McCloskey to A. B. Woodward, Detroit, June 10, 1808; Woodward Papers, Burton Historical Collection.

[10] A. B. Woodward to Thomas Jefferson, January 9, 1809; Jefferson Papers (microfilm), Alderman Library, University of Virginia.

[11] George McDougall to A. B. Woodward; Colonel Matthew Elliott to A. B. Woodward, August 16, 1810; Robert Forsyth to A. B. Woodward, August 19, 1810; Woodward Papers, Burton Historical Collection.

Chapter VIII

[1] Jenks, William L.: Augustus Elias Brevoort Woodward, in *Michigan History Magazine,* Vol. IX, p. 517.

[2] Woodward, A. B.: *Considerations on the Substance of the Sun;* Way and Groff, Washington, 1801; p. 23.

[3] Ibid, p. 22.

[4] Ibid, p. 77.

[5] Ibid, p. 84.

[6] Rufus, W. Carl: Introduction to facsimile of *Considerations on the Substance of the Sun;* W. L. Clements Library publication, University of Michigan, Ann Arbor, 1944.

[7] Bishop, William W.: Judge Woodward and the Catholepistemiad; *University of Michigan Alumnus Quarterly Review;* Vol. LI, No. 24 (July 28, 1945), p. 327.

[8] Ibid, p. 330.

[9] A. B. Woodward to Thomas Jefferson, George-Town, August 16, 1813; Jefferson Papers (microfilm), Alderman Library, University of Virginia.

[10] Woodward, A. B.: *A System of Universal Science;* Edward Earle, Harrison Hall, Moses Thomas, Philadelphia, 1816; p. 252.

[11] Ibid, p. 18.

[12] Ibid, p. 10.

[13] Isbell, Egbert R.: The Catholepistemiad, in *University of Michigan Historical Essays,* University of Michigan Press, Ann Arbor, 1937; p. 163.

[14] Ibid, p. 165.

[15] Woodward, A. B.: op. cit., p. 15.

[16] Bishop, William W.: op. cit., p. 323.

[17] John Adams to A. B. Woodward, Quincy, Massachusetts, November 17, 1824; Woodward Papers, Burton Historical Collection.

[18] Thomas Jefferson to A. B. Woodward, Monticello, March 24, 1824; Jefferson Papers (microfilm), Alderman Library, University of Virginia.

[19] Ten Brook, Andrew: *American State Universities;* Robert Clarke & Co., Cincinnati, 1875; p. 93.

[20] A. B. Woodward: An act to establish the catholepistemiad, etc., University of Michigan Library.

[21] Hinsdale, Burke A.: *History of the University of Michigan;* University of Michigan, Ann Arbor, 1906; p. 11.

[22] Isbell, Egbert R.: op. cit., p. 170.

[23] Hinsdale, Burke A.: op. cit., p. 9.

[24] Farrand, Elizabeth M.: *History of the University of Michigan;* Register Publishing House, Ann Arbor, 1885; p. 9.

[25] Ten Brook, Andrew: op. cit., p. 98.

[26] Ibid, p. 9.

[27] Isbell, Egbert R.: The Universities of Virginia and Michigania; in *Michigan History Magazine,* Vol. XXVI, p. 44.

CHAPTER IX

[1] *MPHC,* Vol. XXXVI, p. 398.

[2] Executive Proceedings of Michigan Territory, January 1, 1818–June 30, 1818; State Department Records, National Archives.

[3] *MPHC,* Vol. XII, p. 639.

[4] Address to the Electors, July 22, 1819 and August 30, 1819; Woodward Papers, Burton Historical Collection, and MPHC, Vol. VII, pp. 526–533.

[5] Lewis Cass to President Monroe, Detroit, September 11, 1819; State Department Records, National Archives.

[6] Solomon Sibley to Andrew G. Whitney, Detroit, November 4, 1820; Sibley Papers, Burton Historical Collection.

[7] Petitions to Congress of the Inhabitants of the Counties of Mackinaw, Brown and Crawford, in the Territory of Michigan, November 5, 1821; in Records of the Seventeenth Congress, Library of Congress.

[8] Lewis Cass to Secretary of State, Detroit, December 5, 1821; State Department Records, National Archives.

[9] Report of a Committee of Inhabitants of Wayne County, November, 1822; Records of the Seventeenth Congress, Library of Congress.

[10] Presentment of the Grand Jury, January 7, 1820; supra.

[11] Memorial to Congress by Inhabitants of the Territory, November 11, 1822; supra.

[12] James D. Doty to Henry R. Schoolcraft, October 25, 1822; Schoolcraft Papers, Library of Congress.

[13] Members of the Michigan Bar to the Secretary of State, December 16, 1823; State Department Records, National Archives.

[14] Reverend Gabriel Richard to Judge Woodward, Washington, January 24, 1824; State Department Records, National Archives.

[15] Governor Cass to Reverend Gabriel Richard, Detroit, February 16, 1824; supra.

[16] Tallahassee in 1824–1825: An unsigned letter in the *Pensacola Gazette,* September, 1825; reprinted in *Florida Historical Quarterly,* Vol. III (October 1924); pp. 38–40.

[17] Hanna, A. J.: *A Prince in Their Midst;* University of Oklahoma Press, Norman Oklahoma, 1947; p. 59.

[18] Rerick, R. H.: *Memoirs of Florida;* Southern Historical Association, Atlanta, 1902; Vol. II, pp. 70–71.

Acknowledgements

ONLY WITH THE generous help of many people was it possible to gather the material from which this book is written. Guidance and advice of others enabled proper interpretation to be made of that material. Among those who assisted are Mrs. Elleine H. Stones, chief, Burton Historical Collection, Detroit Public Library, and her staff of capable aides; Dr. F. Clever Bald, assistant director, Michigan Historical Collections, University of Michigan, Ann Arbor; Mr. Charles Atkins, reference librarian, Port Huron Public Library, Port Huron, Michigan; Mr. John Cook Wyllie, curator of rare books, Alderman Library, University of Virginia, Charlottesville; Mr. Julien C. Yonge, director, P. K. Yonge Library of Florida History, University of Florida, Gainesville, and Dean R. A. Rasco, University of Miami School of Law, Coral Gables, Florida.

The manuscript was read in whole or in part by Mr. Malcolm W. Bingay, editorial director, *The Detroit Free Press;* Mr. Fred Tew, editorial writer, *The Detroit Free Press;* Mr. Colton Storm, acting director, William L. Clements Library, University of Michigan; Professor W. Sprague Holden, Wayne University, Detroit, and Mr. Herbert M. Weil, Detroit.

These few words of appreciation are inadequate, but nevertheless sincere, expression of my thanks.

F.B.W.

Bibliography

MANUSCRIPT COLLECTIONS

Lewis Bond Papers, Burton Historical Collection, Detroit Public Library.

George McDougall Papers, Burton Historical Collection, Detroit Public Library.

William Hull Papers, Burton Historical Collection, Detroit Public Library.

Thomas Jefferson Papers, Library of Congress, Washington.

Thomas Jefferson Papers (microfilm), Alderman Library, University of Virginia, Charlottesville.

William L. Jenks Papers, Port Huron Public Library, Port Huron, Michigan.

Michigan Territorial and Miscellaneous Papers, National Archives, Washington.

Solomon Sibley Papers, Burton Historical Collection, Detroit Public Library.

William Woodbridge Papers, Burton Historical Collection, Detroit Public Library.

Augustus B. Woodward Papers, Burton Historical Collection, Detroit Public Library.

Augustus B. Woodward and related documents, Michigan Historical Collections, University of Michigan, Ann Arbor.

NEWSPAPERS

Detroit Free Press
Detroit Gazette
National Intelligencer
Niles Register
Philadelphia *Aurora*
Pittsburgh *Commonwealth*

GENERAL SOURCES

————: *American State Papers* (Public Lands); Gales & Seaton, Washington, 1832–1861.

Bald, F. Clever: *Detroit's First American Decade;* University of Michigan Press, Ann Arbor, 1948.

Bishop, William W.: Judge Woodward and the Catholepistemiad, in *University of Michigan Alumnus Quarterly Review,* Ann Arbor, Vol. LI.

Blume, William Wirt: *Transactions of the Supreme Court of the Territory of Michigan;* University of Michigan Press, Ann Arbor, 1940.

Bond, Beverly W., Jr.: *The Civilization of the Old Northwest;* The Macmillan Company, New York, 1934.

Bryan, Wilhelmus Bogart: *A History of the National Capital;* The Macmillan Company, New York, 1914.

Burnet, Jacob: *Notes on the Early Settlement of the North-Western Territory;* Derby, Bradley & Co., Cincinnati, 1847.

Burton, C. M.: Scrapbooks, in Burton Historical Collection, Detroit Public Library

————.: Sketch of the Life of Augustus Brevoort Woodward, MSS in Burton Historical Collection, Detroit Public Library.

————.: (comp.) and Burton, M. Agnes (ed.): *Proceedings of the Land Board of Detroit;* Detroit, 1915.

Cabell, N. F.: *Jefferson, Cabell and the University of Virginia;* J. W. Randolph, Richmond, 1856.

Campbell, James V.: *Outlines of the Political History of Michigán;* Schober & Company, Detroit, 1876.

Carter, Clarence E. (ed.): *The Territorial Papers of the United States,* Vols. X-XI; Government Printing Office, Washington, 1942–1943.

Catlin, George B.: Biography and Romance in Detroit's Street Names; *Michigan History Magazine,* Vol. II, Lansing.

————.: *The Story of Detroit;* The Detroit News, Detroit, 1926.

————.: *Columbia Historical Society Records,* Washington, 1901.

Cooley, Thomas M.: *Michigan, A History of Governments;* Houghton, Mifflin and Company, Boston, 1885.

————.: *Dictionary of American Biography* (Dumas Malone, ed.); Charles Scribner's Sons, New York, 1935.

————.: *Dictionary of American History* (James Truslow Adams, ed.); Charles Scribner's Sons, New York, 1940.

Farmer, Silas: *History of Detroit and Michigan;* Silas Farmer & Co., Detroit, 1884.

Farrand, Elizabeth M.: *History of the University of Michigan;* Register Publishing House, Ann Arbor, 1885.

————.: *Florida Historical Quarterly,* Gainesville, Vol. III.

Fuller, George Newman: *Centennial History of Michigan;* Lewis Publishing Company, Chicago, 1939.

————.: *Economic and Social Beginnings of Michigan;* Wynkoop, Hollenbeck, Crawford & Company, Lansing, 1916.

Hamil, Fred Coyne: *The Valley of the Lower Thames,* 1640–1850; University of Toronto Press, Toronto, Ontario, 1951.

Hanna, A. J.: *A Prince in Their Midst, The Adventurous Life of Achille Murat on the American Frontier;* University of Oklahoma Press, Norman, Oklahoma, 1947.

Hayden, Horace Edwin: *A Biographical Sketch of Oliver Pollock, Esq.;* Lane S. Hart, Harrisburg, 1883.

Helm, Lieutenant Linai T.: *The Fort Dearborn Massacre* (Nelly Kinzie Gordon, ed.; Rand McNally Company, Chicago-New York, 1912.

Hinsdale, Burke A.: *History of the University of Michigan;* University of Michigan, Ann Arbor, 1906.

Hubbard, Bela: *The Memorials of a Half Century;* G. Putnam's Sons, New York, 1887.

Hurd, Charles: *Washington Cavalcade;* E. P. Dutton & Co., New York, 1948.

Isbell, Egbert R.: The Catholepistemiad, or University of Michigania; in *University of Michigan Historical Essays* (A.E.R. Boak, ed.); University of Michigan Press, Ann Arbor, 1937.

————.: The Universities of Virginia and Michigania; *Michigan History Magazine,* Vol. XXVI.

James, James Alton: Oliver Pollock, Financier of the Revolution in the West; *Mississippi Valley Historical Review,* January, 1929.

————.: *Oliver Pollock—The Life and Times of an Unknown Patriot;* D. Appleton-Century Company, Inc., New York, 1937.

Jenks, William L.: Augustus Elias Brevoort Woodward, in *Michigan History Magazine,* Vol. IX.

————.: *The First Bank in Michigan;* Port Huron, 1916.

————.: Legislation by Governor and Judges, in *Michigan History Magazine,* Vol. III.

————.: *Michigan Territory Under a British Governor;* Michigan Society, Sons of the American Revolution Year Book, 1919/23.

————.: The Real Origin of the University of Michigan, in *Michigan Alumnus,* Ann Arbor, 1923, Vol. XXIX.

Johnson, Allen (ed.): *Dictionary of American Biography;* Charles Scribner's Sons, New York, 1928.

Lagondakis, Charilaos: Greece and Michigan, in *Michigan History Magazine,* Vol. XIV.

Learned, Henry B.: *The President's Cabinet;* Yale University Press, New Haven, 1912.

Marshall, Thomas Maitland (ed.): *Life and Papers of Frederick Bates;* Missouri Historical Society, St. Louis, 1926.

Michigan Pioneer and Historical Collections (*MPHC*): Wynkoop, Hallenbeck, Crawford Company, Lansing, Michigan; Vols. I-XL.

Moore, Charles: *Governor, Judge and Priest;* DeVinne Press, New York, 1891.

————.: *History of Michigan;* Lewis Publishing Company, Chicago, 1915.

Nicolay, Helen: *Our Capital On The Potomac;* The Century Company, New York and London, 1924.

Pare, George: *The Catholic Church in Detroit 1701–1888;* The Gabriel Richard Press, Detroit, 1951.

Patton, John S.: *Jefferson, Cabell and the University of Virginia;* Neale Publishing Company, New York and Washington, 1906.

Paxson, Frederic L.: *History of the American Frontier 1763–1893;* Houghton, Mifflin Company, Boston, 1924.

Pickens, Buford L.: Early City Plans for Detroit, a Projected American Metropolis; in *The Art Quarterly,* Winter, 1943.

Potter, Justice William W.: The Michigan Judiciary Since 1805; in *Michigan History Magazine,* Vol. XXVII.

Price, Richard R.: *The Financial Support of the University of Michigan; Its Origin and Development;* Harvard University Press, Cambridge, 1923.

Quaife, Milo M. (ed.): *The John Askin Papers;* Detroit Library Commission, Detroit, 1931.

Rerick, R. H.: *Memoirs of Florida;* Southern Historical Association, Atlanta, 1902.

Robbins, Frank E. (comp.): *Records of the University of Michigan;* University of Michigan Press, Ann Arbor, 1935.

Shaw, Wilfred: *The University of Michigan;* Harcourt, Brace & Howe, New York, 1920.

Sheldon, E. M.: *The Early History of Michigan from the First Settlement to 1815;* A. S. Barnes & Company, New York, 1856.

Ten Brook, Andrew: *American State Universities;* Robert Clarke & Company, Cincinnati, 1875.

United States Congress: *House Committee on Affairs in the Territory of Michigan* (Ninth Congress, First Session); A. & G. Way, Washington, 1806.

Utley, Henry M. and Cutcheon, Byron M.: *Michigan As a Province, Territory and State;* Publishing Society of Michigan, New York, 1906.

Wayne County, Michigan: Documents Relating to the Erection of; Burton Historical Collection Publication, Detroit, 1922–23.

Woodford, Frank B.: *Lewis Cass—The Last Jeffersonian;* Rutgers University Press, New Brunswick, 1950.

Woodward, Augustus B.: *Considerations on the Executive Government of the United States of America;* Isaac Riley, Flatbush, New York, 1809.

————.: *Considerations on the Government of the Territory of Columbia;* S. Snowden & Company, Alexandria, 1802.

————.: *Considerations on the Substance of the Sun;* Way and Groff, Washington, 1801.

————.: *Epaminondas on the Government of the Territory of Columbia;* Green and English, George-Town, 1801.

————.: Legislation Relating to the Establishment of the University of Michigan; Burton Historical Collection, Detroit Public Library.

————.: *The Presidency of the United States;* Derick Van Veghten, Washington, 1825.

————.: *A Representation of the Case of Oliver Pollock;* Samuel Harrison Smith, Washington, 1803.

————.: *Supplement to the Representation of the Case of Oliver Pollock;* William Duane & Son, Washington, 1803.

————.: *A System of Universal Science;* Edward Earle, Harrison Hall, Moses Thomas; Philadelphia, 1816.

Index

Abbott, Robert, 6, 11
Adams, John, 153, 185
Adams, John Quincy, 92, 181
Albany Argus, 120–1
Alexandria, Va., 21
American Fur Company, 55
American National Institute, 149
Amherstburg, Ont., 88, 102
Analectic Review, 152
Anderson, John, 69
Angell, James B., 157
Aram, Eugene, 122
Askin Farm, 36, 38
Askin, John, 5
Astor, John Jacob, 142
Atwater, Reuben, 13, 63, 122
Audrain, Peter, 65, 102, 140
Avery, Elisha, 12

Bailey, Theodorus, 90
Baker, Ens. Isaac, 116
Baldwin, Henry, 165
Banks, Enos, 127
Bates, Edward, 13
Bates, Frederick, 7, 13, 36, 49, 50, 60, 65, 72, 76
Bentham, Jeremy, 152, 184
Bishop, William W., 148
Blume, William Wirt, 75–9
Bonaparte, Caroline, 183
Bonaparte, Napoleon, 101, 162, 183
Bradley, Stephen R., 13
Brant, Joseph, 104
Brevoort, Elias, 17, 20
Brevoort, Capt. Henry, 82
Brock, Maj. Gen. Isaac, 109–110
Brookfield, William, 176, 178
Brush, Elijah, 70, 88, 89, 107
Brush Farm, 36
Burr, Aaron, 1, 100–1

Cadillac, Antoine de la Mothe, 4
Call, Richard K., 183
Campbell, Maj. Alexander, 84
Campbell, James V., 24, 112, 116, 160
Cass, Lewis: governor, Mich. Terr., 50, 84, 124–6, 128, 160, 168, 175, 178; blocks Burr conspiracy, 100–1; in War of 1812, 107; supports university, 155–6, 159; promotes political progress, 165–7, 172; opinion of Woodward, 125, 180
Catholepistemiad, or University of Michigania (see also Michigan, University of), 156–164
Catlin, George B., 112
Chartrand, Peter, 5
Chesapeake, U.S.S., 105
Chillicothe, Ohio, 11, 189
Christiancy, Isaac P., 160
Cincinnati, Ohio, 2, 11
Clay, Henry, 71, 105
Clinton, DeWitt, 131
Clinton, George, 11
Columbia College, 18, 145
common law, 78–9
Conrad (?) (Woodward's servant), 143
Considerations on the Executive Government of the United States, 132, 135
Considerations on the Substance of the Sun, 145–8
Cooley, Thomas M., 9, 24, 85, 91
Curry, Peter, 89

Dailey, William, 89
Dearborn, Fort (Chicago), 109, 112
Dearborn, Henry, 104
Denison family, 86–90
Detroit, Mich., 45, 77–8, 97, 104, 155–6, 161, 169, 171, 177, 180–1, 188; Woodward goes to, 1, 7, 189; description, 3, 15, 53, 126–7; destroyed by fire, 3–7, 39; French influence, 16; re-

Detroit, Mich.,—*Continued*
platted, 37, 41, 43, 45; Woodward's plan for, 39–41, 45, 47–9, 50–52; slavery in, 85–6; Indian alarms, 103; in War of 1812, 107–110, 115, 120, 122, 123, 190
Detroit Bank, 55–9
Detroit Gazette, 23, 95, 126, 156, 161, 174, 175
Detroit Lyceum, 143, 161
Dilhet, Rev. Jean, 4, 23
District of Columbia, 25–9, 122
Dodemead, James, 5
Dodemead, James, Jr., 89
Doty, James Duane, 172–5, 177
Downing, Edward R., 186
Duane, William, 140
Dunham, Capt. Josiah, 102–3
DuVal, William Pope, 183, 185
Dyson, Capt. Samuel T., 12

Edwards, A., 128
Egnew, George, 138
Egnew, Samuel, 138
Elliott, Matthew, 88–90, 143
Ely, Ezra Stiles, 82
Emerson, Ralph Waldo, 183
Epistemic System, 152, 154, 162
Erie, Pa., 98, 122

Farley, Capt. John, 128
Farmer, John, 126, 142
Farmer, Silas, 22, 24, 45
Federalist Party, 28–30
Fisher, George, 186
Fisher, Lieut. Otis, 128
Flanigan, William, 56
Florida Advocate, 187
Florida Territory, 181–2, 186
Forsyth, Robert, 143
Forsyth, William, 69
Franklin, Benjamin, 146
French Moral and Benevolent Society, 143
Frenchtown (Monroe, Mich.), 14, 77, 115, 119, 120, 138, 140, 168, 170

Gadsden, James, 183
Gallatin, Albert, 111
Gentle, Adam, 68
Gentle, John, 47, 68
George III, 18
Girardin, Jacques, 6
Girty, Simon, 88
Gooley, Joseph, 128
Governor and Judges: governing body, 8, 10, 14, 36, 53–4, 56, 61, 66, 74–5, 122, 126–7, 129, 154, 156, 160; plan for Detroit, 36–7, 50; land titles, 42–5, 48; difficulties, 53; dissensions, 60; criticism of, 65, 165, 172–3; abolished, 172, 175
Grant, James, 91–2
Greeley, Aaron, 102, 124
Green, Dr. Ashbel, 150
Griffin, Cyrus, 13–14
Griffin, John: territorial judge, 63, 84, 97, 107, 122, 139; appointed, 13; character, 14, 76; signs bank charter, 59; seeks transfer, 64; at Knaggs trial, 70; relations with Woodward, 60, 76, 78, 125; signs university act, 157; absent from legislative board, 169; resigns, 176; attacks on, 95, 174, 176
Griswold, Stanley: territorial secretary, 8, 11, 15, 62, 64–5, 113; character, 12–13; intrigues, 58, 60–1, 63, 100; term expires, 13, 63
Grosse Pointe, Mich., 46

Hale, Nathan, 12
Hanchet, Joseph, 128
Hanks, Lieut. Porter, 82
Harrisburg, Pa., 2
Harrison, William Henry, 5, 11, 106, 115, 122
Harvey, John, 5, 82
Hatch, Rufus, 177
Heward, James, 89
Hickman, Harris, 86–7, 105
Highland Park, Mich., 138
Hinsdale, Burke A., 160, 162
Hoffman, George, 65
Hull, Abijah, 40
Hull, Capt. Abraham, 12, 82
Hull, Ann, 12
Hull, Maria, 12
Hull, William: territorial governor, 1, 11, 15, 50, 60, 65, 75, 86, 101, 115;

character and career, 12, 60, 74; opinion of French, 16; adjusts land titles, 36–7, 42–7; organizes militia, 54–5; and Detroit Bank, 55–9; opinion of Woodward, 59, 62–3; Woodward's opinion of, 60, 63–4, 69; seeks army appointment, 64; pardons Whipple, 68–9; leaves territory, 75, 106; quarrels with Woodward, 55, 61, 63, 107–8; leniency toward Indians, 97; mobilizes militia, 55, 64, 100; fear of Indians, 102–4; commands Northwest Army, 75, 106; in War of 1812, 107–8, 110; surrenders Detroit, 109, 110, 124, 190
Hunt, John, 177
Huntington, Samuel, 13

Indiana, 5, 10, 78–9, 84, 91
Indians, 43–3, 81, 85, 96, 101–4, 107, 112–3, 115, 190
Isbell, Egbert, 151, 161, 163, 164

Jefferson, Thomas, 2, 3, 12, 13, 14, 22, 29, 42, 58, 63, 135–6, 175; association with Woodward, 1, 20, 24, 25, 28, 31, 38, 121–2, 141, 153, 188; and Burr, 2, 100–1; influence on Woodward, 132, 163; comments on *Executive* pamphlet, 133–4; scientific interests, 149, 184; establishes University of Virginia, 163; plan for educational system, 163–4; appointments criticized, 14; death, 185, 186
Jenks, William L., 145
Johnson, Sen. Richard, 180
Johnson, Dr. Samuel, 150

Kentucky, University of, 163
Ketanka, 96
Knaggs, Whitmore, 69–71, 118, 174

Ladies Society, 143
Lafayette, Gen., 183
Langdon, Austin, 89
Larned, Charles, 169
Lawrence, Amos, 139
Learned, Henry B., 136
Legislative Board (see Governor and Judges)
L'Enfant, Charles Pierre, 20–1
Leopard, HMS, 105
Lexington, Va., 20
Liberty Hall Academy, 20
Linnaeus [Carl von Linne], 149
Livingston, Robert Gilbert, 18
Locke, John, 2, 149
Lundie, Ens. John Stowe, 81–4
Lyon, Lucius, 138

Mackinac (Michilimackinac), 14, 15, 42, 77, 105, 107–8, 168–9
Macomb, Gen. Alexander, 142
Macomb County, Mich., 168
Macomb Farm, 36, 38, 50
Macomb, William, 8, 85
Macon, Edgar, 186
Madison, James, 11, 24, 44, 50, 58–9, 61, 101, 110, 121–2, 134, 186
Maisonville, Victoire, 140
Malden, Fort, 80, 84, 88, 107, 115
Mansion House, 137
Marietta, Ohio, 2, 11
May, James, 7, 66, 113, 137, 176
Mechanics Society, 143
Meldrum, George, 6
McCarthy, Johnsy, 170
McCloskey, James, 140, 169, 176
McDonnell, John, 179
McDougall, George, 65, 105, 118, 142
McGurk, James, 31
McKee, Alexander, 88
McKenney, John, 176
Michigan Territory, 30, 50, 73, 99, 100, 144, 153, 180, 188; establishment, 1, 2, 11, 36; inhabitants, 14–5, 39, 80, 131; early conditions, 14, 54; American occupation, 15, 79, 85, 87, 91; land titles, 41–5, 137; unrest in, 46–7, 101; government, 8–9, 12, 53, 64; judiciary, 76–80; slavery, 84–6, 91; Indian alarms, 101–4; repeal of establishment act urged, 113; description 1814, 124; migration, 125–6, 131; Indian title to, 126; education in, 141, 154–164; social and economic development, 55–6, 59, 75, 127–9, 155, 165, 170; congressional delegate, 165–6; elections, 166–171; judicial reform, 171–5; reorganiza-

Michigan Territory,–*Continued*
tion, 166, 175; Americanization of, 189–90; British occupation, 110-120; laws, 54, 66, 75, 97; in War of 1812, 104-6, 107–9, 122-3
Michigan, University of (see also Catholepistemiad), 160, 162, 191
Monroe County, Mich., 126, 169–9, 171
Monroe Doctrine, 93
Monroe, James, 92, 114, 117, 119, 120, 126, 136, 176–8, 180–1
Monticello, 20, 26, 31, 121, 122, 175
Montieth, Rev. John, 155–6, 159
Morrison, ________, 81–3
Muir, Capt. Adam, 81–3
Muir-Lundie Case, 80–84, 174
Munro, Robert, 4, 5
Murat, Achille, 183–4, 186

National Intelligencer, 6, 28, 73, 187
Navarre, Marianne, 141
Navarre, Monique, 140–1
Navigation Act, 18
Nicholas, Cary, 181
Nolan, Thomas, 81
Northwest Ordinance (see Ordinance of 1787)
Northwest Territory, 10–11, 75, 78–9, 85–6, 97, 114, 122, 169, 189, 190, 192

Oakland County, Mich., 169
Olmstead, Frederick Law, Jr., 41
Ordinance of 1787, 9–10, 63, 66, 78, 84, 87, 90–1, 172

Palmer, F. T. & J., 128
Pattinson, Richard, 88–91
Pensacola Gazette, 182
Perry, Oliver Hazard, 122
Philadelphia Aurora, 48–9, 82, 134, 140
Pickens, Buford L., 40–1
Pindar, Charles, 183
Pittsburgh Commonweath, 47, 49, 72
Pittsburgh, Pa., 2
Poindexter, Rep., 113
Pollock, Oliver, 31–5
Pontiac, 101
Pontiac, Mich., 139
Presidency of the United States, The, 135–7
Proctor, Gen. Henry, 110–115, 117–9, 120
Prophet, The, 103–4
Put-in-Bay, Battle of, 122

Quebec Act, 18

Reed, Thomas B., 102
Rerick, R. H., 186
Richard, Rev. Gabriel, 4, 5, 6, 23, 36, 125, 154–6, 159, 178, 180
River Raisin, 14, 63, 115, 117, 118, 124, 125
River Raisin Massacre, 115, 119, 120, 180
River Rouge, 81, 124, 128
Robinson & Martin, 6
Rockbridge County, Va., 20

St. Anne's Church (Detroit), 3, 4, 159
Sandwich (Ontario) Canada, 5, 88, 107–8
Sault Ste. Marie, 14
Schoolcraft, Henry Rowe, 128, 174
Scott, Dr. William McDowell, 89
Seek, Conrad, 82–3
Selkirk, Lord Thomas Douglas, 91–2
Seward, William H., 92
Sibley, Solomon, 96, 105, 169–171, 175, 177
Silvester, Ann (mother of Woodward), 17
Smith, Thomas, 38
Smyth, Richard, 88–9, 105
Smyth's Tavern, 65, 66, 175
Stamp Act, 18
Stead, B., 127
Stelle's Tavern, 25
Stephens, Blackhall, 108
Supreme Court (Michigan Territory), 76–8, 94–7, 122, 171–3, 175, 185
System of Universal Science, A, 150, 157, 158–9, 160

Tallahassee (Fla.), 181–3, 185–8
Tecumseh, 103–4
Ten Brook, Andrew, 162
Ten Thousand Acre Tract, 38, 138

Thibault, Joseph, 6
Thorn, William, 128
Tippecanoe, Battle of, 106
Tocqueville, Alexis de, 184
Traquhair, Earl of, 13
Trowbridge, C. C., 98
Tucker, Mrs. Catherine, 86–7
Tucker, William, 86
Tunnicliff's Hotel, 25
Tuttle, Capt., 82

Underground Railway, 91

Vincennes (Ind.), 11, 14, 189
Virginia, University of, 163

Walk-in-the-Water, 126
Washington, D.C., 1, 2, 20–1, 25–6, 29–30, 38–9, 44, 64, 113, 121, 125–6, 177, 180–1
Wayne County, Mich., 127, 168–9, 171
Whipple, Maj. John, 68, 114, 174
White, Margaret, 4
William and Mary College, 13
Williams, John R., 169
Wilson, George Ewing, 69
Winchester, Gen. James, 115, 117–8
Wing, Austin E., 22
Witherell, James, 60, 68, 70, 76, 94–5, 97, 107, 109, 125, 174, 176–7
Woodbridge, William, 14, 122, 125, 155–7, 159, 166, 167–9
Woodward, Augustus Brevoort: early life, family and education, 17–20, 21, 98, 145, 186; in Washington, 20–21, 25–30; admitted to bar; 21; appearance, 21–22; character, 19, 22–5, 59, 62, 97, 125–6, 167, 176, 184, 189–191; notebook, 19, 21, 38; property, 20–21, 137–9, 180; militia officer, 25, 54–5; goes to Detroit, 1, 7; chief justice, 1, 8, 76, 185; attacks on, 23, 46, 48, 95, 97–8, 171–8, 190–2; at Frenchtown, 62–3, 138, 140; seeks office, 1, 64, 166, 178, 181; on slavery, 86; American ideals, 98–9, 189–90; explores wilderness, 126; plan for Niagara canal, 129–131; love affairs, 139–141; as public figure, 141–4; a Mason, 143, 184; intemperance, 177, 180; testimonial to, 179; friendship with Murat, 183–4; death, 186–7; influence, 144, 190; legal practice, 30; defends McGurk, 31; represents Pollock, 32–5; judicial career and conduct, 71, 76–7, 94–7, 176, 190; dominates court, 76, 125; relies on grand jury, 98; codifies laws, 60–61; shocked by lawlessness, 67; assaults on, 68–71; threatened by mob, 88; Indian trials, 96; decisions, 86–7, 90–1, 92; conducts Muir-Lundie trial, 83–4; abolishes foreign laws, 79–80; defends Knaggs, 118; Florida district judge, 181, 182, 185–6; opinion Ordinance of 1787, 10, 189; political philosophy, 26–8, 29–30, 46, 132–4, 135–6, 137, 166, 188–9; candidate for delegate, 166–171; defended, 121, 179, 192; legislator, 74, 76, 84; impeachment, 72–3; president Detroit Bank, 56–9; advocates acquiring Canada, 92–3; reports conditions in territory, 100–1, 105–6, 117, 125; and Indian alarms, 64, 101, 104; and Burr conspiracy, 1, 100–1; advocates oriental trade, 135; urges tariff revision, 134; encourages domestic industry, 128; proposes Indian treaties, 126; term of office expires, 175; reappointment opposed, 175–6; leaves Detroit, 180; writing, 26, 131, 132, 135, 145, 150; scientific interests, 145–154; 184; devises Epistemic System, 152; adjusts land titles, 36–8, 42–50; plan for Detroit, 39–41, 47, 50–52, 188; suggests campaign against British, 105; in War of 1812, 106–118, 190–1, aids prisoners, 112, 115–6; loyalty, 111, 113, 119, 121, 174, 191–2; member peace celebration committee, 123; interest in education, 154–6, 162–3, 164; writes Catholepistemiad act, 157; lays university cornerstone, 159; relations with settlers, 7, 16, 45–6, 114, 116, 118, 125, 178–9, 192; association with Jefferson, 1, 20, 24, 25, 28, 30, 121, 131–2, 133–4, 149, 153, 163–4, 184, 188; association with Richard, 23,

Woodward, Augustus Brevoort:—
Continued
141, 154, 156, 180; relations with Hull, 55, 59, 60–1, 62–4, 69, 107–8; relations with Cass, 125–6, 180; relations with Griswold, 58, 61, 100; relations with Witherell, 60, 94, 174; relations with Bates, 7, 13, 49, 65, 72, 76; letters to and from, 46, 49, 56, 59, 61, 62, 63, 65, 67, 71, 72–3, 90, 92, 93, 102, 105, 108, 111, 112, 113, 117, 118, 119, 120, 121, 124–5, 133–4, 136, 139, 140–1, 142, 149, 153, 180
Woodward Avenue, 47, 65, 188
Woodward Code, 60–61
Woodward, John, 17–8, 98
Woodward, John Jr., 186
Woodward, Maria, 21
Woodward Plan, 38, 39–41, 47, 50–2, 63, 188
Woodwardville, 138
Woodworth, Benjamin, 123, 127, 179
Woodworth, Samuel, 127
Worthington, Thomas, 73

Ypsilanti, Alexandre, 138
Ypsilanti, Demetrios, 138
Ypsilanti, Mich., 138

Zion Lodge, 143